ULVERSTON
AN ENGLISH MARKET TOWN THROUGH HISTORY

The erratic spelling of Ulverston over the centuries, with the final 'e' only being dropped in the 19th century, is matched by the range of theories on the name's origins. The name is in two parts, and 'ton' is usually thought to be the Anglo-Saxon suffix denoting a settlement. However, some argue that this was originally 'stan', referring to a large stone which once stood at the foot of Soutergate and is now partly buried in the Tank Square roundabout. The first part could refer to a proper name or, in some opinions, to the animal wolf. Thus, Ulverston could be the settlement of Ulf or Ulfere (or any other variation) or where the 'Wolfstone' was, depending on your preference.

ULVERSTON

AN ENGLISH MARKET TOWN THROUGH HISTORY

Helen Shacklady

H
HANDSTAND PRESS

Published by Handstand Press
East Banks, Dent, Sedbergh. Cumbria.
LA10 5QT

First Published in 2016

Second Edition

Designed & set by Russell Holden ~ Pixel Tweaks, Ulverston
Unless otherwise stated, the photographs in the book were taken by Russell Holden

Printed in Great Britain by Biddles, Kings Lynn, Norfolk.

ISBN: 978-0-9576609-4-6

Front cover. Ulverston from Birkrigg (Photo Russell Holden)
with section from County Palatine Map of Lancaster 1771.
Back cover, Ulverston market day circa 1980 (Photo Dave Abbott)
with Ulverston Market Charter.

H
HANDSTAND PRESS

Acknowledgements

Many people have contributed to this book with information, encouragement and illustrations. Thanks go to Caitlin Barratt of the Dock Museum, Barrow-in-Furness; Jill and the helpful staff at Ulverston Library; Deborah Walsh of the Armitt Museum, Ambleside; Glenn Lang, Michael Stephens, Susan Benson, Selena Kendall and Sonya Waplington from the Archive and Local Studies Centre, Barrow- in-Furness; Francesca Halfacre at the Cumbria Archives Centre, Carlisle; Dan Elsworth of Greenlane Archaeology, Ulverston; John Garbutt; Sarah Holmes; Irvine Hunt; Neil Honeyman; Denis McGeary; Jane and Mark Carson and Pete Langley who drew the black and white illustrations.

Anyone writing about Ulverston depends on the work of other local historians, including Jennifer Snell, Rob McKeevor, the late Ian Lewis of the Swarthmoor Hall History Group whose lectures provided background information and especially Jack Layfield, who sadly passed away before this book was finished. Thanks also go to Ian McNicholl for lending books and sparking ideas. Special gratitude goes to Peter Lowe, who has put up with endless questions and been generous both with his time and in providing the cover image and other illustrations from his collection. Any faults in the book are the responsibility of the author and not of these patient informants.

Russell Holden set out the book and took many of the photographs with his customary expertise and enthusiasm, and the author would like to thank Liz Nuttall of Handstand Press for persuading her to attempt this history and for editing her ramblings with skill and forbearance.

To the people of Ulverston

CONTENTS

Introduction

On the surface Ulverston seems a typical English market town both in the story of its growth over the centuries and in the challenges it faces today. Mentioned in the Domesday Book of 1086, in the twelfth and thirteenth centuries it was developed by its Norman overlords into a borough and a market and, like many other centres, received its formal market charter during the reign of Edward I (1272 - 1307). Relatively populous and busy at the beginning of the fourteenth century, it suffered a decline after the Black Death, bouncing back as a significant market in Tudor and Stuart times. Growing prosperity from trade and the beginnings of industrialisation led to a boom in the eighteenth century, and by the end of the nineteenth century it had the characteristics of any Victorian town with its railways, heavy industry, packed terraced streets and smarter houses for the well-off. In common with other towns Ulverston has faced the changes brought about by two world wars, widespread demolition in the 1960's, and recent revolutions in shopping habits which threaten the very existence of its ancient market.

Yet in many ways Ulverston is not like any other town, and has a unique story to tell. Its position on Morecambe Bay made it a port for many centuries; it was involved in the iron industry from at least the Middle Ages; it played an important role in the establishment of Quakerism and has its own internal history of colourful lives and events. Although local historians have produced invaluable books on aspects of Ulverston's past, the only overall history of the town remains Henry Birkett's *The Story of Ulverston: A Short History* published in 1949. A native of Ulverston who loved the town and who could draw on a vast depth of local knowledge and a wide array of contacts, Henry Birkett is a hard act to follow. In this book I take a slightly different approach by looking at Ulverston's story in the context of English history to understand its connection with wider events. Charting its development through history, I show how Ulverston gained the particular character which distinguishes it from other similar small towns and makes it such a special place.

Helen Shacklady, Ulverston 2016.

• I •

Very Early History

Over five thousand years ago a dog dragged a red deer bone along the Furness shore near the present day village of Bardsea. With any luck it was able to settle down and gnaw at it in peace before leaving it to sink in the mud. There it lay undisturbed until it was discovered, complete with tooth marks, by archaeologists in the 1990's. Unfortunately, even the most up-to-date archaeological techniques cannot tell us whether the people who went to the bother of hunting the deer in the first place were miffed at the bone's disappearance or whether this was a very early example of suppertime for man's best friend. Still, we can be reasonably sure that in the very distant past, not so far from where people sit and enjoy ice-creams today, men and women were eating venison and looking out over Morecambe Bay to the same hills on the horizon.

It is easy to assume that the history of Ulverston is the story of countless forgotten generations, like these hunters, whose names have long been lost and who left only traces of their lives. Ulverston is famous for being the birth-place of Stan Laurel and of pole-vaulting; it cannot claim to be the seat of kings, the site of major battles or the cradle of the Industrial Revolution. Yet when we dig a little deeper we find that its past is not one of complete obscurity and it has had its fair share of inhabitants whose influence lasted well after their deaths. We can also see that looking

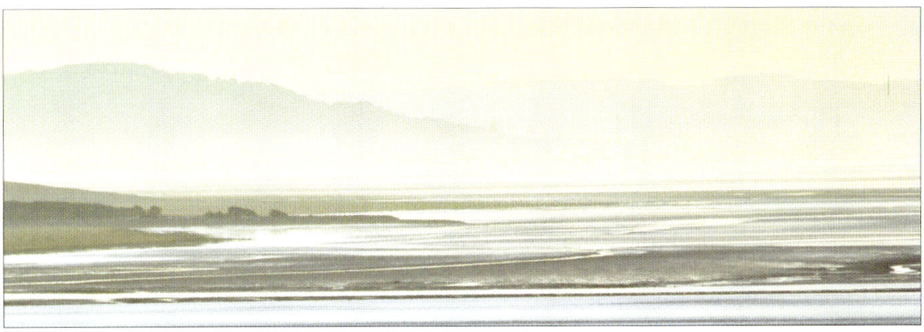

at the history of one small town in the context of wider events gives us a unique window into the past, and that changes elsewhere in the country reverberated in what is sometimes seen as an out-of-the way place. Visible evidence of Ulverston's past is found in its surroundings, surviving older buildings, the canal and the railway, and there is plenty more which can be glimpsed briefly, just as the covered streams which once ran open through its streets come unexpectedly to the surface behind odd walls and in the backs of gardens.

The everyday trip to Ulverston from Lancaster by rail can take us backwards and forwards in time, and for a visitor this is probably the best way to come to the town, although maybe not on the last train on a Saturday night. The line, itself a miracle of Victorian persistence and engineering ingenuity, sets off under the crag where the Romans built a fort and where the Pendle witches were held in the forbidding castle prison. When the tide is high it is a journey which seems more on water than on land, as the train floats over mosses and salt marsh and waves swirl a few yards below the track on the two great viaducts over the Kent and Leven estuaries. Then it isn't hard to picture Norse longships slinking up from the Irish Sea, and if you pass the ruins of Arnside Tower on a winter's sunset with its empty windows a fiery red it is as though raiders have turned up one last time to set the roof ablaze and make off with the cattle. As the train leaves Cark behind and Ulverston comes into

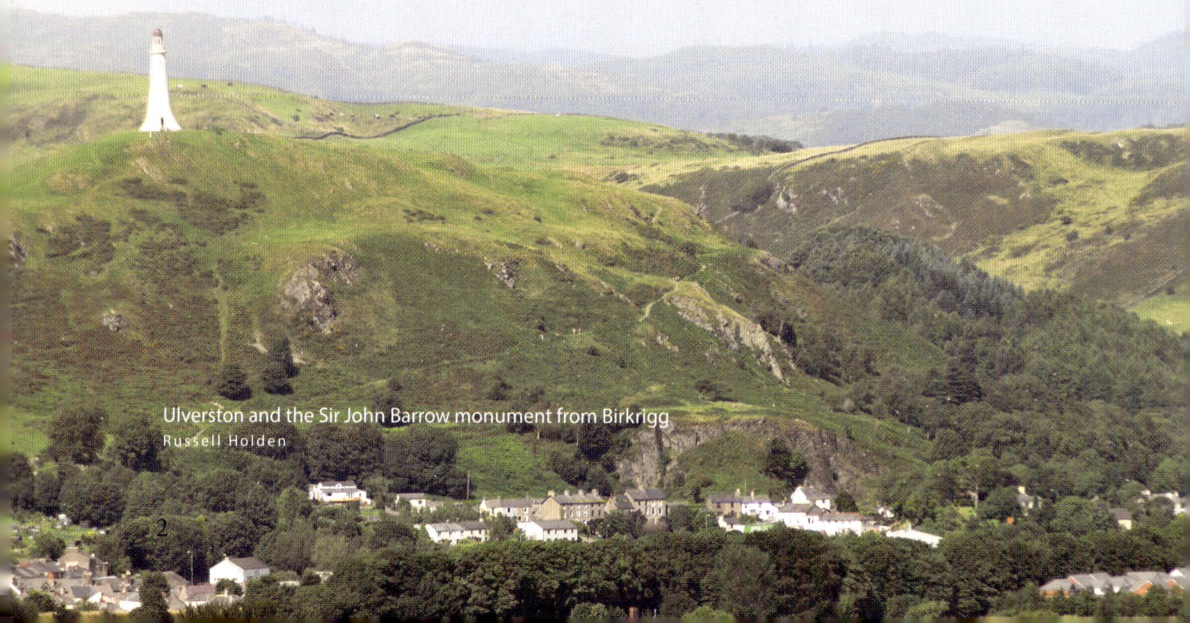

Ulverston and the Sir John Barrow monument from Birkrigg
Russell Holden

view, framed on one side by Birkrigg Common with its pre-historic burial sites and on the other by the white finger of the newly restored Sir John Barrow Monument, one can sense the relief felt by travellers over the centuries who made this journey by boat or, when the tide was out, by horse, cart and foot over the shifting sands of the bay.

Anyone could be forgiven for thinking that this lovely train ride is taking you through an untouched green and pleasant corner of rural England. A hundred years ago, though, it would have looked quite different. What are now sleepy platform stops were larger stations with complex sidings; Carnforth was an important junction and even Arnside had a branch line leading off to Sandside and then to the west coast main line. It would come as a shock to a modern traveller to see the amount of heavy industry in the shape of ironworks, lime works and quarries along the line, and Ulverston itself would have looked far from picturesque as the train came closer. Some might think the large GlaxoSmithKline plant a bit incongruous in the approach to a small country town, but it is nothing compared to the scale of the North Lonsdale ironworks which then occupied the site. Men toiled in the raw face of Plumpton quarry on the shore to the left of the viaduct, and present day fields were criss-crossed with railway tracks leading to the quarries, to Haverthwaite and through the ironworks to Conishead. With steam and smoke from industry and train engines, not to mention hundreds of domestic fires, hanging in the air, it all might have looked very grimy to twenty first century eyes. While new housing is gobbling up the fields around Ulverston at an alarming rate, nature has reclaimed many of the old industrial sites, and it is very rare nowadays for a passenger to get off the train choking and covered in smuts. Even before the railways and ironworks, Ulverston had its share of industries and the now quieter canal, where swans and moorhens nest, was alive with coastal shipping and workshops. As with anywhere else in England, we would have to travel back many thousands of years in the Furness peninsula to find a near-pristine landscape, although we might not be exactly thrilled with what we would find at the end of the last Ice Age.

The first thing to notice, apart from the cold, would be that the Irish Sea wasn't where we would expect. 12,000 years ago Morecambe Bay was dry land, the fells were permanently under snow, there were glaciers in the high valleys and any flat land would have looked like the Siberian tundra does today, with herds of reindeer and elk. Even in this gloomy scene there were people, surviving by hunting and living in caves which, thousands of years later, have given up their stone tools and the bits and pieces of rubbish they left behind. In contrast, by 8,000 BCE the landscape was more congenial. The temperature had gone up, melting the snow and glaciers, and the sea had risen to fill Morecambe Bay. Deciduous forest covered most of the land and people were out and about, fossicking for shellfish and hunting red deer, wild cattle and pigs, the elk having gone the way of the tundra. Traditionally, British pre-history has been divided into neat time periods each with their distinct characteristics, and this was the Mesolithic era when people were hunter-gatherers. It was followed in around 4,000 BCE by the Neolithic Age, marked by the appearance of agriculture and settled communities. These Stone Ages came to an end in about 2,000 BCE with the dawn of the Bronze Age, which in turn was followed in circa 450 BCE by the Iron Age.

Pre-history Timeline

Palaeolithic	Mesolithic	Neolithic	Bronze Age	Iron Age
Pre c. 10,000BCE	c. 10,000-4,000 BCE	c. 4,000-2,000 BCE	c. 2,000-450BCE	c. 450BCE-43AD
People living on Morecambe Bay	Hunting and fishing	Farming, Langdale axes produced	Birkrigg Stone Circle built in stone	Iron made in Furness?

Despite this tidy framework, it quickly becomes clear to a non-specialist that our knowledge of what really went on in pre-history is patchy and confusing, so that the Roman invasions of the first century AD are often greeted with a sigh of relief as the beginning of 'proper' history as we know it. However, it would be a pity to write off pre-Roman Furness and fast forward to more organised times if only because the area around Ulverston is relatively abundant in evidence of pre-historic activity, and there is probably a lot more which has either been destroyed or is waiting to be discovered.

Modern archaeologists are of the opinion that there was more continuity and overlap than was previously thought between the neat time periods outlined above. In Furness it is possible that the coming of the Neolithic Age didn't mean that people suddenly started living in one place: even if they now had domesticated animals, they probably continued to move up and down valleys between summer pastures higher up and more sheltered winter settlements. The Gleaston valley, which runs from Urswick Tarn, a few miles from Ulverston, down to the coast may have been such a route, used over many centuries. Conversely, although it was in the Neolithic era that large areas of deciduous woodland were cleared, either for grazing or for crops, there is some evidence that back in Mesolithic times woodland was being burned, perhaps to create glades to make hunting easier. Life for Furness folk in the Neolithic Age was undoubtedly hard and uncomfortable, yet we shouldn't think of these early inhabitants as primitive people blindly scavenging a meagre living in isolation from the rest of the world. This becomes clear when we look at one of the less dramatically obvious wonders of the Neolithic era: the production and distribution of stone axes from Cumbria.

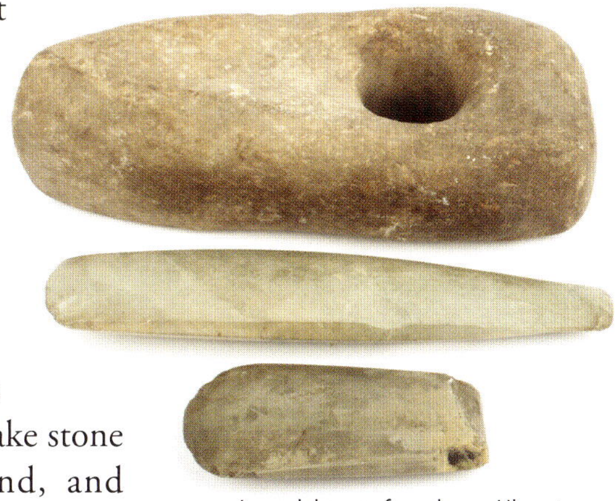

Langdale axes found near Ulverston
Courtesy of The Dock Museum, Barrow-in-Furness

As early as 3800 BCE people started using a particular hard volcanic rock occurring in outcrops high up in the Lakeland fells to make stone axes ideal for clearing woodland, and archaeologists describe the sites where these axes were chipped out as 'axe factories'. The most famous is the Great Langdale axe factory on the steep slopes of Pike o'Stickle, where axes were roughed out before being transported to other sites to be ground and polished. Comparatively large numbers of these axes have been found in Furness, and there may have been a finishing site at Stainton, not far from Ulverston. Moreover the axes have not just been found in Cumbria but as far afield as southern England, the Isle of Man and Ireland, suggesting that people were organising production and long distance trade with all the enthusiasm we associate with much later societies.

The other better known wonder of the Neolithic and early Bronze Ages is of course the stone circles, whose enduring hold over the popular imagination does not diminish. Up to fifty stone circles can be found in Cumbria, making it something of a circle hot spot, and a small yet beautifully situated circle lies not far from Ulverston on the south-east side of Birkrigg Common overlooking Morecambe Bay. We can assume that stone circles were not randomly placed on any suitable piece of land with a nice view. The circles we see today may have been built on sites which were already significant, to mark real or metaphysical border points on established routes where people from different communities met to trade objects and information. The presence of axes in or near some circles suggests that during the hundreds of years of axe production the circles were intimately connected with this trade, and that stone, and later bronze, axes had a profound ritual significance.

The stone circle on Birkrigg is unusual in that it was built in two concentric stone rings, although only the inner ring remains in place today. It was excavated and the finds recorded in the early part of the

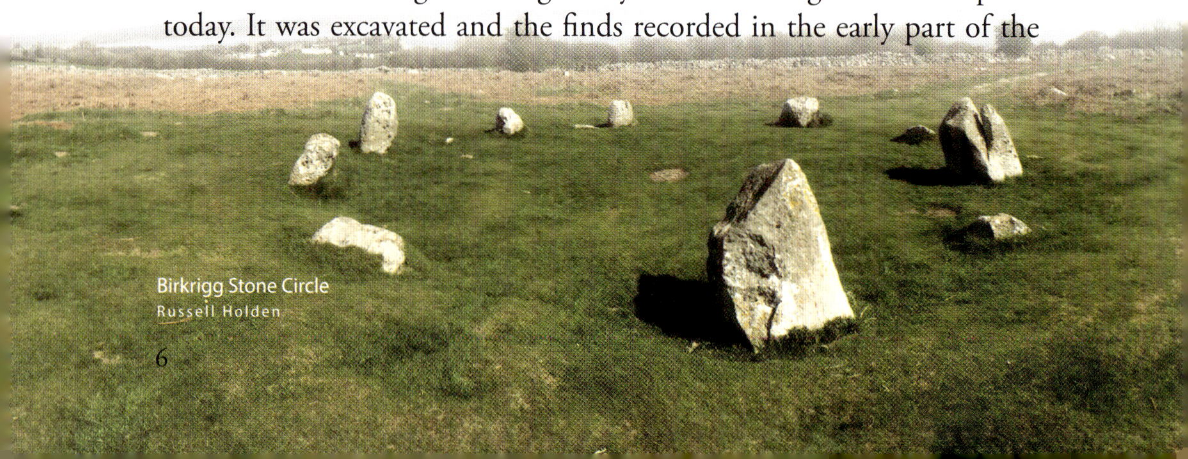

Birkrigg Stone Circle
Russell Holden

last century. In the inner circle two layers of blue-rag cobbles were found under which lay the remains of five cremated burials. Three of the burials appear to have been cremations above shallow pits, one lay under a large stone and the fifth lay in an early Bronze Age urn buried upside down. Three intriguing objects were found between the inner and outer circles: a pear-shaped stone which might have been a pestle; a stone which might have been shaped to use as a palette and a piece of red ochre. It is assumed that these objects were used for rituals, but we may never know why these particular people were buried in the circle, or the relationship, if any, between these burials and other Bronze Age burial sites on the common. If the stone circle site had not been disturbed by this earlier excavation, a modern dig with its more sophisticated methods might have told us more.

Even more enigmatic than the stone circle is the site of Skelmore Heads which lies a short distance north-west of Birkrigg Common, just above Great Urswick. This is marked on Ordnance Survey maps as an ancient fort, and for a long time it was believed to have indeed been a late Bronze Age or Iron Age defended position. Nowadays, in view of a likely Neolithic burial mound situated close by, some archaeologists believe it is a much older site; an enclosed space used over many centuries for gatherings and rituals before being bolstered by earthworks in the later Bronze Age. Archaeological investigations haven't turned up any signs that people lived there, but four stone blades were found in a limestone gryke in the 1950's, and a hoard of

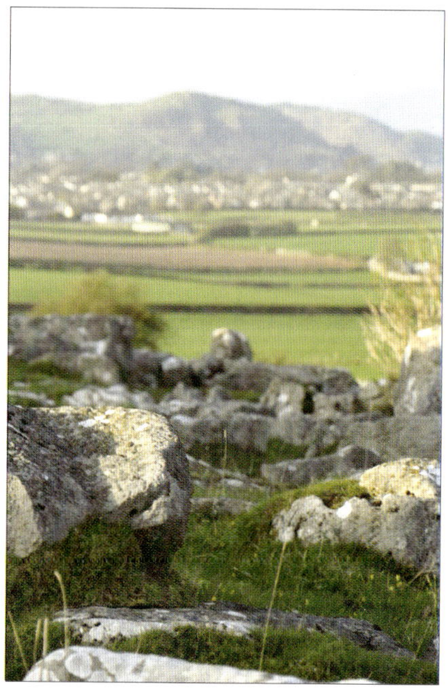

Ulverston from Skelmore Heads

six bronze axes was found in a similar fissure. It is believed that deliberately placing axes in the ground was an important ritual act throughout the Neolithic and Bronze Ages, perhaps making Skelmore Heads another site of ceremonies. If you stand on top of the flattish mound, you can look one way down to Urswick Tarn and beyond to the coast where the Gleaston valley opens up, then turn round 180 degrees to see Ulverston nestled in its hollow. Since the Gleaston valley seems to have been an important route in pre-historic times, it is easy to imagine Skelmore Heads as a meeting place for people coming up from the coast one way and down from the fells the other, a place for exchanging goods and news and cementing bonds through rituals, rather than as a stronghold against attacks.

It would be misleading to think that Morecambe Bay and the Irish Sea were barriers to communications in pre-historic times. Until the coming of the railways it was easier to travel by sea than over land, so the Furness peninsula was slap-bang in the middle of the historic equivalent of the M6. Connections between Furness and the outside world are shown by the trade in axes. During the Neolithic era stone axes were taken to Ireland, and later on it appears that trade went the other way, since three of the bronze axes found at Skelmore Heads are of Irish design, as are

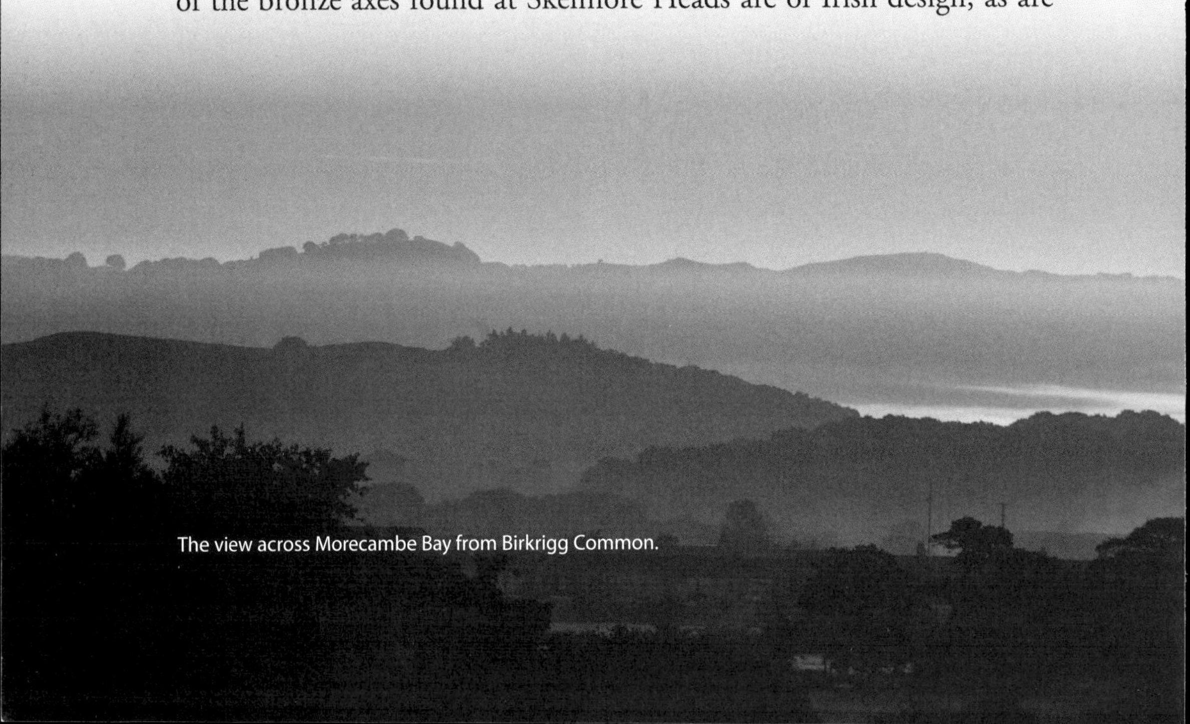

The view across Morecambe Bay from Birkrigg Common.

other bronze axe finds in Furness. The route to Ireland was most likely via the Isle of Man which on a clear day can easily be seen from Birkrigg Common. The view from here is a wonderful panorama all the way around from Black Combe through the Lakeland fells to Ingleborough and the Lancashire moors. In the right conditions the hills of northern Wales can be made out with the naked eye, so pre-historic people would have had a pretty good idea of the world beyond Furness.

Morecambe Bay also has the advantage of its low tides making travel across the sands possible, far more convenient than trudging through boggy mosses all the way around the coast. People in the past had plenty of time to observe the natural world and to work out how to cross the sands safely, so the routes across the bay, which were well-established by the Middle Ages, are probably very ancient indeed. However, archaeologists believe that for some reason, in the later Bronze Age contact with Ireland diminished while contact with eastern Yorkshire increased, and that people living around Morecambe Bay started to develop a distinctive culture of their own. These people were the precursors of the Setantii who occupied these areas during the Iron Age and at the time of the Roman invasions.

Several sites in Furness have been identified as Iron Age settlements, most notably the site of 'stone walls', the remains of an enclosure and a stone round house, near Little Urswick. The big question is whether people in Furness discovered as early as this that substantial amounts of iron ore, which they could turn into iron, lay underground in the peninsula. This ore was haematite, a particularly rich form of ore containing up to 70% metallic iron, much sought after because of the technical difficulty of smelting iron. Unlike other metals, workable iron cannot be made by simply heating ore in a container over a roaring blaze until molten metal can be poured off. All iron ores are oxides, iron

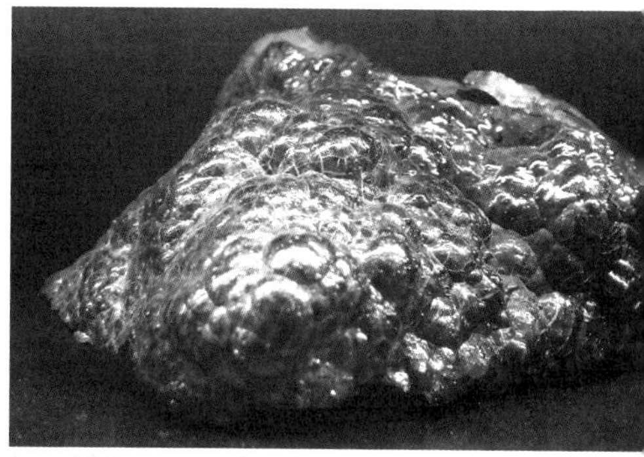

Iron rich haematite, found in Furness and much in demand through the centuries. Library Photo

combined with oxygen, and are also mixed in with other materials such as sand or clay and other chemicals, in various combinations. To make iron, the oxygen and unwanted materials have to be eliminated in a chemical reaction. It is thought a process to achieve this was discovered over four thousand years ago in the Middle East, although this technology probably didn't reach Britain until around 450 BCE. It was found that if small pieces of iron ore were put in a furnace with charcoal, and bellows were used to encourage the charcoal to burn at a high temperature, after several hours a piece of iron would form. This 'direct reduction' process produced iron which was strong in tension and which could be re-heated, hammered and shaped to make tools and weapons far superior to those of bronze. In England the clay furnaces came to be known as bloomeries, with the pieces of wrought iron produced being called blooms, and since bloomeries were small, iron was scarce and highly prized. On the other hand, iron production only needed iron ore, wood for charcoal, and clay, so once the know-how reached Britain, an iron industry was quickly established, mainly in the Weald area of Sussex and Surrey.

Historians haven't always agreed on when iron smelting began in Furness. Thomas West in his '*Antiquities of Furness*', the first real history of the area, believed that iron was made in Furness in pre-Roman and Roman times, while Henry Barber in his Victorian and idiosyncratic '*Furness and Cartmel Notes*' of 1894 gives a couple of examples of how nineteenth century iron miners penetrated 'old men's workings'. In one case they found a 'rude iron implement' and in another a skull which Barber proclaimed was of an Ancient Briton. The magisterial Alfred Fell in his 1908 '*The Early Iron Industry of Furness and District*' seemed quite convinced that no-one smelted iron in Furness before the Normans while, later on, JD Marshall in his 1958 '*Furness and the Industrial Revolution*' cited Urswick 'stone walls' as a place where there is evidence of Iron Age working of iron. It is likely that any pre-Roman, and indeed Roman, iron working sites were obliterated by later medieval mining and smelting activities, so this question remains open. Iron mining and smelting is a thread which runs through the history of Furness, and the drive to exploit this precious resource was certainly one of the factors which shaped Ulverston's history.

No-one so far has been able to settle the debate over the extent of Roman settlement in Furness. When the Romans invaded southern England in 43 AD it is likely that the Setantii of Morecambe Bay had come under the loose control of the Brigantes, the most powerful tribal grouping in northern England, whose base was in the area north of York. Cartimandua, the 'queen' of the Brigantes, appears to have been happy to make an alliance with the Romans, giving them security against an attack from the north while they established themselves in the south. It appears that Cartimandua fell out with her ex-husband who opposed the Romans, so the Brigantes started fighting amongst themselves. This drove the Romans to campaign in the north in 69 AD, again in 71-84 AD and once more between 90 and 130 AD until all of northern England was brought into the Roman Empire. The Romans built roads and a series of forts from Lancaster through the Lakes, notably at Kendal, Ambleside and Hardknott Pass, and until the disintegration of the empire in the fourth century AD, Furness was, nominally at least, part of their world of central heating, good roads and regular baths.

Thomas West's theory that the Romans came to Furness rests on the notion of a Roman road constructed from the point at which the route over the sands came ashore at Conishead through Lindal to Dalton, where a Roman fort was built. Henry Barber picked this up, noting that the Romans used Cartmel and Furness as a short-cut between Lancaster and Carlisle, and even Alfred Fell agreed that the road and the fort at Dalton were Roman. Later historians poured cold water on these ideas, preferring the theory that the Romans ignored Furness altogether. Now historians are inclining back towards the view that even if the fort at Dalton was never Roman, there was certainly contact between Romans and people living in Furness. Before the roads into northern England were finished, the Romans may well have moved up the coast by boat and landed at various points on Morecambe Bay, and since they transported material up Windermere to build the fort at Ambleside, they may have had some kind of camp at Newby Bridge. Later on in the third century AD they rebuilt the fort at Lancaster and organised ships to defend the coast against Irish and Pictish raiders, and it has been suggested that they may have had a base near where Barrow is today, as part of these coastal defences. Roman coins, including one dating from 67 AD, before the major campaigns in the north, have been found in Furness, and recent finds like this highlight how incomplete our knowledge is of Furness during the Roman era. We might think that by the end of the fourth century AD people in Furness were pleased to see the backs of the Romans with their taxes and general bossiness. However, it could have been a case of out of the frying pan and into the fire as England faced new invaders, and any semblance of central government disappeared.

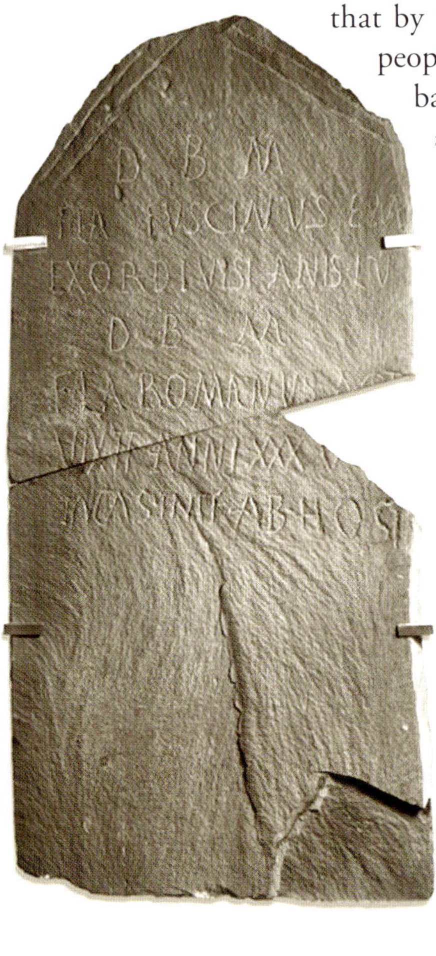

Roman gravestone from Ambleside.
The inscription reads 'To the Gods of the underworld, Flavius Fuscius, retired from the Centurionship, lived 55 years. To the Gods of the underworld, Flavius Romanus, clerk, lived 35 years, killed in the camp by the enemy'.
The Romans may have encamped at Newby Bridge while material was sent up Windermere to build Ambleside Fort.

Gravestone from Ambleside Roman Fort on display at the Armitt Museum and Library,
Courtesy of the Armitt Trust.

• II •

The Birth of Ulverston

From the Dark Ages to the Norman Conquest

For some, the years before 1066 are a historical black hole best left alone until proper history resumed with the Norman Conquest. For others they are the centuries during which, after a series of invasions, an English nation was born and grew to maturity only to be stolen by the thuggish Duke William, who wiped out an entire native aristocracy and turned a population of free-born Englishmen into serfs. Although there is debate about how many Angles, Saxons, Jutes and Frisians flocked into England in the fifth and sixth centuries AD, we know this was a pretty grim time for native Britons unless they managed to escape to one of the Celtic enclaves in Wales, Cornwall or the Cumbrian mountains. There is evidence that the population fell, Romano-British towns were mostly abandoned and woodland cleared in Neolithic times grew back. On the bright side, by the end of the Anglo-Saxon period Ulverston had come into existence, and so had all the English institutions which loom large when we look at Furness in the Middle Ages. An idea of monarchy in which a king had to be consecrated by an archbishop had developed, and there were greater and lesser landowners, courts, shires, hundreds, manors and boroughs. The Church, answerable to the pope in Rome, was strong and wealthy with its bishops, parishes and monasteries, and there were written lists of landholdings in the shires, without which the Normans' Domesday Book could not have been put together. While we are uncertain what kind of people lived where in Furness during Roman times, by contrast we know that just before the Norman conquest places like Ulverston, Aldingham and Dalton were recognisable settlements where land was owned by named individuals, and from then on, we can start to rely on written records rather than educated guesses to work out what was happening.

It is well outside the scope of this book to describe the growth of the Anglo-Saxon kingdoms, but a quick dash through these centuries will help to set the scene for Ulverston's eventual emergence as a medieval borough. Through all this period, and indeed for some time after the Norman Conquest, Furness together with most of what is now Lancashire was a border area, caught first between the Celtic and Anglo-Saxon worlds and later between the Anglo-Saxons, the Norsemen and the Scottish kingdoms. After the Romans left Britain, it is likely that Furness was included in the fifth century British kingdom of Rheged, which stretched from Galloway into Lancashire. However, Rheged didn't last long, since early in the seventh century most of its territory was swallowed up by the Anglian kingdom of Northumbria. Northumbria was one of the most enduring of the Anglo-Saxon kingdoms which rose and fell in a shifting patchwork, as territories expanded under powerful rulers and shrank after their deaths. Even in these times, this seeming chaos of small kingdoms rising and falling might not have been all-embracing. At a local level, the Anglo-Saxons had a definite system of landholding and obligation to whichever overlord happened to gain control. For the Anglo-Saxons, the basic unit of land was the 'hide', notionally the amount of land it took to support a free farmer and his household, probably around 120 acres. Each hide owed the local ruler a tax, which could be in the form of produce like grain or eggs or honey. Hides were grouped together in multiples of ten, and ten hides together might owe something more specialised, like a horse. Ten groups of ten households made up a hundred, an administrative division which survived for centuries.

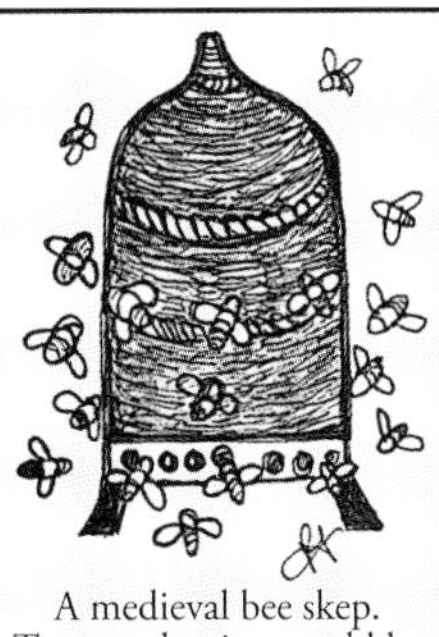

A medieval bee skep. Taxes at the time could be paid with produce such as grain, eggs or honey.

The early seventh century saw a change in the Anglo-Saxon kingdoms: the conversion of kings, queens and their courts to Christianity. This started with King Ethelbert of Kent, who was converted in 597 by Augustine, sent to England by Pope Gregory. Ethelbert gave land in Canterbury to the Church for a cathedral, and Augustine became the first archbishop of Canterbury. Other Anglo-Saxon kings, including the rulers of Northumbria, followed suit and became Christians in the following decades. However, Celtic Christianity, as opposed to the Roman Church, also seems to have been spreading in Wales, Scotland and north-west England, especially since the founding of a monastery on Iona by St Columba in the 560's. The Roman Church was hierarchical, with the pope at the top, then bishops running dioceses from cathedrals in the middle and priests running parishes at the bottom. Celtic Christianity seems to have been looser, based around wandering saints and monks who formed small cells and informal monasteries, and the two different traditions followed different rites. A synod was convened in Whitby in 664 to thrash out the differences between these two versions of Christianity, and since the most powerful figures argued for accepting the pope's authority and following the practices of the Roman Church, this is what happened. The upshot was that Anglo-Saxon rulers began to use the literate clergy to write down laws based on those in areas of Europe where the pope had authority, and although it was to be centuries before England was fully politically united, the Church was a constant throughout its different kingdoms. The Church needed kings for land and protection, and kings needed the Church to give them status and to provide educated men to help them run their little kingdoms. So, the Roman Church started to gain the wealth and influence it enjoyed in England until the reign of Henry VIII. Bishoprics and parishes were established, and in Northumbria the great monasteries at Lindisfarne and Jarrow became centres of learning and culture equal to anywhere else in seventh and eighth century Europe.

How these developments played out in Furness is a matter of conjecture, partly arrived at by looking at place-names. The word for 'church' in Celtic languages is 'ecles', taken from the Latin 'ecclesia', and place-names which include 'ecles' or its variations, like Ecclerigs near Broughton-in-Furness, are interpreted as places where there was a Celtic Christian place of worship. Perhaps a transition between Celtic Christianity and the Roman Church in the area can be glimpsed. One of the most intriguing Anglo-Saxon finds in Furness is a fragment of a stone cross discovered in the church at Great Urswick during restoration work in 1911.

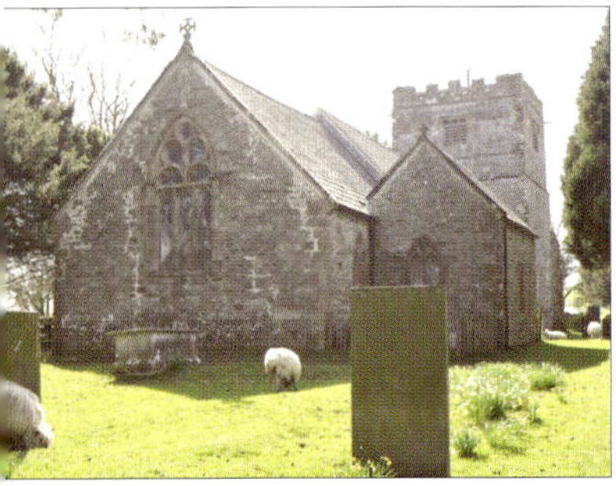

The church at Great Urswick which may have been a Celtic Christian centre.

This fragment has a panel of runic inscription above the top halves of two sculptured figures, their bottom halves and the rest of the cross having been lost. This discovery has been exhaustively analysed by historian Steve Dickinson, who published his conclusions in *'The Beacon on the Bay'*. He believes that Great Urswick was the site of a major Irish/Celtic Christian monastery which was 'taken over' by the Roman church some time after the Synod of Whitby. Whether or not one agrees with his conclusions, it is likely that the Roman church moved into sites where Celtic Christians had been active. In non-religious settlements, places ending in 'ham' and 'tun', such as Ulverston and Aldingham, which were both in existence by 1066, denote Anglo-Saxon settlements. We don't know when these settlements first appeared in Furness, and if Anglo-Saxon settlers established new centres, or took over existing Celtic

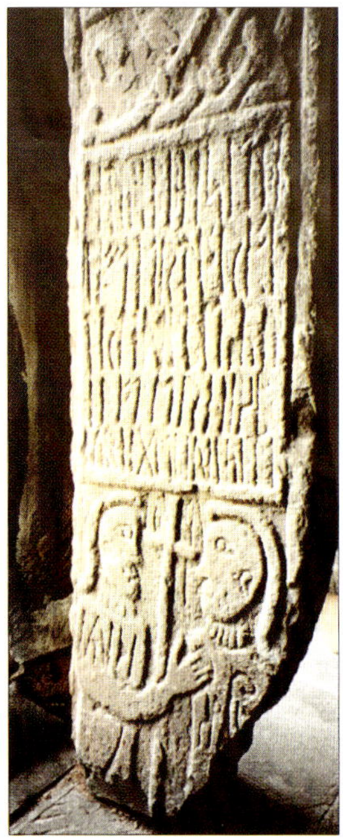

Runic panel and figures from the cross discovered at Great Urswick church in 1911.
Courtesy of Steve Dickinson

landholdings and renamed them, while keeping to boundaries which had been in place for centuries. It is generally accepted that Ulverston is named after a person, and was the 'tun' of an Ulf or Ulfere. If this isn't vague enough, everything got even more complicated with the arrival of the Vikings in the ninth century.

By the beginning of the ninth century, the Anglo-Saxon kingdoms of Northumbria, Wessex, Mercia and East Anglia were wealthy and internationally respectable. This relatively peaceful state of affairs was upset when the Vikings came on the scene. We tend to use the word 'Viking' pejoratively to describe the people from Denmark and Norway who wreaked havoc during raids on the English coast before settling in the country. A number of historians are of the opinion that the Vikings have been given a bad press. They weren't wild men hell-bent on pillage, rather they were skilled farmers and craftspeople and exceptional navigators and traders, whose only crime was to run out of space in their homelands. The truth may be that they were both, since the word 'Viking' means 'pirate', which doesn't describe ethnic origin like the word 'Dane'. It is thought that Danes and Norwegians sent out their surplus testosterone-charged young men to raid wealthier lands to bring back cash and loot. If they could, they settled down to make new colonies. A generation later, another crop of second sons and wild young things set out, and the process would start again. However well-behaved the Danes and Norwegians were in their own homes, this was of no comfort to the monks of Lindisfarne and Jarrow in 793 and 794 when the Vikings stormed in, murdering, laying waste, destroying precious books and carrying off treasure. Viking raids on England continued through the ninth century and culminated in 865 when a huge Danish army led by Halfdan and his ominously-named brother, Ivar the Boneless, invaded East Anglia. Saxon resistance crumbled, the kingdoms of East Anglia, Mercia and Northumbria were overrun and in the end, only Alfred, the ruler of Wessex and famous cake-burner, was left to hold the fort. After Alfred defeated the Danes in 878, the Danish leader Guthrum converted to Christianity, yet the Danes remained in England from the Thames to the Tees in the area which became known as the Danelaw. Alfred's house of Wessex became in effect the royal house of the English, and for over a century, until the Danish Cnut became king of England, power ebbed and flowed between the Wessex kings, the Danes and their client 'kings' in the Danelaw, the Scots, and Norsemen from Ireland.

After the Danes had overrun Northumbria, they installed a client local 'king', and though later Wessex Saxon kings received homage from the rulers of Northumbria, areas in the Danelaw operated a separate administrative and legal system. Who exerted meaningful control in Furness in all this confusion is anyone's guess. In the Danelaw, the Saxon 'hide' became a 'carucate', and the division of a shire, the 'hundred', became a 'wapentake'. Since carucates and wapentakes turn up in Furness in later records, it must have been part of the Danelaw at some point. Although it is well-known that Norsemen settled in Furness and Cumbria, these people were probably not Danes but Norwegians by origin. Norwegians had raided Ireland in the ninth century, eventually founding a Norse settlement at what is now Dublin, and from here they

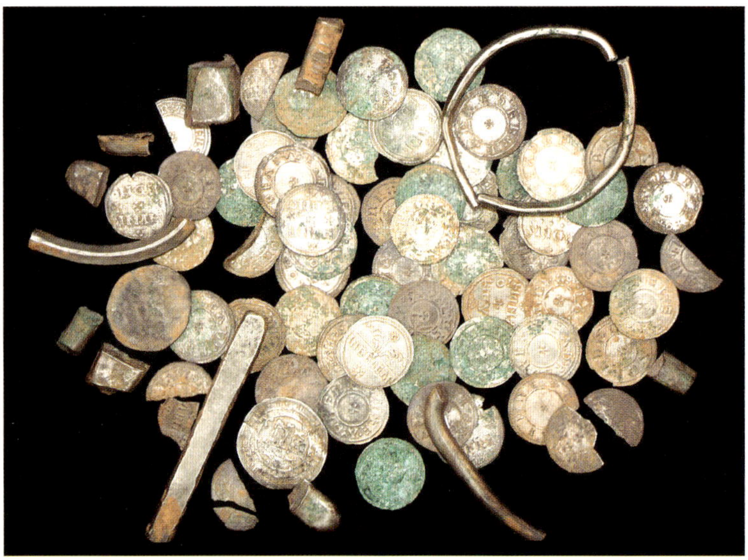

The Viking Hoard of silver coins, ingots and arm-rings or ring money found in Furness in 2011.
Courtesy of The Dock Museum, Barrow-in-Furness

launched raids on the Irish Sea coast of Lancashire. There is a story that in around 902 AD, the local ruler of Mercia and his wife negotiated a deal with Norsemen from Ireland allowing them to settle in Lancashire. Since the Irish made periodic attempts to boot the Norsemen out, this also encouraged them to try their luck in north-west England.

Whether they took over Anglo-Saxon settlements in Furness by force or were given land that was underused, they left a legacy of place-names. Ireby and Ireleth are likely places where Irish Norsemen settled down. Words like thwaite, beck, dale, fell, force and nes (a headland) are Norse, as are place-name endings like erg, scale, set and side, which all indicate grazing land, hence Satterthwaite, 'the clearing by the summer pasture'. Lying between the great Norse settlements of York and Dublin, Furness must have been drawn into a web of trading and cultural links, and the recent discovery of a Viking hoard in the area is evidence of this.

Distracted as we are by the Norman Conquest of 1066, it is easy to overlook our Norse connections and the fact that the Anglo-Saxon era ended in 1016 when the Danish ruler, Cnut, became King of England. This subjugation of England into the Norse empire, and the forging of the fateful link between the English crown and the Dukes of Normandy, who were themselves descended from Rollo, a Viking raider, were results of the reign of the luckless Wessex king, Aethelred the Unready (978 – 1016). ('Unready' meant 'badly advised' rather than always running late.) During his reign invading Danes came back with a vengeance. Aethelred was forced to pay them off with the notorious Danegeld, even fleeing to Normandy for a time, where he married the Duke's daughter, Emma. Aethelred's handing over of massive sums of cash to the Danes was of no avail, and on his death the Danish Cnut (1016 – 1035) was crowned king of England. England might have

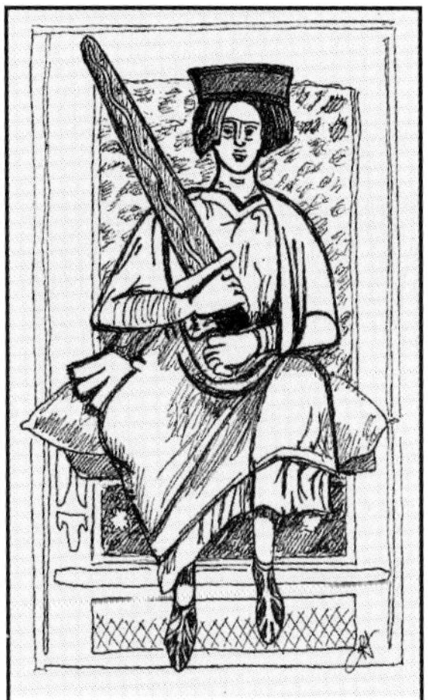

Aethelred the Unready.
His death in 1016 marked the end of the Anglo-Saxon era.

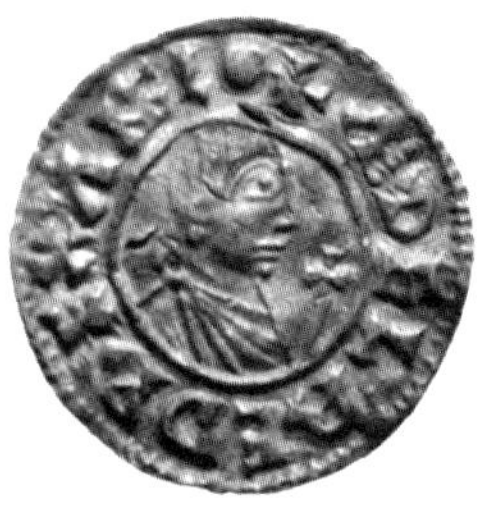

Aethelred

Silver pennies of Aethelred the Unready and Edward the Confessor. The Anglo-Saxons were the first to produce the silver penny which constituted the primary unit of coinage in England for approximately 500 years.

Library Photos

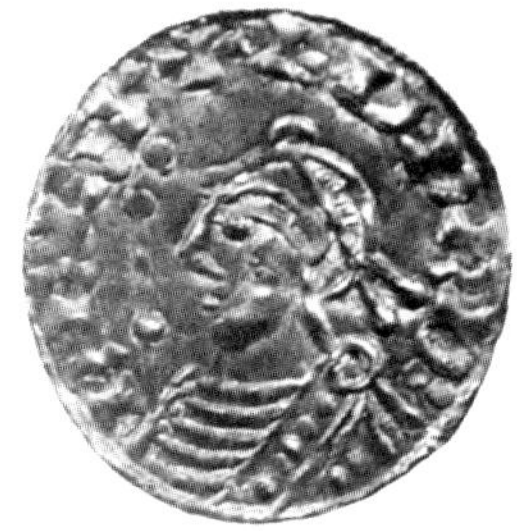

Edward the Confessor

remained in the Norse empire if Cnut's sons hadn't died in 1040 and 1042 respectively, at which point the English turned back to the house of Wessex and elected Edward, the son of Aethelred and Emma of Normandy as king. Edward the Confessor (1042 – 1066) was half-Norman, had spent most of his life at the Norman court, and brought a posse of French-speaking courtiers across the Channel with him.

This didn't go down at all well with English nobles, such as the powerful Godwine and his sons. One son, Harold, succeeded his father as Earl of Wessex, and another, Tostig, became Earl of Northumbria, the earldom which included Furness. It was a falling out between these two brothers which had momentous consequences. The Northumbrians, who accused Tostig of murder, marched south in force demanding his removal, and Harold took their side, sending his brother into exile.

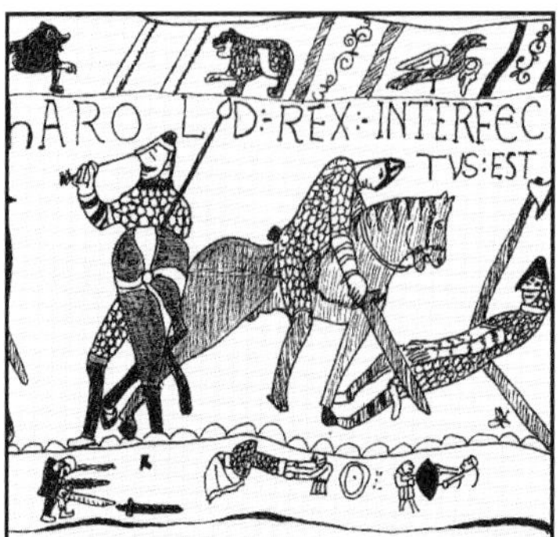

Harold at the Battle of Hastings from the Bayeux Tapestry

This came back to bite Harold when Edward the Confessor died in 1066. The Norman version of events was that the childless Edward the Confessor had promised Duke William of Normandy the English crown, and that Harold had acquiesced. This doesn't seem to have concerned the English royal council, the witan, which elected Harold king and ignored William's furious message when he heard the news. The rest of the story is well known. While William was breathing fire on the French side of the channel waiting for the wind to change, Tostig and the Norwegian Harold Hadrada, who also had an obscure claim to the English crown, landed in Northumbria and took York. Harold rushed his army north and defeated Tostig and Harold Hadrada at Stamford Bridge, only to hear that William had managed to cross the Channel. One can only feel sorry for Harold who had to hotfoot it back to the south coast, where it was no wonder that William won the decisive battle near Hastings, the final blow to Anglo-Saxon England.

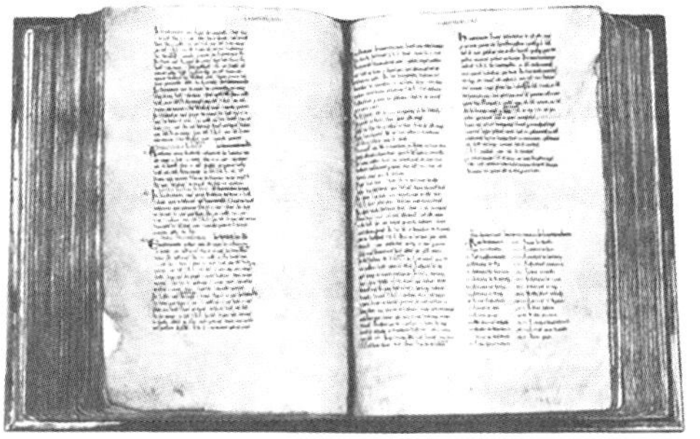
The Domesday Book

The best picture we have of Furness before 1066 comes from William the Conqueror's Domesday Book. Domesday Book was not only a survey of who owned what in 1086, it also listed settlements with their size, owners and rating for tax during Edward the Confessor's reign before the Conquest. Domesday shows that although we know so little about events in Furness during the turmoil of these struggles for power, people there were not left to themselves in some kind of primitive anarchy until the Normans came along bringing law and order. In the tenth and eleventh centuries England was wealthy, which is why it was so attractive to Danes and Normans, and its rulers had developed efficient systems to exploit this wealth, an efficiency spurred on by the Danes' demands. Kings had a 'shire-reeve' or sheriff in each shire to organise collecting taxes and to preside over the shire court where the king's justice was dispensed, and kings sent these sheriffs their orders in royal writs sealed with wax. Kings also had a clerical staff to keep proper records, mainly rolls with lists of the hides or carucates in the different shires, noting which lands the king personally owned and how much tax was owed from each landholding. These Anglo-Saxon records were probably copied by the Norman compilers of the Domesday Book.

In the Domesday Book the 'vills' or agricultural settlements in Furness during Edward the Confessor's reign were counted as part of Yorkshire because Lancashire didn't exist as a county until the late twelfth century. These pre-Conquest settlements fall into two categories. The first is a whole string of vills belonging to the manor of 'Hougun', whose exact location is unknown although the consensus seems to be that it was somewhere near Dalton. Some places mentioned, like Dalton, Roose, Newton, Leece, Gleaston, Marton, Stainton and Pennington still exist today, while others like Hart and 'another Leece' have disappeared without trace. One vill was Oregrave, a hint that iron ore was being mined before the Norman Conquest. The manor of Hougun stretched to the settlements of Whicham, Bootle and Kirksanton in Cumberland, and at the time the list was compiled the whole lot belonged to Earl Tostig, presumably while he was Earl of Northumbria before he was sent into exile. The second category is settlements which didn't belong to this large manor. These were Aldingham, where someone called Earnwulf had six carucates, Ulverston where Thorulf also had six carucates, Kirkby where Dubhan had six carucates and Dendron whose owner is not named. One odd feature is that these separate settlements are not listed straight after the manor of Hougun. Between the two categories is a list of places including Kendal, Helsington, Old Hutton and Burton in Kendal, which suggests that administratively speaking Furness wasn't treated as a discrete area. This continued after the Norman Conquest, when the barons of Kendal had claims on Ulverston. Ulverstonians today who are not overjoyed at coming under the Kendal dominated South Lakeland District Council should perhaps blame a connection which was made many centuries ago.

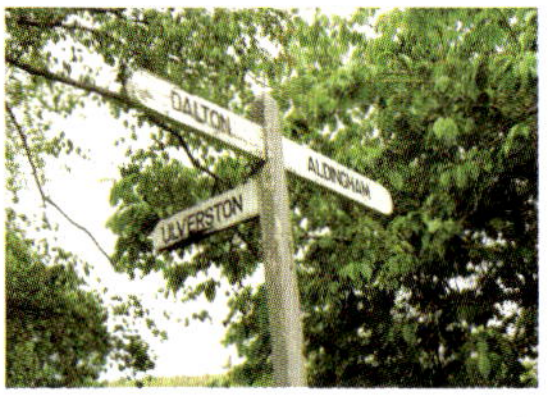

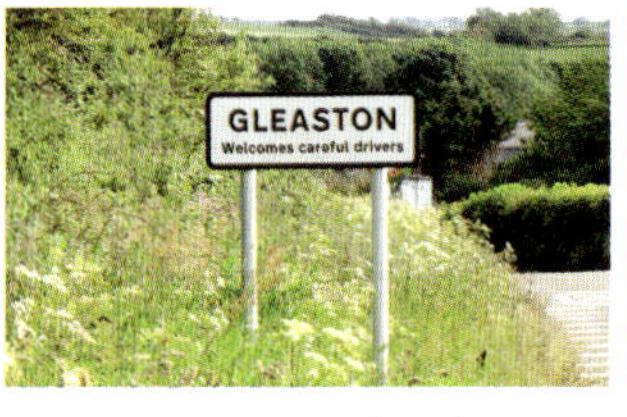

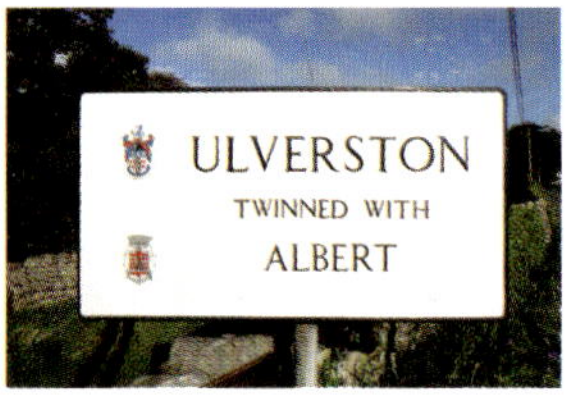

Many settlements in Furness pre-date the Norman Conquest,
with the suffixes 'ham' and 'ton' denoting Anglo-Saxon settlements.

The Domesday Book listings show how the countryside had become more organised by later Anglo-Saxon times, with villages and manors having developed from the original pattern of independent farmers or 'ceorls' each having their own separate hide.

While it is easy to identify Earl Tostig as a pre-conquest landowner, identifying Thorulf of Ulverston is another matter, and it is usually assumed that he was a local 'thegn' (landowner). It is also nearly impossible to say whether Ulverston before the Norman Conquest was more than a few houses and agricultural buildings. In the tenth and eleventh centuries thegns founded parish churches to serve their households and workers, and it has been suggested that half the parish churches in existence in 1700 were founded before 1066. It is almost certain that the large Ulverston parish, which extended from the Leven estuary to Langdale, existed before the Conquest, and while it is usually accepted that the town's parish church is a Norman foundation, it would not be surprising if a church of some kind existed in Ulverston before this.

By the end of the twelfth century Ulverston had become a medieval borough, a type of settlement originating in the fortified strongholds or 'burhs' established by King Alfred. Paid for by local landowners, they were built to provide safe defendable centres in case the Danes turned up uninvited. Landowners put up buildings in the burhs on plots of land called tenements, using them to store produce which they could then sell. In the tenth and eleventh centuries some of these burhs grew to become small towns with regular markets, and there is a school of thought that many markets, like Ulverston, which received formal charters in the thirteenth century are in fact much older. It may be that Ulverston, positioned on a cross-roads and close to the shore for easy communication, had a church and a market before the Norman Conquest, and that there was more continuity between Anglo-Saxon and Norman times than is usually assumed.

• III •

EARLY NORMAN FURNESS

By 1200 Ulverston was a borough with an established woollen industry and by 1300 it had an official market charter, so was well on the way to becoming a recognisable town. The story of Ulverston's growth in the centuries after the Norman Conquest is often overlooked. This may be because of the pre-eminence of Furness Abbey, which was founded in 1127, and also the tendency to ignore the dynamism of the Middle Ages. The Middle Ages were more than a procession of interchangeable and forgettable kings, knights galloping around in armour and muddy serfs toiling away at the bottom of the heap: they were a time of economic and political change, and this is reflected in Ulverston's development.

At first, the Norman Conquest seemed a complete disaster for much of northern England. Having crowned himself king in Westminster Abbey on Christmas Day 1066, William returned to Normandy, and as soon as his back was turned, the English started muttering behind it.

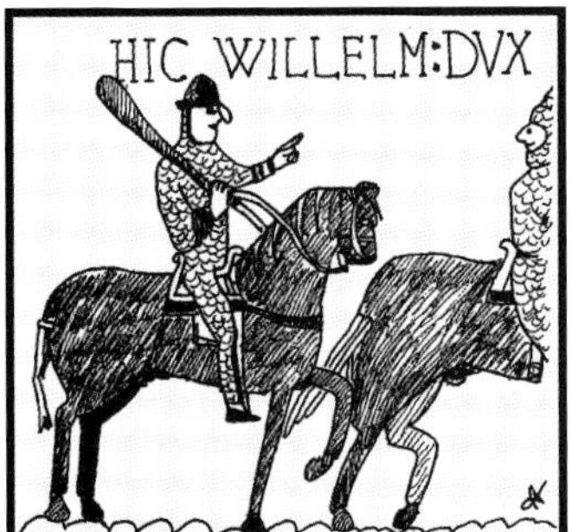

William the Conqueror. From the Bayeux Tapestry

People perhaps hoped that his reign, like Harold's, would be a temporary blip before normal service was resumed under the Wessex kings. In 1069, a great-grandson of Aethelred the Unready, Aedgar the Aetheling, who had actually been proclaimed king in 1066 but never crowned, came out of exile in Scotland to York to lead William's opponents in Northumbria. They were soon disabused of any notion that William would be reluctant to defend his conquest. Back from Normandy, he moved north, defeated Aedgar and his allies, and proceeded to lay waste the area between York and the Tees with unprecedented ferocity. Villages were burned, crops and food stores destroyed, livestock killed and ordinary people left to starve. This was the 'Harrying of the North', which even in those brutal times was seen as a terrible act, leaving village after village to be recorded as 'laid waste' in the Domesday Book. After snuffing out other opposition in Cheshire and the Fens, William set in motion one of the biggest land grabs ever. Anglo-Saxon and Anglo-Danish landowners were replaced by Normans, Flemings and Frenchmen who wanted their reward for sticking their necks out and supporting William's less than watertight claim to the English crown. Moreover, native English culture was systematically suppressed, as Anglo-Saxon churches were demolished and rebuilt, and most Anglo-Saxon church feast days abolished. To stamp their authority, Norman landowners built castles, usually a mound (motte) and an outer compound (bailey), from where they could enforce their rule over the natives. Finally, in 1085 William began the survey which resulted in that great gift to historians, the Domesday Book of 1086, an exhaustive survey of exactly who had owned what in England before his conquest and who owned it now. William died in France in 1087 having seen through twenty one years of profound change in England, although there is little evidence of any of this change in Furness.

There is no evidence that Furness was 'harried', indeed we cannot be sure that a single Norman set foot there during the reign of William the Conqueror. Although the entries for Furness in the Domesday Book come under the heading 'The King's Lands in Yorkshire', the book doesn't mention any Norman, French or Flemish landowners, and only gives details for pre-Conquest settlements. Some older books about Ulverston say that Domesday names a Gospatric as the holder of six carucates in Ulverston and that he was a Norman. However, the 'Oulston' that this entry refers to is a settlement elsewhere in Yorkshire, not Ulverston in Furness. It is unclear, therefore, how much authority William the Conqueror actually had in Furness, especially since much of what is now

Cumbria was claimed by the Scottish kings. It is possible that the Domesday Book compilers copied entries for Furness from the Anglo-Saxon records and hoped for the best.

It was probably not until the reign of William's successor in England, his son, William II (1087 – 1100), usually known as William Rufus, that the Normans gained any meaningful control in Furness. Although William Rufus was nagged by the church for running a degenerate court and forced the country to pay a high price in taxes for his general extravagance, he led a successful expedition north in 1092, driving Malcolm III of Scotland out of Westmorland and Cumberland, and building a castle at Carlisle to move the border with Scotland to beyond the Solway. Even after this, there is not much evidence that Normans found their way into Furness, and working out who was given land there is difficult. One version suggests that William Rufus granted Roger de Poitou, who already held the area between the Mersey and the Ribble, another block of land north of the Ribble as far as the Lune. Roger de Poitou built a castle at Lancaster and from there he was also able to take control of Cartmel and Furness, using the long-established route over Morecambe Bay. For the first time, all the land from the Mersey to Furness was held by one major overlord. This holding, which became known as the 'Honor of Lancaster' was the basis for the future county of Lancashire, and because of this grant Furness became part of the county, where it remained until the counties were reorganised in 1974. We have little evidence that Roger de Poitou, who held land all over England and in France, ever came to Furness in person, but in any case he lost all his land in England in 1102. When William Rufus was shot in a controversial hunting 'accident' in 1100, his younger brother Henry rushed to get himself crowned king in England, rather to the annoyance of William the Conqueror's eldest son, Robert Curthose, who, so far, had had to make do with being Duke of Normandy. Roger de Poitou picked the wrong side when he supported Robert Curthose's bid for the English crown, and Henry I (1100 – 1135) confiscated his English estates, including the Honor of Lancaster, which he kept for himself for the moment.

To complicate matters, the Norman barons of Kendal claimed lordship in Ulverston, and encouraged its medieval development, although the origins of this claim are obscure. The first Norman baron of Kendal was Ivo de Taillebois. William Rufus is said to have granted Ivo a huge estate which included Amounderness (the area between the Ribble and the Lune), the barony of Kendal and the south west corner of Cumberland, and Ivo may have latched on to a pre-Conquest link between Ulverston and Kendal.

It was not until Henry I's reign that the first identifiable non-Anglo-Saxon or Anglo-Danish landholder appeared in Furness, and he had no discernible connections with the barons of Kendal . This was Michael le Fleming, whose name is a bit of a giveaway to his origins, to whom Henry granted the manor of Aldingham at some time between 1107 and 1111. Aldingham manor took up a large chunk of the southern part of the Furness peninsula, extending on the coast from the Walney channel around Rampside to Aldingham and inland to Sunbrick and Great Urswick, and either the original Michael or his son built a motte at Aldingham.

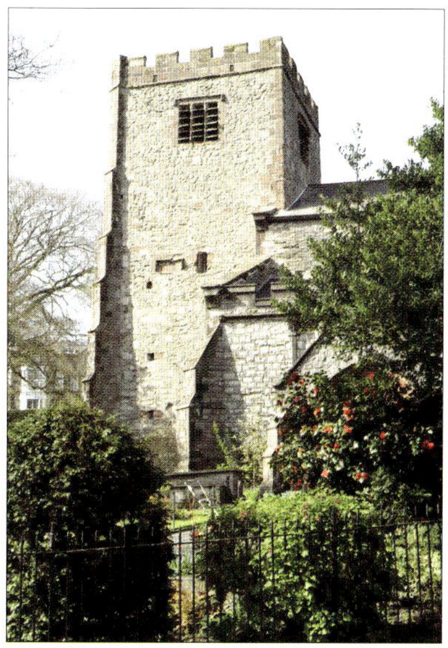

Ulverston Parish Church, believed to have been founded in 1111.

It is not known for certain who originally built Ulverston parish church which, by long tradition, was founded in 1111, and has a Norman doorway. There was a Saxon church in Great Urswick, a church which is sometimes described as the 'mother' church of Ulverston's. Perhaps Michael le Fleming was the landlord who rebuilt them both to emphasise a break from the past. Alternately, it could have been Ivo de Taillebois or one of his successors as barons of Kendal who was the Norman founder of Ulverston church. Interestingly, like the church at Great

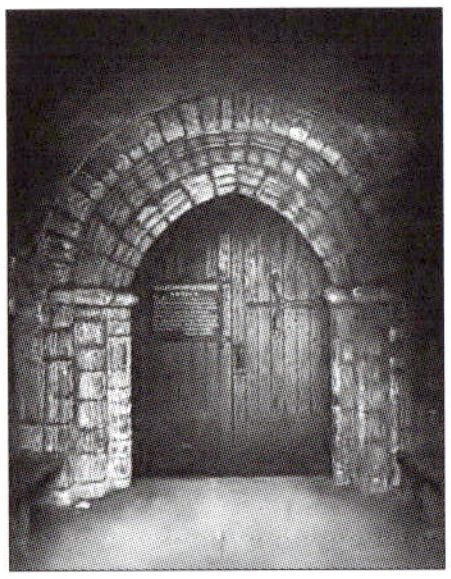

Norman doorway
Ulverston Parish Church

Urswick, the parish church in Ulverston was built on the edge of a tarn. This might be a coincidence, or it might be that these were two similar ancient religious sites by stretches of water, taken over by the Christian church, first Celtic, then Anglo-Saxon and then Norman.

The picture of landholding in Furness becomes clearer after 1127, the year of the foundation of Furness Abbey. The significance of this foundation, and the power that came to be exercised by the abbots over the peninsula, cannot be overestimated. In the twelfth and thirteenth centuries, as the abbey grew to become one of the largest monasteries in England, it was not only the dominant landowner in Furness but also an institution which strived to preserve a monopoly over legal and economic life in the area. It was during these centuries that Ulverston was established as a medieval borough, and in the records we catch a fleeting glimpse of an ongoing struggle between Ulverston's secular landlords and the abbey over who had control of what, the kind of struggle between the Church and laymen which was going on all over England.

With its four-hundred year history of empire-building, interminable land disputes and sometimes less than charitable acts, Furness Abbey is worthy of a full volume to itself. It was founded by Count Stephen of Boulogne and Mortain, a grandson of William the Conqueror through his daughter, Adele, who had married Stephen of Blois. Count Stephen was brought up at the English court, and was a favourite nephew of Henry I, especially

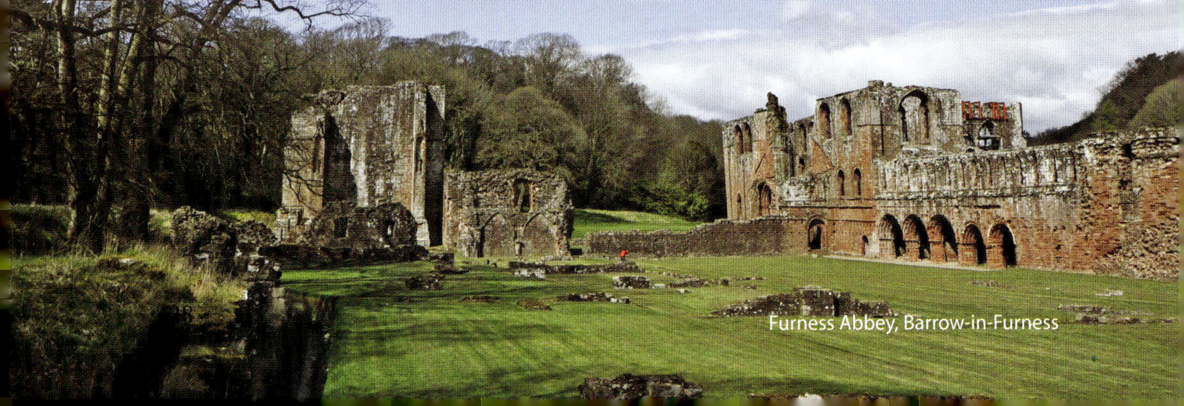

Furness Abbey, Barrow-in-Furness

after Henry's only legitimate son was drowned in the wreck of the White Ship in 1120. Henry I granted Stephen the Honor of Lancaster, adding to the estates he already held in England and those he owned in France, which had been increased by his marriage to Matilda, the heiress to Boulogne. Before 1127, Count Stephen had given land outside Preston to a group of monks from the monastery at Savigny in France, and he then gave this group most of Furness for a new monastery. Like other monasteries in the Middle Ages, Furness Abbey was not so much a place of solitary piety and prayer as a complex business and cultural enterprise. The Church was an integral part of any medieval European regime. It was a great landowner, owning over a fifth of the land in England, and its upper echelons in Normandy and England were a home for Norman aristocrats, making it difficult sometimes to see much difference between fighting bishops like Odo, William the Conqueror's half-brother, and other leading magnates. Kings, who needed literate advisors and administrators, would not have been able to rule without the Church's co-operation, and since the Church was almost the only source of education, it was clerics who were the lawyers, accountants and secretaries in an England where land and tax arrangements were heading for mind-boggling complexity. Kings and magnates, like Count Stephen, also founded monasteries in part as a penance for their undoubted sins, believing that having clerics dedicated to praying for your soul and the souls of your relations was a necessity rather than a luxury. However, although the reforming movement in monasticism placed an emphasis on persuading rulers and aristocrats to found monasteries in isolated areas, this was not necessarily a withdrawal from the world and its temptations. Instead, it could be seen as part of a drive to bring outlying areas into the civilised world and to exploit their resources, rather like multinational corporations moving into developing countries.

A glance at Stephen's charter for Furness Abbey shows that he was not giving a few monks a quiet corner for a life of prayer and contemplation; it is more like a licence to take control of Furness and its potential riches. This charter gives the abbot the forest of Walney and Furness (not forgetting the hunting rights), Dalton, Stephen's lordship of Furness with its inhabitants and everything in it, including Ulverston, and a fishery at Lancaster. Stephen specifically excluded Michael le Fleming's land from his grant, but otherwise the abbot was given the rest of Furness and, which is equally telling, the rights to hold a court, raise taxes on wheat ground in his mills, try peasants and administer justice to thieves. These were extensive powers, and the civil war which followed Henry I's death in 1135 probably enabled the abbot to consolidate them.

Although Henry I had made vigorous attempts to impose royal justice and centralise power in England, this was threatened by the uncertainty over who would succeed him to the throne. None of his string of illegitimate sons could realistically be considered, and his only other legitimate child after his son William drowned was his daughter, another Matilda (not to be confused with Stephen's wife), who had married first the emperor Henry V and then Geoffrey, heir to the Count of Anjou. Henry decided that Matilda, usually called the Empress Matilda after her first marriage, should be his heir, and he insisted that all the leading nobles, including Stephen, take an oath that they would accept her as ruler of England after his death. However, as soon as Henry died, Stephen broke this oath and claimed the English crown for himself, even though he was on shaky ground since he had an older brother, and, oath-breaking aside, was hampered by a lack of the inner ruthlessness vital for success as a medieval king. The following nineteen years were dubbed 'The Anarchy' by Victorian historians as England suffered a protracted civil war between Stephen and Matilda, during which the nobles frequently swopped sides, and in one memorable episode Matilda made a daring escape from Oxford in the dead of winter, wrapped in a white cloak for camouflage. It wasn't so much the fighting between the two sides which was the problem as the breakdown of royal authority and the dearth of proper justice. The crown lost its monopoly

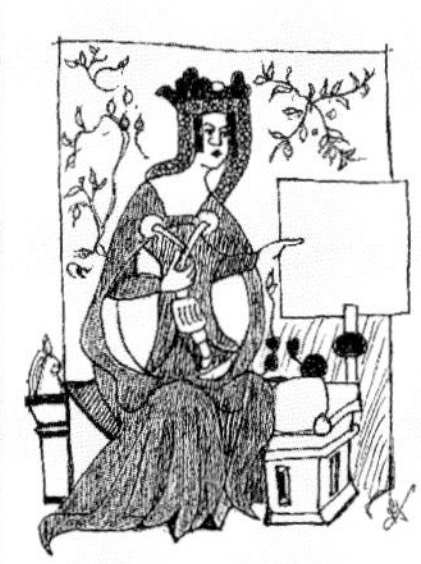

The Empress Matilda who fought Stephen for the crown of England

in minting coins, and some landholders built unlicensed castles, pillaged the countryside and terrorised its inhabitants so that, in the famous quote, 'men said openly that Christ slept and his saints'.

The civil war affected Furness directly when David I of Scotland took advantage of the conflict to move into northern England. Although he lost the Battle of the Standards in 1137, he succeeded in the following peace negotiations when Stephen granted him the former earldom of Northumbria. Thus, for nearly two decades Furness was part of the Scottish kingdom. While there is no reason to assume that people were any worse off under David I than they would have been under Stephen or Matilda or a rapacious baron, it means that during its formative years Furness Abbey was not under the English crown's authority, and the abbot could probably do as he pleased. Maybe we shouldn't be too indignant about Furness being handed over to the Scottish king for a while. At the time, Europe didn't consist of sovereign states with fixed borders, and the concept of nationality as we understand it didn't exist. David I of Scotland had been brought up at the English court, and when he succeeded to the Scottish crown he gave estates in southern Scotland to Normans like Robert de Brus (or Bruce) who also had land in Brix in Normandy and Cleveland in Yorkshire. A family like the de Brus's would owe allegiance to the English king for their English estates, to the Scottish king for their Scottish land and to whoever ruled Normandy for their French lands, a pattern which continued down the centuries. Furness Abbey certainly continued to have very close ties with Scotland in the twelfth and thirteenth centuries, with the abbot being consecrated at Melrose in 1211.

The monks of Furness also quickly built up links across the Irish Sea. In 1134, before the civil war in England, King Olaf granted land on the Isle of Man to the abbey for a daughter house, and he also gave the abbey control over who should be bishop of a new islands diocese, that of 'Sodor' (or the Hebrides) and Man. Furness Abbey had a market on the Isle of Man, and as late as 1228 a King of Man, Reginald, was buried in the abbey. At its height, the abbey's influence stretched all the way from

Yorkshire, where it had tracts of grazing land, to Ireland, where it had four daughter houses. The more we look at it, the more Furness Abbey appears as the centre of a network of trading and cultural ties which may have existed before, in the days of Norse dominance. The one early potential glitch in the abbey's autonomy was in 1148, when three other English Savigniac monasteries joined the Cistercian order, and the abbot, Peter, not happy with this development, hurried to Rome to appeal against Furness Abbey following suit. His case was lost, and under a new abbot, Richard of Bayeux, the abbey became Cistercian, although this doesn't seem to have made much practical difference to the abbots' status as virtually independent rulers in Furness.

The civil war in England limped to an end in 1153 when Stephen accepted Henry, the son of the Empress Matilda and Geoffrey of Anjou, as his heir, and on Stephen's death in 1154, Henry was crowned king at Westminster. The first Plantagenet king, Henry II (1154 -1189) was a very different kettle of fish from Stephen. Immensely charismatic, intelligent, energetic and prone to awe-inspiring tantrums, he was determined to restore the power of the monarchy in England as well as to keep hold of the huge swathes of territory he had inherited in France from his father. His wife, Eleanor of Aquitaine, was equally formidable. Married to Louis VII of France, she had led troops on the Second Crusade and was to govern Aquitaine independently. When she clapped eyes on the much younger Henry at the French court in 1151 she fell in love on the spot, divorced Louis and married this short, red-headed dynamo, eventually bearing him eight children. Although in later years this was a family for whom the term dysfunctional could have been invented, at their zenith Henry and Eleanor were the original power couple of Europe, ruling from Scotland to the Pyrenees and organising their domains with a relentless attention to detail, an attention which was felt in Furness.

Once he was king, Henry II moved quickly to assert his authority over the magnates who had had a free rein in the civil war, forcing them to surrender their unlicensed castles. He then took advantage of the death of David I of Scotland to regain the north of England, including Furness. He emphasised that it was the king who was the source of justice in England, developing the Chancery as an office where standardised royal orders or writs were written out, sealed with his seal and sent all over the country, so that his order still prevailed while he was rushing around on the continent. Where Henry II eventually came unstuck was in his efforts to establish the king's authority over the Church. The Church had its own system of law, canon law, and medieval minds had to mull over the knotty problem of the line between the king's justice and that of the Church, especially since the Church was an international body with the Pope at its head. The Church held that if a cleric committed a crime, he should be dealt with by the Church, not by civil courts, and neither was it at all clear who should arbitrate in a dispute, about land for example, between a layman and a cleric. Henry II wanted jurisdiction over all disputes about land and taxation, and control of the Church became the nub of the long-running conflict between him and his former great friend and ally, Thomas Becket. After accepting the Archbishopric of Canterbury Thomas Becket came to assert that the Church should not be subject to the king. In 1170, four knights, acting on words spoken by Henry in a tantrum while he was in France, crossed the Channel and murdered Thomas Becket in his own cathedral. Henry never fully recovered from the opprobrium heaped on him for this crime, and had to back off from taking on the Church. The core problem was never fully resolved, and it is in Henry II's reign that we first see arguments on the ground between the barons of Kendal and the Church, as represented by Furness Abbey, over who owned what in Furness.

Most of what we know about Furness in the Middle Ages comes from surviving records of court cases and charters and from Furness Abbey's own Coucher Books. These medieval records were systematically collected and analysed by the indefatigable editors of the Victoria Histories of the Counties of England, a massive project originally dedicated to Queen Victoria. The Victoria County History for Lancashire alone runs to eight volumes, and while these are a vital treasure trove of information, because of the fragmentary nature of surviving records, it is sometimes difficult to see exactly what was going on. The picture of landholding in Furness shows that the traditional pyramid diagrams of the 'feudal system' with the king at the top, a few great magnates underneath, more barons under the magnates and a mass of peasants at the bottom is an inadequate way to describe the way even important figures had a patchwork of holdings with more than one superior landlord. We can see that although Ulverston had been given to Furness Abbey in its original charter, the de Lancastre family, who were lords of Kendal, also claimed to be lords in Ulverston, even if it was stressed at times that they were tenants of the Abbey for this part of their landholdings. The implication of this is that Ulverston and the surrounding countryside were places worth having.

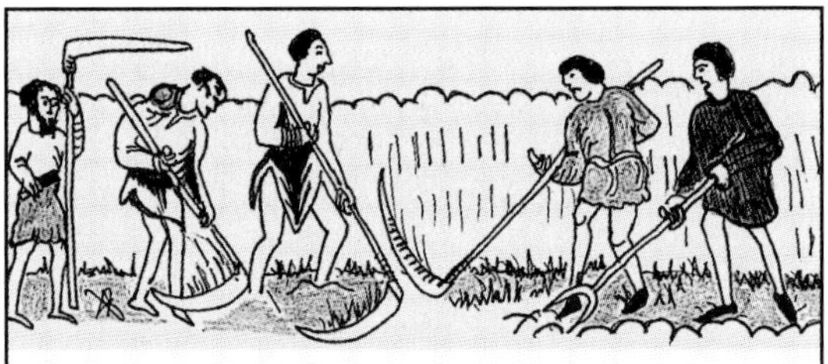
A typical early medieval harvest scene.

The de Lancastres were a grand family, firmly placed in the complex web of marriages and landholdings which glued the English crown and the aristocracy together. The first de Lancastre to be named in connection with Furness is William de Lancastre, a son of Gilbert de Lancastre and Godith, a daughter of Fulk FitzReinfred, a name which will crop up again. William de Lancastre lived from about 1100 until 1170, and married Gundred de Warenne, whose grandfather, William de Warenne, was very eminent indeed. He had fought at Hastings and had been rewarded with large estates in Sussex, Norfolk and Yorkshire and with the title of Earl of Surrey. Since surnames were a somewhat fluid concept at this time, it's not always easy to identify exactly who was descended from whom and why they held the lands they did, but the records show that at some point between 1150 and 1155, William de Lancastre was granted a large holding in Kendal, Lonsdale and Horton-in-Ribblesdale.

Thomas West states that William was directly descended from Ivo de Taillebois, the first Norman lord of Kendal, although not all historians agree. What we do know is that there must have been some argument rumbling on between William de Lancastre and Furness Abbey over who had control over the Furness fells, because in 1162 Henry II confirmed an agreement between the two sides which carved up the fells. The Abbey ended up with the eastern part between Windermere and Coniston Water, including Hawkshead and the present-day Grizedale Forest, and William had the western half. He had to pay the Abbey twenty shillings a year, but could still go hunting in the eastern part, which neatly illustrates one of the aristocracy's priorities. Whether Henry II personally supervised the agreement or whether his Chancery rubber-stamped it with his seal, it is a good example of his government in action, using his authority to make such agreements official so they would hold up if they were revisited by later generations, which this one was.

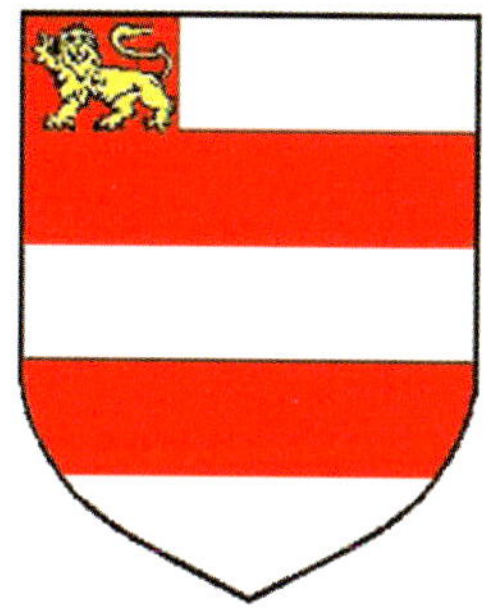

The de Lancastre coat of arms

The de Lancastre gripe with Furness Abbey didn't stop them following other noble families in giving generously to other ecclesiastical concerns. William gave Cockerham further south in Lancashire to monks from Leicester. His son, another William and usually called William de Lancastre II to avoid even more confusion, founded Cockersands Abbey on the shore south of Lancaster and gave land to the parish church in Kendal. More pertinently, William de Lancastre II was the benefactor of what became Conishead Priory, a religious house less than two miles from Ulverston. This house was probably originally founded as a hospital by Gamel de Pennington, whose family might possibly have held land in Furness since before the Conquest. The story goes that it was founded as a hospital because Furness Abbey definitely didn't want another religious establishment on their patch. Whatever the truth of this earlier foundation, William de Lancastre II gave the house all of Conishead, the church in Ulverston, 40 acres in Ulverston's fields, a salt works and the rights to cut peat, use pasture, feed pigs in the woods and take timber in 'the wood of Furness and manor of Ulverston'. Before William de Lancastre II's death in 1184, the house was promoted to a priory, and became a house of Augustinian canons, clerics who lived together in a community even though they were not monks. Founding a canons' house was seen as the next best thing to founding a monastery, and was a cheaper option, and one can't help wondering if William de Lancastre II was cocking a snook at the Abbey by giving rights over land which he held from the Abbey to a different religious order. Certainly the scene was set for a plethora of disputes which are such a feature of the records, and while the first two William de Lancastres remain somewhat shadowy figures, we know a lot more about the next lord of Kendal and holder of the manor of Ulverston, the entrepreneurial Gilbert FitzReinfred.

• IV •

THE BOROUGH OF ULVERSTON

Sometime between 1184 and 1186 Henry II wrote to his 'dear son' Richard in France to tell him that he was giving William de Lancastre II's daughter, Helewise, together with all her inheritance to an officer of his household, Gilbert son of Roger FitzReinfred. Among the witnesses to this grant was Geoffrey, another of Henry II's sons. The apparently amiable tone of this family message is somewhat ironic, given that for the last ten years or so Henry and his wife and sons had been fighting each other in various combinations over who was to inherit what of Henry's huge territories.

These violent disagreements and Henry's complete estrangement from Eleanor continued until Henry II died in France in 1189, having been defeated by Richard. All the same, the new king, Richard I (1189 – 1199), confirmed that the lucky Gilbert could have Helewise de Lancastre's hand in marriage. Helewise was the only legitimate heir of William de Lancastre II and, as was the lot of heiresses to large estates, had been made a ward, in this case of William Marshal, one of Henry II's right hand men, until a suitable husband could be found. It's hard to find any reference to Gilbert FitzReinfred before this, although with such a distinctive name he was surely related to Godith FitzReinfred, William de Lancastre I's mother and hence Helewise's great grandmother. We needn't assume that Helewise was a doormat: like many aristocratic

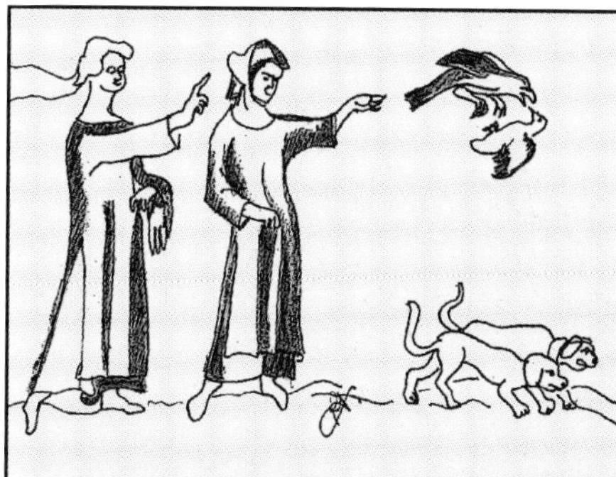

A medieval depiction of ladies hunting.

women she may have played an active role in running her inheritance. We know she had her own seal, separate from that of her husband, for official correspondence. Still, it is Gilbert FitzReinfred's name which turns up most in records of their tenure of Kendal and Ulverston, and these records tell a story of a baron doing all he could to develop his estates while trying to satisfy the king's endless demands for money.

It is difficult to understand why Richard I is generally regarded as a 'good king', unlike his brother who succeeded him in 1199 and who is immortalised as 'Bad King John' (1199 – 1216). Richard spent only about five months of his ten year reign in England and never bothered to learn English. His passion was for the Crusades, which cost a packet and failed to recapture Jerusalem. Moreover the English people were forced to pay a vast ransom when he was captured by the Holy Roman Emperor on the continent. With what might be seen as a touch of ingratitude, he spent the second half of his reign fighting in France. In spite of his absence, the government of England did not collapse. The institutions set up by Henry II ran on in the capable hands of Eleanor and of Richard's chief minister, and survived attempts by John to take over behind Richard's back.

From the records of Gilbert's activities as baron of Kendal, we see that the life of a medieval baron wasn't all wearing shiny armour and going off hawking in the afternoon. Gilbert cannot have been unique in his efforts to make money from his estates and find ways to raise cash for Richard I. There are a number of accounts of how he paid the king lump sums in return for certain privileges (for example being excused ongoing taxes levied on cattle), and how he bought fisheries which, along with forests, were desirable assets. Significantly, in 1190, soon after his marriage to Helewise, he paid Richard I for permission to hold a market every Saturday in Kendal. In the twelfth and thirteenth centuries, the population was growing and trade was increasing, and these are the centuries when many such market charters were granted. If a charter was granted to a landlord allowing him to hold a market in a settlement, it doesn't necessarily mean that there hadn't been a market there before.

What these charters meant was that lords could take over earlier more free and easy arrangements, since if a local lord controlled a market he could count on a regular income from stall rents and tolls on the goods sold. Barons like Gilbert realised they could make money from towns and markets and did what they could to develop them, as we will see when we look at Gilbert's borough charter for Ulverston. It is probable that like many other settlements Kendal had had a market for centuries outside the parish church. After 1066 the parish church was granted to the Abbey of St Mary's in York, so any money made there would have gone to the Abbot, not to a secular landlord. It may be no coincidence that in both Kendal and Ulverston the medieval market place is a fair distance from the parish church, leading to the conclusion that once Gilbert had his charter for Kendal he set up his new market well away from the church's land. A similar process may well have taken place in Ulverston, although Ulverston didn't get a formal market charter until nearly a century later.

Gilbert may not have asked for a market charter for Ulverston, but in about 1200 he gave it a borough charter which granted the 'free burgesses' of Ulverston various privileges and spelled out what they had to pay for them. This charter can be seen as part of Gilbert's efforts to make money, and is full of interesting phrases telling us a lot about Ulverston at the turn of the twelfth and thirteenth centuries. It was mentioned earlier how some of the fortified 'burhs' of Alfred the Great evolved into the forerunners of towns, and these boroughs gained a separate legal status. Within the boundaries of a borough the land was divided up into sections known variously as tenements, tofts or burgage plots which the people who owned them could use as gardens or places to keep horses, sheep, hens and pigs. However, the owners of these plots, who were usually called burgesses, were free men, rather than serfs, could buy and sell their plots as they wanted, and had other privileges, including the right to trade without paying market tolls. Burgesses were predominately craftspeople and merchants, and lords, from the king down to barons, supported existing boroughs, or created new ones, because burgage plots brought in more rents than agricultural land. This helped to encourage manufacturing and trade, and landlords gave the sought-after burgage plots with their associated privileges to their friends and members of their households, and encouraged craftspeople to settle in their boroughs.

Gilbert's charter states that he is confirming liberties to 'my free burgesses of Ulverston', which could be taken as implying that the burgesses were already there and that he was not creating a new borough. Notwithstanding this, it is clear that not everyone in Ulverston was a free burgess: burgesses were to be allowed to cut peat and enjoy common pasture 'with the other inhabitants of Ulverston'. In general, they were to have the same terms and conditions as burgesses throughout England in other boroughs 'belonging to the king, earls and barons'. In particular, Gilbert's burgesses could buy and sell their tofts at will, as long as they paid the rent, and could take wood from Gilbert's woods under supervision from his foresters, but they still had to pay the same rate as everyone else to have their corn ground at Gilbert's mill.

The charter is very specific about the terms for selling ale. Although the burgesses could sell it for a higher price than the burgesses in Appleby, they had to sell it cheaper to Gilbert. In addition they were to give him forty days credit for anything he bought from them. Along with bread, ale was the most important commodity in medieval England, being almost the only drink available for most people as water was considered unhealthy. It was brewed from barley and, since hops were not introduced into England until the fourteenth century, had to be brewed every few days, a job which was often done by women. Gilbert was obviously not doing Ulverston's burgesses any favours when it came to bread since he kept his bakehouse to himself, and it seems that people had to pay once to get their corn ground and again to have it baked. A significant detail in the charter is that Gilbert held on to his 'dyeing house' and 'fulling mill'. This is a very early reference to the woollen industry on which much of England's prosperity in the Middle Ages was based.

Not for nothing does the Chancellor of the Exchequer sit on a woolsack; wool was England's largest export for many hundreds of years. In the twelfth and thirteenth centuries most of the wool exports were unworked fleeces, and foreign buyers bought up years' worth of fleeces in advance, particularly from great abbeys like Furness Abbey. From the presence of a dye-house and a fulling mill, where woollen cloth was finished so that it would retain its texture and shape, we can see that the manufacture of woollen cloth was established in Ulverston even at this relatively early date. Although it would be too much to describe Ulverston as a full-blown manufacturing centre at this time, it was definitely more than just a farming community, and its textile industry of later centuries had deep roots indeed.

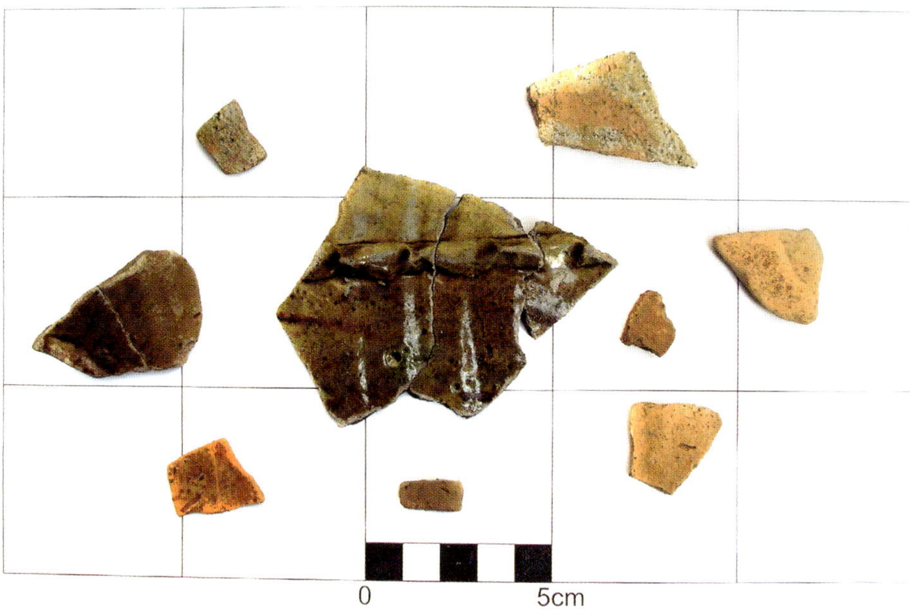

Early pottery fragments dating from the twelfth to the mid-thirteenth century found near present-day Stanley Street. Archeologists believe they are evidence of a medieval road which linked Soutergate to a market in the Gill.
Courtesy of Greenlane Archaeology

The charter also tells us that Gilbert was administering justice in Ulverston. He set a fixed fine for bad-mouthing the lord of the manor and guaranteed that burgesses could have their cases heard in his court without any penalty. We know from other records that he had a court and a gallows in Kendal, giving him power of life and death over malefactors brought before him. What Furness Abbey, which had its own court, thought about this is not recorded, although the issue came up again later in the thirteenth century when it obviously rankled with the abbot that Gilbert's successor, William de Lancastre III, had put up his own gallows in Ulverston. We get a definite sense from the records that Gilbert and Furness Abbey were competing for resources in Furness, and that neither side was happy with the 1162 division of the fells. One account says that Prince John, acting in Richard I's absence, had given all the fells back to the Abbey, and Gilbert had retaliated by stealing 1,000 of the abbey's sheep, upon which the monks offered 500 marks to bring the dispute to an end. All of this makes one wonder how Gilbert dealt with thieves in his court.

In 1196 the agreement of 1162, which had been given the royal seal of approval, was revised. It looks like Gilbert and Helewise lost out in the new agreement: they retained the western part of the fells but could no longer hunt in the eastern part, they had to guarantee that they would let the monks go through Ulverston to reach their fishery on the Crake, and they still had to pay rent to the abbey for Ulverston and the fells. The fact that they had to guarantee to let the monks through Ulverston hints that there might have been some not so neighbourly disputes over rights of way. Gilbert also seems to have pushed his luck with the abbey by getting involved in the iron business. A record quoted in Fell's *'The Early Iron Industry of Furness and District'*, says that Gilbert admitted,

> *'that the mineral ore which I take at Oregrave I have by the grace and will of the lords the Abbot and Convent of Furness, nor have I nor do*

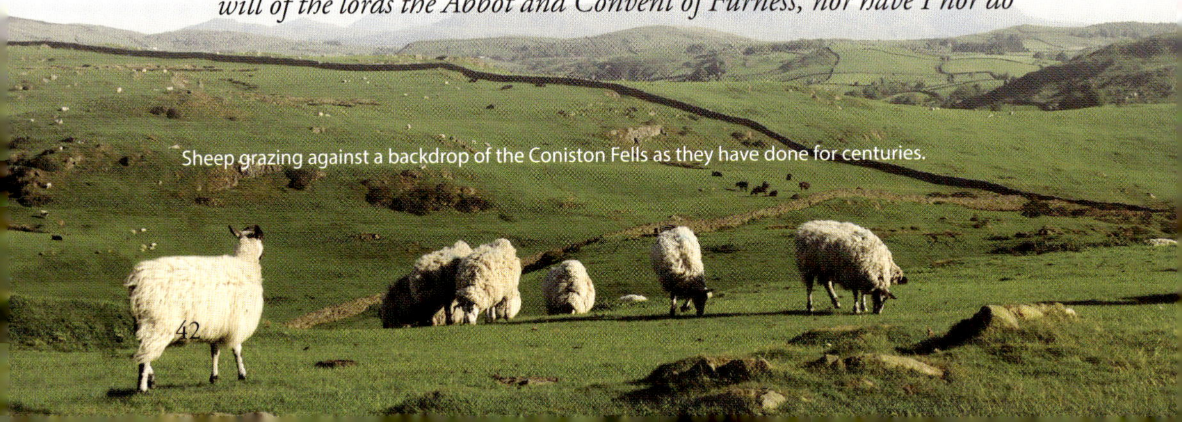

Sheep grazing against a backdrop of the Coniston Fells as they have done for centuries.

I claim any other right of taking mineral there save only of their mere grace and will',

which suggests another attempt by the abbey to put him in his place. Maybe the iron ore of Furness was one of the reasons the barons of Kendal were so keen to pursue their claims there. Furness Abbey also had issues with the de Lancastres' pet project, Conishead Priory. The priory canons had been claiming that a chapel at Hawkshead belonged to them, while the Abbey claimed control over the churches in Ulverston and Pennington as daughter churches of Urswick. In what could be interpreted as an outbreak of common sense, in 1208 the priory was given the closer church in Ulverston, and the abbey was given the chapel at Hawkshead.

Although constant arguments like this over land and rights were an everyday feature of medieval England, Gilbert FitzReinfred came unstuck during the political turmoil at the top towards the end of John's reign. It might have looked like business as usual back in 1199 when Richard I died. Gilbert paid John, Richard's heir and successor, to have his charters detailing his possessions confirmed, yet by 1216 in the last year of King John's reign, Gilbert was in the position of having to find the enormous sum of 12,000 marks and hand over child hostages, including his own grandson, to free his only legitimate son, another William, from John's prison. Gilbert and his family had become embroiled in the conflict between John and the barons, of which Magna Carta was a part. Because John's wars were mostly failures, he was resented far more than Richard I had been. By 1204 he had managed to lose the English crown's possessions in Normandy, Brittany and Anjou, and so had to turn the screw more tightly in England to make up for his lost estates. His flip-flopping over the church led to more resentment and the threat of an invasion by France. After he attempted to impose his authority on the church and then confiscate all its property, the pope not only excommunicated him but suggested that Philip Augustus, the king of France, should invade England in what he would bless as a crusade. John performed a complete U-turn and more or less turned England into the pope's fief by acknowledging him as his overlord and promising to pay him a substantial fee each year. The final straw for the barons was a disastrous expedition in France in 1214. They saw the money extorted from them go up in smoke, and openly turned against John, presenting him in 1215 with their demands in the document which became known as Magna Carta. This 'Great Charter' was the most comprehensive effort yet in England to work out what the king and his subjects should expect from each other. It is rightly famous for the clauses which form the bedrock of modern human rights legislation, namely that no free man could be imprisoned without proper legal process and that justice could not be sold, delayed or denied. It has to be said that these clauses were not uppermost in the minds of the bishops and barons who compiled the charter: the first clause states that the church in England should be free from interference by the king, and the second relates to curbing the amount heirs had to pay the king when they took over their estates. When Johns' new ally, the pope, declared that Magna Carta was null and void, the barons invited Philip Augustus's son, Louis, to come to England and be king. However, John died in 1216 in the middle of this conflict, and the barons came together to support the accession of John's son, Henry, a child of nine, in the hope that this would be a fresh start.

John's supporters captured Gilbert's son, William, in 1215, and he was not released until 1217 after Henry III (1216 -1272) acceded. William's story illustrates the occupational hazards of being a baron. The huge amount he owed to the crown for his release, including debts to Aaron and Samuel, Jews in York, and David, a Jew in Oxford, was still hanging over him when he died in 1246. Persecution of Jewish moneylenders who had bankrolled the building projects of kings, magnates and Cistercian Abbeys increased in the thirteenth century, and the crown took over their assets, so as late as 1270 two of William's heirs still owed the crown £3196 0s 7 1/2d each. We have to admire the precision of the medieval accountants who worked out this debt to the last halfpenny. Before he died in 1220, Gilbert FitzReinfred saw his heir finally safe, and William, who took the de Lancastre name from Helewise, is usually known as William de Lancastre III to distinguish him from his grandfather and great grandfather.

The records don't tell us much about Ulverston while William de Lancastre III was baron of Kendal. He was active in national affairs, popping up at Henry III's court in Bedford in 1224, in Shrewsbury in 1234, overseas in 1242 and in Wales on Henry's business in 1245. Once Henry III had come of age his long reign was marked by the perennial conflict between the crown and the barons, since in spite of his promise to uphold Magna Carta, Henry's natural tendency was to rule autocratically. This came to a head in 1234, the year in which William de Lancastre III was sent to Shrewsbury, although it's not clear whether William supported Henry or sided with the other barons on this occasion.

We tend to imagine medieval England as a country where communications were poor and somewhere like Furness well beneath the radar of kings. This is contradicted by a bizarre report in 1236 when William was ordered to send to Henry III 'the sturgeon taken on the sea sands' despite its being found in the 'liberty' of Furness Abbey, (a 'liberty' being an area whose owners had certain rights). How Henry III heard about this sturgeon, and what state it was in when he received it, we shall never know. The strange episode might be an example of Henry III trying to throw his weight around, since it was an obscure point of medieval law that sturgeon and whales found on land belonged to the crown, whereas if they were found at sea they belonged to the finder.

Because many of the surviving records from the Middle Ages are records of court cases, we are left with the impression of a society obsessed with legal niceties. In legal documents, such as Ulverston's borough charter and the very similar charter given to the burgesses of Kendal by William de Lancastre III, every possible 'i' was dotted. The same goes for William de Lancastre III's grant to Conishead Priory of a share in the Furness iron industry, which was obviously well-established by now. William gave the priory *'one acre of land next the stream which runs next the house of Richard le Turnour for a forge with a yard and for building other houses there necessary to it. The mine in Plumpton where they best and most easily may seek for it. Dead wood in Blawith to burn coals wherever they may be found. And free ingress and egress for two horses with men to carry the mine without any molestation. And with grass for the said horses as well within Plumpton as without.' (Thomas West)*

What would happen if the priory tried to use more than two horses it doesn't specify. This is probably the first written reference to iron mines at Plumpton just outside Ulverston, and shows how iron was being smelted using charcoal (coals) made in woods some distance from the borough.

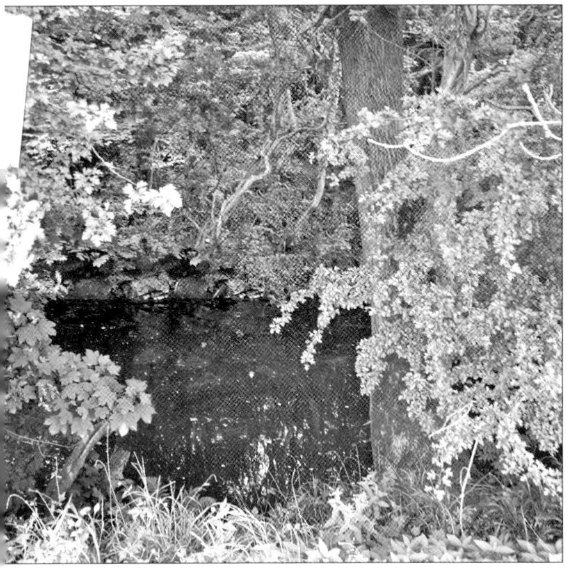

Iron ore pit at Plumpton, probably worked from the Middle Ages until the nineteenth century.

William seems to have enjoyed good relations with Conishead Priory and, along with a veritable crowd of knights, relatives and household officials, the prior was at William's deathbed on November 28th 1246. Unfortunately for anyone trying to make sense of who owned what in Ulverston over the next hundred years or so, William died childless and the de Lancastre estates were split up, leading to all sorts of complications. Before we look at how the seeds of future confusion were sown, it is worth having a stab at imagining what Ulverston looked like in the middle of the thirteenth century.

If we are familiar with its modern built-up streets, and the A590 which has sliced through the town sweeping away all in its path, it isn't easy to picture a much greener and more cultivated area, crossed by streams and with fewer buildings. The earliest map of Ulverston, dating from 1832, shows what was still a small town clustered around a crossroads at the Market Cross. The general consensus is that the two routes, which run very roughly north to south and east to west and which meet to form this crossroads, are very ancient, and that the bones of the medieval street plan have survived in the town centre north of the A590. The north to south route comes from Broughton-in-Furness down present day Soutergate and along King Street to the crossroads where it turns into Queen Street and heads south towards Urswick. The east-west route comes from the Leven Sands up Market Street, and after the crossroads becomes Daltongate, the old road to Dalton. The tenements or burgage plots were probably arranged along these roads, at a slight distance from the Parish Church which stands apart to the north east of the crossroads.

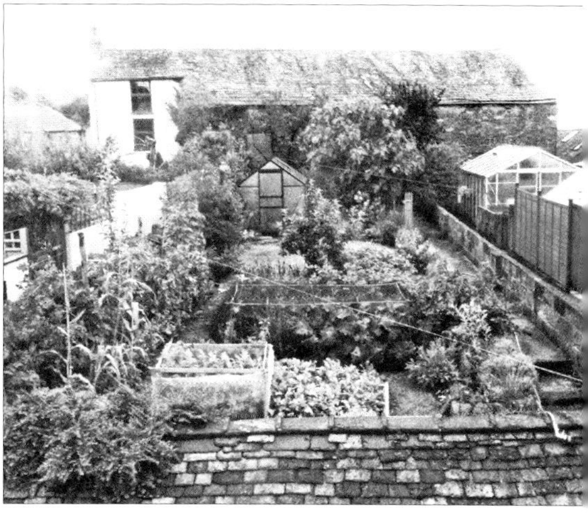

A rear garden on Soutergate. Its location and shape suggest the site of a medieval burgage plot. Barbara Cushnie

Burgage plots were long and narrow, and it is believed that in different boroughs all over England and Scotland they were marked out with a standard measuring rod of 16 feet 6 inches. The most common breadth of a plot was one and a half rods, or 24 feet 9 inches, and they were usually about 400 feet or 120 metres long, extending from a road to the borough boundary which could be a ditch or a hedge. Somewhere under the buildings we see now must be the old burgage boundaries, and looking, to take one example, at the long thin gardens between the houses on the east side of Soutergate and Back Lane leads us to think that these may be the remnants of burgage plots. Nowadays we expect to see the fronts of houses along our streets, but houses on medieval burgage plots were often built with their gable ends facing the road. Private alleys running at right angles to the road led to the open spaces behind the houses, and main doors and windows opened on to these alleys.

Sometimes local regulations forbade burgesses to have doors or windows in the back walls of their houses, to prevent them spying on their neighbours or chucking the contents of their chamber pots into the next door property, which must have been the medieval equivalent of sneaking your rubbish into someone else's wheelie bin. If you walk up Soutergate today, you will notice a house, next to the old Bugle Horn inn, with a gable end facing the road, which was possibly built on the 'footprint' of a thirteenth century burgess's home.

Medieval Ulverston had at least two mills and it would be fascinating to know where the grain and fulling mills were located. James Park's *Some Ulverston Records* contains a wonderful map showing all the streams running through Ulverston in the first half of the nineteenth century before the railways came, together with some of their attendant dams and mills. The way the main stream through the centre of town divides, joins up and divides again may differ from the route it took in William de Lancastre III's day, since within fifty years of his death we have written evidence that people diverted a mill stream and built a new mill. On the other hand, medieval mills were built on good sites, and all over the country later mills were erected on the sites of much earlier ones. Town Mill on Mill Street, which branches off at the foot of Soutergate, operated as a grain mill in Ulverston until modern times, and in 1832 there were two mills on the Ellers (one on the opposite side to the mill still standing), one out of town on what is now Old Hall Road, previously Ure Mill Road, and one at Low Mill near Outcast in the opposite direction.

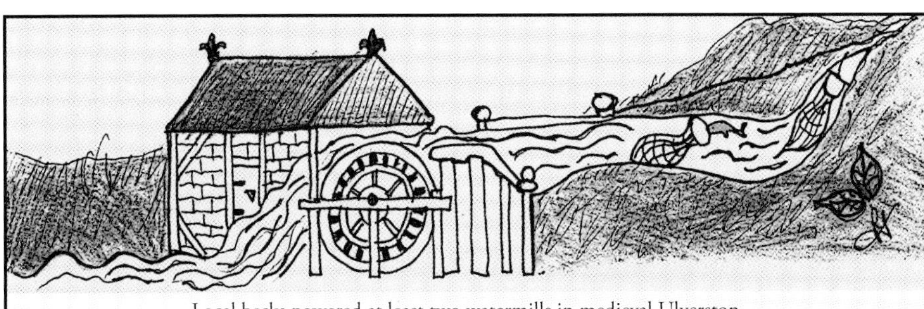

Local becks powered at least two watermills in medieval Ulverston.

Perhaps lying beneath two of these are the mills Gilbert FitzReinfred was determined to keep to himself.

The accounts in the Victoria County History of competing claims in Ulverston at the end of the thirteenth century and in the first half of the fourteenth century almost defy untangling, and involve a cast of colourful characters arguing with each other against a backdrop of political change in England and wars with Scotland. It is important to remember that when Ulverston is referred to in records of arguments between William de Lancastre III's heirs, this doesn't cover only the area we know as the town today. William's estates in Furness extended right up to Blawith, so his various heirs weren't squabbling over a small patch of land.

William de Lancastre III was the only surviving legitimate son of Gilbert FitzReinfred, yet he had two sisters who reached maturity, and all three siblings had been married off into prominent families. William was married to Agnes de Brus, and one of his sisters, Helewise, to Peter de Brus. They came from the same original family as Robert the Bruce, the king of Scotland who later caused such havoc in Furness, and may have been sister and brother. Helewise and Peter de Brus had one son who died childless and a clutch of daughters who also married well. One of these, Margaret, married Robert de Ros, the baron of Wark in Northumberland, who in turn was descended from an illegitimate daughter of King William 'The Lion' of Scotland. Another of Helewise's daughters, Lucy, married the splendidly named Marmaduke de Thwenge. The de Ros and de Thwenge families seem to have been close, and in later years not so keen on the descendants of William's other sister, Alice. She was married to William de Lindsay (or de Lyndseye) of Lamberton in Berwickshire, and their grandson (or son, the records are difficult to follow) married Ada de Balliol, sister to John Balliol who was king of Scotland before Robert the Bruce. William de Lancastre III was not only baron of Kendal, a landholding which extended as far as Windermere and included villages around Kendal, but also had extensive estates in Wyresdale between the Ribble and the Lune. On his death, the bulk of all this property was divided between his sisters, Helewise de Brus and

Alice de Lindsay, (or, rather, their husbands), so their descendants had plenty to argue about as their families expanded through the generations. In Ulverston the picture was even more complicated. While the de Brus and the de Lindsay heirs later pop up with claims in Furness, William also seems to have divided Ulverston between one of his knights, Lawrence de Cornwall, and a certain Roger de Lancastre, who is described as William's illegitimate half- brother. For the latter half of Henry III's reign it is this Roger de Lancastre who appears as the chief landlord in Ulverston, although the records don't have much to say about him during these years.

When William de Lancastre III died in 1246, England was enjoying rare years of internal peace, and Henry III had just embarked on his project to build Westminster Abbey. This calm wasn't to last. From the late 1240's onwards Henry III demanded more taxes from his subjects, and the money was mostly wasted on foreign adventures like the unlikely, expensive and unsuccessful scheme to have his son, Edmund, made king of Sicily. Henry also showered favours on his wife's relatives, the Savoyards, and on his half-siblings from his mother's second marriage, the Lusignans, while sinking further into debt with the Pope and other leading European families. The barons' resentment of Henry III's taxes and 'foreign' favourites grew, and eventually found a leader in Simon de Montfort, a significant figure in the development of the English parliament. 'Parliaments', or gatherings of bishops and barons which met on specific occasions, were beginning to appear, and a parliament in Oxford in 1258 came up with the idea that real power should be wielded by an elected council of fifteen men who in turn would be answerable to a parliament which met three times a year. In 1264 de Montfort and his supporters defeated Henry III at Lewes, forcing him to agree to these novel proposals, and in the following year de Montfort took the critical step of expanding parliament to include knights from the shires and burgesses from the most prominent towns. All this was scuppered by the inability of de Montfort and his followers to behave much better in practice than Henry III's favourites, and the heir to the throne, Henry's son Edward, defeated and killed de Montfort at Evesham, restoring power to the monarchy. Little evidence of these momentous events appears in the records about Ulverston. There is a report that some of the landlords in Furness supported Simon de Montfort against Henry III, although they wisely changed sides before the battle of Evesham. About the only thing they have to say about these years in Ulverston itself is that Roger de Lancastre gained a charter of 'free warren', which meant that he could hunt rabbits and hares without being prosecuted, not, as might be thought, that it was open season on rabbits for everyone in Ulverston. It wasn't until the action-packed reign of Edward I (1272-1307) that we see a lot more evidence of disputes in Ulverston between the descendants of William de Lancastre III's various heirs, and return to a sense of players in these dramas having some involvement on the national stage.

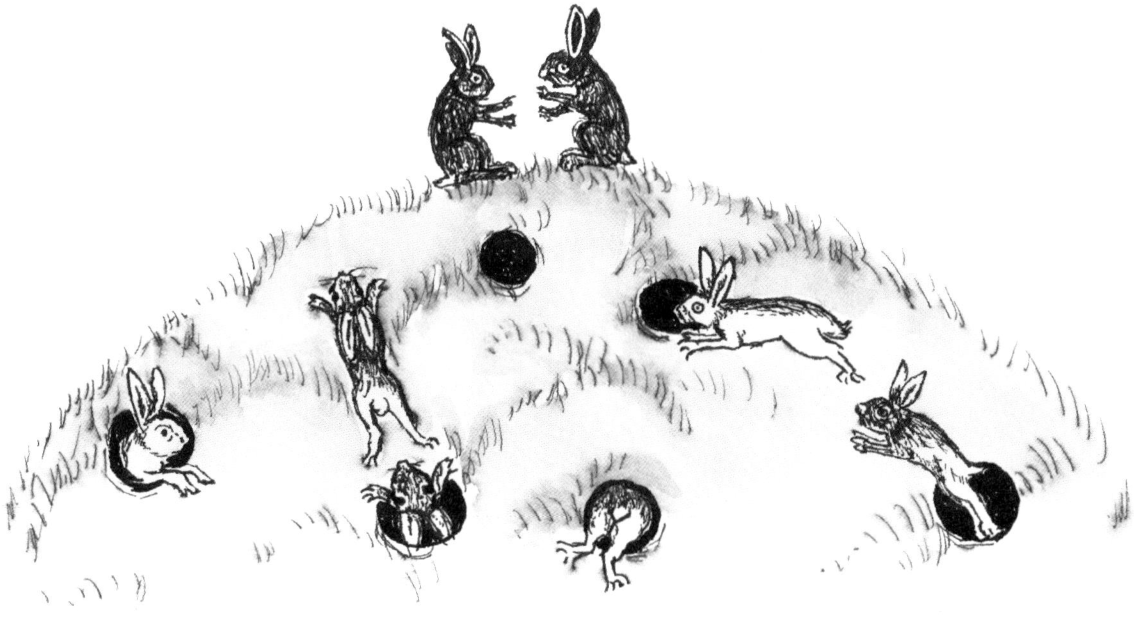

Rabbits were an important part of the medieval diet. Hunting in warrens was restricted by law. Records show Roger de Lancastre was granted a charter of 'free warren' in the 13th century.
Sketched by Mary Andrews from an original medieval drawing.

• V •

ULVERSTON

IN THE HIGH MIDDLE AGES

The late thirteenth century was a time when the climate was slightly warmer than it is now, and England's population peaked to a level which some historians believe was the maximum which could be supported by pre-industrial agriculture, not reached again until the end of the eighteenth century. Although more land was being brought into cultivation to support the growing population, 'land hunger' and disputes over nearly every acre were defining characteristics of the age. This is reflected in records of Ulverston for the reign of Edward I (1272 – 1307) where we are suddenly faced with a mass of detail about legal rows over property and rights.

In these records people who were not major landowners start to appear, like Adam, son of Roger de Holland, who in 1276 accused the Abbot of Furness Abbey of taking some of his common pasture. Another 1304 case, not so different from a 'neighbour from hell' spat we might read about today, involved William, son of Alexander de Lindeby, who complained that the de Cornwall family had put up a hedge which blocked the way from his house to the Leven sands. The de Cornwalls argued that the path they had blocked was not for carts, as William de Lindeby claimed, but for pedestrians or horsemen who dismounted and led their steeds. They won their case. Local historians are still scratching their heads over the boundaries of the de Cornwall estate which passed to the de Nevill (or Neville) family in the first half of the fourteenth century.

The Victorian police station and court across the A590 at the bottom end of Market Street were built in 1872 on the site of Neville Hall, the manor house for this estate and shown in an early photograph as a sixteenth or seventeenth century building. It is possible that Neville Hall was built on the site of a hall belonging to the de Cornwall family, and that several layers down under the Victorian buildings lie the remains of Ulverston's first manor house.

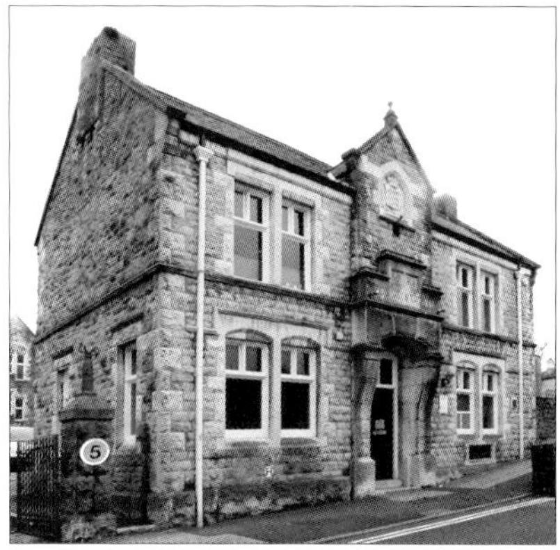

Ulverston police station built by the Victorians in 1872 on the site of Neville Hall. The manor of Nevill Hall originated in a grant by William de Lancaster to his knight Lawrence of Cornwall in the mid 13th century.

The thirteenth century arguments over property in Ulverston show it to be a busy place with cultivated 'plough lands', tenements, pastures, woods, mills, bake-house, dye-house and forges. As well as its cloth and iron industry, Ulverston was also making salt, essential in medieval England for preserving meat, fish, butter and cheese. Records mention a salt pit, which gives us a clue of the way it was being made. In coastal areas salt was extracted from evaporated brine, and since even in the better climate of the thirteenth century the sun wasn't hot enough to be relied on, brine was evaporated over fires in shallow pans. The brine could be concentrated first by trapping sea water in lagoons, or by using pits, known as kinches. Sand impregnated with salt was put into pits, water was poured through it and the resulting brine was collected in a cistern. This method was used in the Solway Firth and in Lincolnshire, and maybe in Ulverston as well.

Getting a grip on who was entitled to what in medieval England and curbing abuses of power by the great lords and barons must have been like trying to nail jelly to a wall, which doesn't mean that Edward I didn't give it a go. He seems to have tried to be a great king, modelling himself on the ideal of kingship represented by the seal of his great grandfather Henry II, with its depiction of a warrior king defending his people on one side and a wise king dispensing justice on the other. To appease the barons he pardoned many of de Montfort's former supporters, and then organised an investigation into abuses of power all across the country. His aim was to restore royal authority, so that no-one, high or low, could escape his jurisdiction. He followed this by enacting new statutes, passed by parliaments consisting of barons, knights and burgesses, to bring order to everything from trade to the way land was held and the privileges enjoyed by landholders, including religious houses. From now on landholders, even in Furness, could not escape Edward's determination that they should be able to demonstrate that they had legal warrants for the privileges they claimed.

In the early part of Edward I's reign, Roger de Lancastre appears as the main mover and shaker in Ulverston, in spite of the grant to Lawrence de Cornwall. He seems to have done a deal with the de Brus heirs, the descendants of William's sister, Helewise, and the de Lindsay heirs, the descendants of his other sister, Alice, to have the de Lancastre part of Ulverston to himself. In 1282 Roger de Lancastre and the Abbot of Furness made an agreement, and Roger paid homage to the abbot in Cartmel church for his holding in Ulverston. Like Gilbert FitzReinfred earlier in the century, Roger de Lancastre seems to have been interested in developing Ulverston, and he is remembered for obtaining a market charter from Edward I in 1280. This charter gave him permission to hold a market in Ulverston every Thursday and a fair once a year between 7 – 9 September. It might well be that Ulverston had had a market of some kind before this, probably in the open space of the Gill. While working on a site in Stanley Street, Greenlane Archaeology found evidence of a medieval road which may have connected Soutergate with the Gill and have been used to bring animals into the Gill for market. On the road, the archaeologists found pottery dating from the twelfth to the mid-thirteenth century, well before the date of the charter.

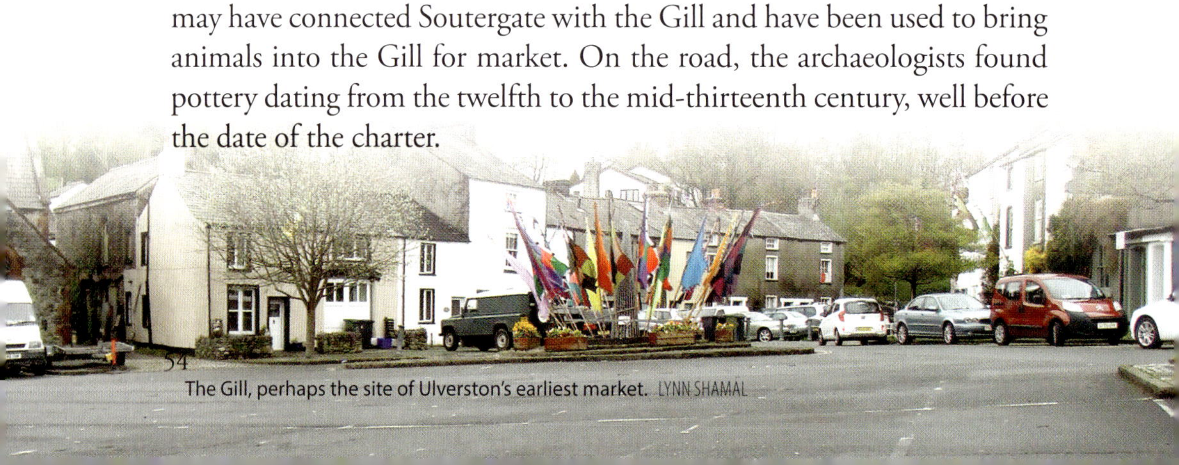

The Gill, perhaps the site of Ulverston's earliest market. LYNN SHAMAL

THE ULVERSTON MARKET CHARTER

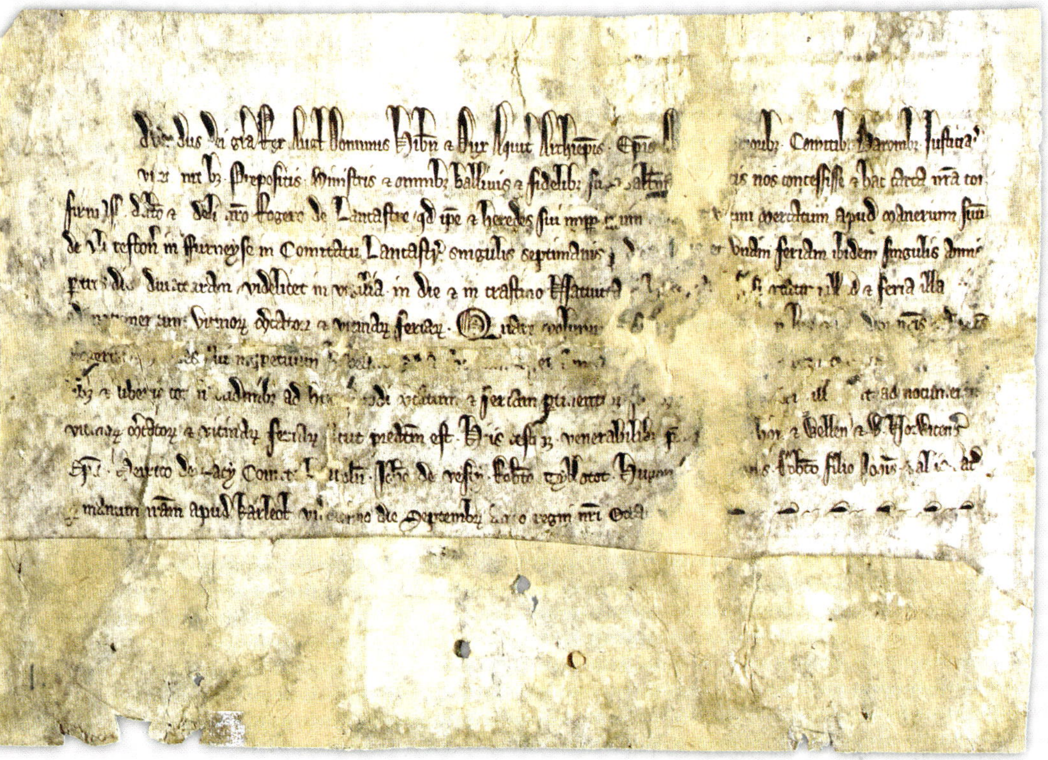

Edward, by the grace of God, King of England, Lord of Ireland, and Duke of Aquitaine to Archbishops, Bishops, Abbots, Priors, Earls, Barons, Justices, Sheriffs, Officials and all his Bailiffs and faithful mon greeting. Know that we have granted and by this our charter have confirmed to our beloved and faithful Roger de Lancaster that he and his heirs for ever shall have a market at his manor of Ulverston in Furness in the County of Lancaster on Thursday of each week, and also every year a fair lasting three days, that is to say on the Vigil - the day and the morrow of the nativity of the blessed Mary (7,8,9 September) unless this market and fair are to the damage of neighbouring markets and fairs. Wherefore we will and firmly command for us and our heirs that the aforesaid Roger and his heirs for ever shall have the aforesaid market and fair at his manor with all the liberties and free customs appertaining to the same market and fair unless this market and fair are to the damage of neighbouring markets and fairs as aforesaid.

These worthy fathers being witnesses
Robert - Bishop of Bath and Wells, William - Bishop of Norwich, Henry de Lacy - Earl of Lincoln, John de Vescy, Robert Tybltot, Hugh, son of Otto, Robert - son of John and others.

Given under our hand at Carlisle, the eleventh day of September in the eighth year of our reign.

Whether or not there had been a market before 1280, the formal charter was an important milestone and continues to be celebrated every year in the Charter Festival. In 1285, in another indication of the town's improved status, Roger de Lancastre lifted various feudal duties from Ulverston's burgesses, putting them on a par with Kendal's burgesses. It is often thought that the Abbot of Furness objected to Ulverston having a market because it drew trade away from the Abbey's own market in Dalton, forcing Ulverston's market to lie dormant until the Dissolution of the Monasteries. However, this is contradicted by records which state that in 1387 a later lord of the manor, Sir Robert de Harrington, obtained confirmation of the charter allowing the market and the fair. The permission was investigated again in 1498 and 1500, suggesting that Ulverston's landlords carried on holding a market whatever the Abbots of Furness said.

Roger de Lancastre's death in 1291 was the catalyst for a spate of claims and counter-claims over property in Ulverston. Moreover, in 1292 landlords in Furness, including even the mighty Furness Abbey, were required to satisfy Edward I's government of their entitlement to the powers they exercised, with the justices in Lancaster hearing their response to the king's writs of 'quo warranto' (roughly translated as 'by which authority') which had winged their way north. Roger de Lancastre's son and heir, John de Lancastre, had to prove that he could hunt rabbits and hares, and although this seems trivial to us now, it demonstrates what a prize the right to hunt was at that time. Furness Abbey had much to prove, especially in the role it had assumed of law enforcer in Furness. The Abbot was persuasive, and it was agreed that he could still have a gallows in Dalton and deal with thieves, as well as hold on to the rights of wreckage and lost property and be excused from attending county and shire courts. He

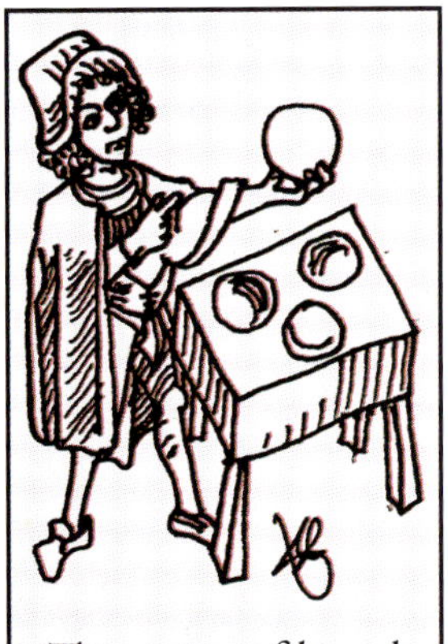

The assize of bread
forerunner of our trading standards legislation.

could also keep any money made from the assizes of bread and ale. In the thirteenth century bread and ale were so important as staple foods that local laws had developed to enforce some basic quality control. These were formalised by Henry III, who regulated the price, weight and quality of bread and ale, and imposed fines on unscrupulous bakers and brewers. It was these fines which the Abbot could hang on to. However it was decided that the bailiffs of Aldingham and Ulverston could also have a court for the assize of bread and ale in their area, and that the lords of these manors could deal with thieves. The idea that the lord of the manor of Ulverston could put up his own gallows, as William de Lancastre III had done, seems to have been successfully opposed by the Abbot.

If the Abbot and the lords of the manor in Ulverston were mostly in control of what we would call criminal justice, it was the assizes in Lancaster who had to deal with the fall-out of the division of Ulverston between John de Lancastre, the de Cornwall family, and William de Lancastre III's other heirs. In 1292 a set of cases centred round the grain mills in Ulverston might give us some pointers on where these early mills were. Since everyone needed to have their grain ground, grain mills were good little earners, and landlords could make tenants 'pay suit to', or use their particular mill, with home grinding outlawed. It looks like the estate which William de Lancastre III bequeathed to Lawrence de Cornwall included Ulverston's grain mill, and, not to be outdone, Roger de Lancastre, had built another one. Lawrence de Cornwall's and Roger de Lancastre's heirs were both called John, which is confusing, and it seems that John de Cornwall went to court to try and make people use his mill rather than the newer one. His patience

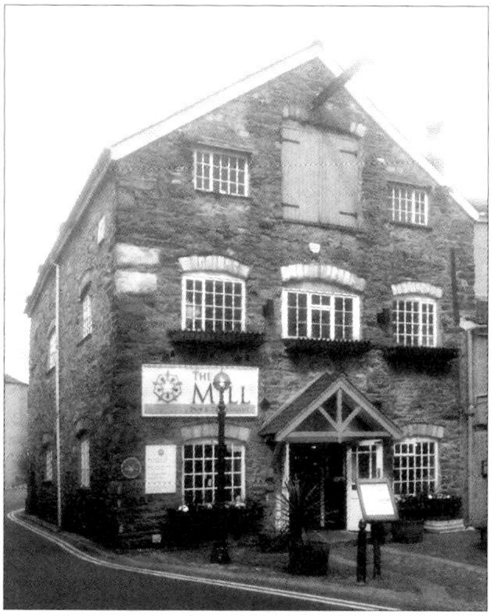

The former town grain mill on Mill Street, Ulverston, now a public house.

was tried further by a group of men who diverted the mill stream to the new mill as a favour to John de Lancastre while he was off campaigning in Scotland, and John de Cornwall successfully claimed damages against them. If the de Cornwall estate was centred on where Neville Hall later stood, maybe Ulverston's original grain mill was on the Ellers, where there was a large mill of one sort or another until the twentieth century. The site of the Town Mill on what is now Mill Street might have been where John de Lancastre built his new mill. It is even possible that this was the time when the stream which flows through the Gill was originally split in two so that it flowed past the new mill. John de Cornwall and John de Lancastre also clashed over pasture, another common cause of arguments, and it is noticeable that the women of the two families were not afraid to demand their rights. In 1294 a Richard de Cornwall's daughter, Maud, successfully claimed 'messuages' (houses with their outbuildings and gardens) and land in Ulverston from Roger de Lancastre's widow, Philippa. Maud pointed out that this property was her own inheritance from her mother, Mabel, who in turn had received them from her father, William de Skilmeresford, on her marriage to Richard de Cornwall. It was common at this time for a father to hand over land and houses to his new son-in-law when his daughter was married on the understanding that this property would revert to his daughter on her husband's death, and this was probably how Mabel came to own the property in her own right.

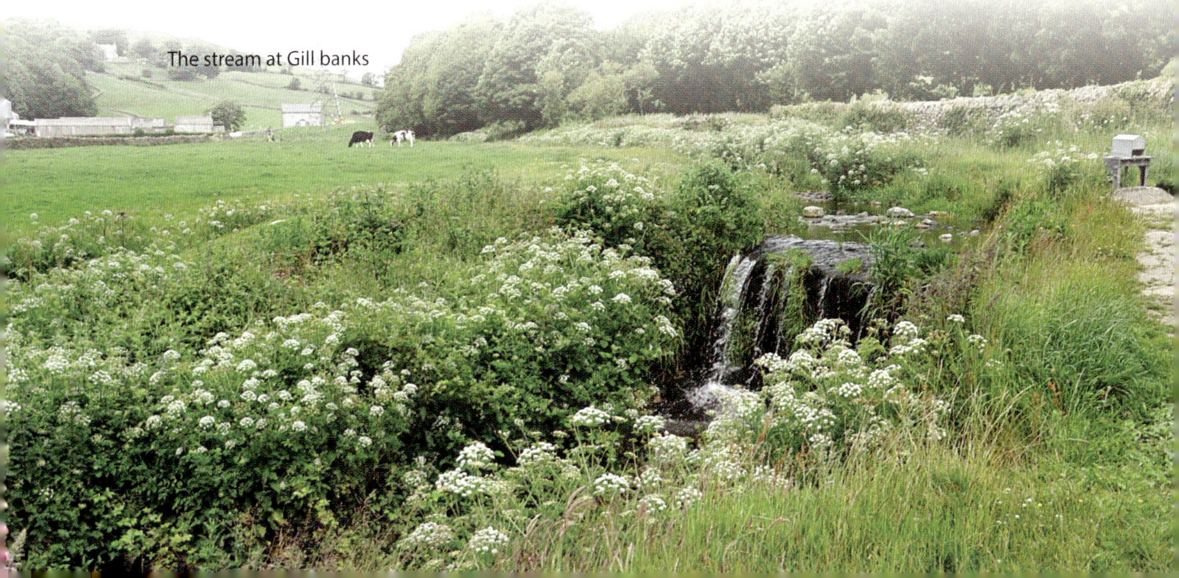
The stream at Gill banks

The claims of women to inheritances are brought into more focus by the sudden appearance in the records of Ingram de Gynes and his wife Christiana de Lyndsey, a dynamic if not grasping duo, who succeeded in muddying the waters of who owned what in Ulverston. Ingram and Christiana's greed for property in Ulverston shows us how fluid the concept of nationality was in the Middle Ages, since we wouldn't call either of them 'English'. Christiana was very well connected in the Scottish upper classes. She was either the grand-daughter or great grand-daughter (the records are hard to follow) of William de Lancastre III's sister Alice, who had married William de Lindsay of Berwickshire. Christiana's father was another William de Lindsay and her mother was Ada Balliol, sister to John Balliol who was briefly king of Scotland. Ada and John Balliol's mother was the grand Dervorgilla of Galloway, benefactor of Balliol College in Oxford and a descendant of David I of Scotland. Christiana's husband, Ingram de Gynes, was the second son of the Comte de Gynes in France, and one account states that the king of Scotland himself arranged this marriage.

Christiana and Ingram seem to have been hell-bent on pursuing any claim they might have to property in England. In the records dealing with Kendal a notice appears for the year 1284, remarking that Hugh de Lowther and Gervase de Whitby were the attorneys for Christiana and Ingram who were in Scotland, suggesting that the couple were not going to let sleeping dogs lie even though they weren't living in England. At the same time, they were not so quick to pay their debts. In the 1290's the master of the Knights Templar in England was chasing them for rent arrears, and the archdeacon of York was waiting for Ingram to settle a bill of £24 which he owed. Whatever arrangement Roger de Lancastre had made with William de Lancastre III's other heirs, now that Roger was dead, Christiana was claiming her share, and she and Ingram wanted John de Lancastre to give them their half of various land and houses, a mill, a salt pit, a bakehouse and two forges. While the case was being heard, Ingram was sitting on the bench with the justices, which suggests a touch of intimidation from a forceful aristocrat. The couple won their claim, and in 1296 were nagging John de Lancastre for a partition of the woods they jointly held in Ulverston, while a note from 1297 says that Ingram de Gynes and John de Lancastre held Ulverston between them. If this wasn't enough for John de Lancastre, whose inheritance must have been shrinking before his eyes, Conishead Priory successfully claimed some common pasture from him, Ingram and Christiana. In addition, the Prior alleged that Lawrence de Cornwall had taken over three acres which belonged to 'his' church in Ulverston. These are just a fraction of the lawsuits flying round, and since there is no reason to assume that circumstances in Ulverston were unusual, the Lancaster Assizes must have been incredibly busy with similar squabbles going on all over Lancashire. These lawsuits are an indication of pressure on the land, and one can't help noticing that the Prior of Conishead agitating over three acres is a far cry from Furness Abbey claiming all the Furness fells a century or so earlier. Meanwhile, rumbling in the background to this vying for land and assets, were Edward I's wars with Scotland, which were to have dreadful consequences for Furness.

Depending on your point of view, Edward I was either the first king to put the 'Great' into Britain or an intolerant warmonger whose actions cast a baleful shadow over the political structures and attitudes of the United Kingdom. There is no doubt that he played an important role in fostering the rule of law and in developing parliament as an assembly of knights and burgesses without whose consent taxes could not be raised. On the more unattractive side, in 1290 he was quite comfortable with expelling the Jews, whose financial expertise had propped up the crown since the Norman Conquest and who had been suffering increased persecution in the thirteenth century. He also had a burning ambition to exert the English crown's authority beyond England, starting with Wales. In 1279 he marched into Wales, crushing the semi-independent Welsh princes, building the great castles we see today, and imposing English law on the Welsh. After a Welsh rebellion in 1282, Edward decreed that opposing the king was treason, and instituted the barbaric punishment of hanging, drawing and quartering for such crimes. Having dealt, satisfactorily in his mind, with Wales, he then turned his attention to Scotland.

The relationship between England and Scotland was complex. Although Scotland had had its own monarchy for centuries, the English and Scottish royal houses had intermarried for almost as long. Since Scottish kings also had extensive estates in England for which they paid homage to the English king, in some respects they were subjects of the English crown. At the same time, Scottish rulers saw themselves as the equals of English kings by virtue of being monarchs in Scotland. One gets the feeling that Edward I had no patience with such subtleties, and wanted to establish once and for all that he was the top dog. After the death of Alexander III of Scotland in 1286, the only obvious Scottish heir was Margaret, 'the Maid of Norway', and Edward decided that she should marry his eldest son, also Edward. Unfortunately, Margaret died in 1291, leaving a number of claimants to the throne, upon which Edward announced that he had the right to decide which one should be king. In the end, he chose Christiana de Lyndsey's uncle, John Balliol, who happened to have large estates in England. Although John Balliol was crowned king of Scotland, Edward made it clear that he saw himself as Balliol's superior lord and could use English courts to administer justice in Scotland. In the end, Edward's heavy-handedness was all too much for Balliol and the Scots who rebelled, upon which Edward did a repeat performance of his invasion of Wales. He stripped Balliol of his symbols of office and had the Stone of Scone, upon which all kings of Scotland had been crowned, taken off to Westminster. This did not stop the Scots under William Wallace resisting his rule, especially his taxes. Edward might have thought he had put an end to this trouble when he captured and executed William Wallace in 1305, but Robert the Bruce crowned himself king of Scotland in 1306 and carried on fighting the English. Edward was on his way to campaign yet again against the Scots when he died in 1307, leaving a legacy of violent antipathy between the two crowns which would last for centuries.

With their Scottish connections through marriage, the descendants of William de Lancastre III's sisters were maybe typical of northern upper class families where there was considerable blurring between who was English and who was Scottish; and the de Lancastre heirs did not escape involvement in Edward's wars. John de Lancastre fought for Edward I in Scotland. He was at the siege of Caerlaverock Castle south of Dumfries in 1300, and it might have been because of this service that he was made a knight. Marmaduke de Thwenge, who had married William de Lancastre III's niece, Lucy de Brus, seems to have had a torrid time. He was captured following an English defeat outside Stirling and was kept in Stirling castle until 1299. Luckily for him, he escaped the fate of one of Edward I's tax collectors whom William Wallace allegedly skinned to make a scabbard for his sword. Christiana de Lyndsey, the most 'Scottish' of all the de Lancastre heirs, seems to have been a born survivor. Her uncle John Balliol's loss of the Scottish crown and the subsequent rebellions appear not to have affected her hold on her property in Ulverston. Later on in the fourteenth century there was obviously a lot of bad feeling between Marmaduke de Thwenge's son and Christiana's son, and one wonders whether the origins of this hostility lay in the Scottish wars whose ups and downs seemingly left Christiana unscathed. Nevertheless, the unintended consequences of Edward I's belligerence towards the Scots hit Furness with a vengeance during the reign of his son and successor, Edward II (1307 – 1327).

Edward I and his son were chalk and cheese, so much so that as Edward II's reign wore on there were rumours that he was a changeling, swapped at birth for the true heir. While Edward I was the kind of indomitable force we can imagine rising at dawn champing at the bit to smite his enemies, Edward II was more the sort who liked nothing better than a lie-in followed by a day of messing about in boats or hanging out with workmen thatching roofs. In itself his lack of his father's furious drive might not have been unwelcome to the nobles and lesser folk who had paid dearly in taxes and their lives for Edward I's constant wars. Unfortunately, Edward II had a blind spot with which modern psychologists could have a field day, namely his tendency to become passionately attached to favourites whom no-one else could stand, and to shower them with titles, gifts and power. His first and most well-known favourite was Piers Gaveston, the son of a squire, with whom he became inseparable. The exact nature of their relationship might not have been such a problem if Edward hadn't put the great nobles' noses completely out of joint by trying to rule with Piers rather than with them.

On-going arguments between Edward II and his nobles were not just a faraway political stand-off with no relevance to Furness. One of Edward II's most vocal critics was his cousin Thomas, Earl of Lancaster and holder of the Honor of Lancaster, who had taken part in Edward I's campaigns in Scotland. Men like John de Lancastre and Marmaduke de Thwenge who had interests in Furness were counted as his 'followers'. With no standing army, medieval kings relied on the great magnates and the quasi-private armies they raised from lesser noblemen and tenants, and when John de Lancastre was fighting in Scotland it was probably in the Earl of Lancaster's army. The Earl of Lancaster was prominent in the killing of Piers Gaveston in 1313, when the nobles and bishops managed to capture the unfortunate favourite, subject him to a show trial and have him beheaded. Marmaduke de Thwenge was once more in hot water, since he is named as one of the five hundred followers of the Earl of Lancaster whom Edward II, through lack of support, was forced to pardon, not that he ever forgave Gaveston's killers.

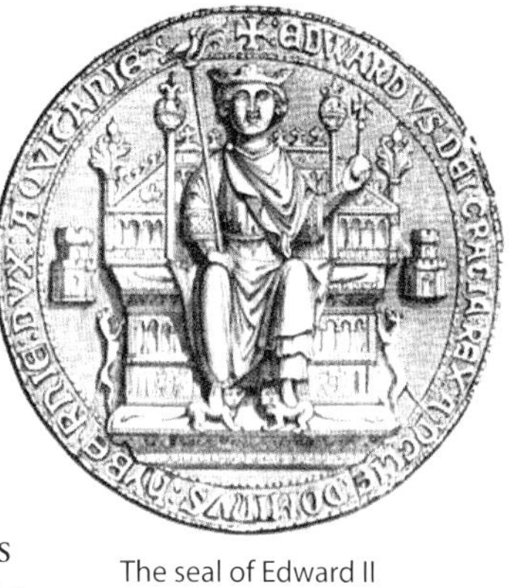
The seal of Edward II

Maybe in an effort to redeem himself after this humiliation, Edward II decided to lead an expedition into Scotland against Robert the Bruce who had been busy driving the English from castles and raiding across the border. This campaign was a disaster for Edward, ending as it did with the resounding Scottish victory at Bannockburn from which he fled, leaving most of his army to perish. With no more strings to his bow he had to accept the nobles' control, and the Earl of Lancaster, who had missed the Scottish campaign, became increasingly powerful.

As if to prove that it never rains but it pours, the climate was now changing for the worse. There was a bad harvest in 1314, and this was followed by two years of wet weather when crops rotted in the fields. The result was a terrible famine in England. Grain prices rose, many poorer people who were unable to sell land to buy food starved, and any further expeditions against the Scots were stymied because there were no provisions for an army. We are unable to tell from the records how widespread the famine was in Furness, and although there are accounts that the Abbot was able to import grain from Ireland in times of need, since Ireland was also suffering, this might not have happened. Famine was not the only cause of misery. The Earl of Lancaster and the other magnates seem to have been powerless to prevent Robert the Bruce who, like most medieval rulers, was never averse to kicking an enemy when he was down, sending raids into northern England with impunity. In 1316, having allegedly been bought off by a bunch of nobles holed up in Richmond Castle, the Scots moved west and descended on Furness. According to reports they laid waste and burnt everything as far as Furness, then carried away all the goods they could manage, killing or taking prisoner anyone who put up a fight. They were especially pleased with the iron they found and spirited off to Scotland with no-one to stop them. We don't know if the local landholders, who could raise armed men, offered any resistance, went to ground or were dancing attendance on the Earl of Lancaster who was following his own agenda.

There is evidence that the Earl of Lancaster, whose private estates were left suspiciously untouched by Scottish raids, was conniving with Robert the Bruce, and neither he nor Edward II come out with much credit from these years. Edward found new favourites in the unpleasant father and son combination of the Despensers, powerful and unscrupulous Marcher lords, and was especially captivated by Hugh Despenser the Younger, who seems to have been a particularly unsavoury character even by the standards of the time. Thoroughly miffed, the Earl of Lancaster rebelled openly in 1321, only to be defeated at the Battle of Boroughbridge. He was taken prisoner, 'tried' much as Piers Gaveston had been by a tribunal who knew the verdict before they had started, and executed near Pontefract Castle in 1322. This is the date which is etched in all the histories of Furness as the year of Robert the Bruce's 'Great Raid', and it is not hard to see the connection between the two events. While the English were riven with internal strife, Robert the Bruce led an army south through Cumberland and across the Duddon Sands into Furness. At least the Abbot of Furness showed some initiative. He met Robert the Bruce, took him back to the abbey and paid him a huge ransom of £10,000 to protect Furness from more burning and plundering. He saved the abbey, yet the Scots still rampaged through the rest of the area as they had done in 1316 before proceeding further on into Westmorland and Lancashire where they helped themselves to 'gold and silver, animals, church ornaments, bedding and linen'. There then followed one of the more shameful episodes of Edward II's reign in his treatment of Andrew Harclay, the Earl of Carlisle who, even though he was a former follower of the Earl of Lancaster, had been instrumental in defeating him at Boroughbridge. Andrew Harclay realised that the English were on a hiding to nothing in trying to fight Robert the Bruce, and made a truce agreement with him, to spare northern England from further destruction. Out of what looks like spite, Edward II had Harclay arrested and hung, drawn and quartered as a traitor. A few months later, he made his own truce with Robert the Bruce.

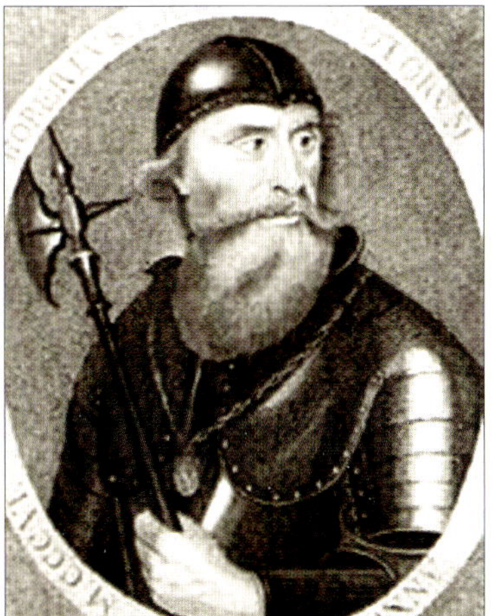

Robert the Bruce
Library Image

The horrible fate of a man who had helped him get rid of one of his most inveterate enemies just about sums up Edward II, and his days were numbered. Isabella, his queen, managed to wangle a trip to her royal relatives in France where she teamed up with Roger Mortimer, a Marcher lord ousted by the Despensers. In a remarkable display of stupidity, Edward sent their eldest son, another Edward, across to join her. With the trump card of the teenaged heir to the throne in their hands, and the support of young Edward's future father in law, the Count of Hainault, Isabella and Mortimer crossed back to England in 1327. Isabella met with no resistance and succeeded in deposing her husband and having her son crowned as Edward III. Edward II was captured and imprisoned in Berkeley Castle where he was most likely murdered, although there were rumours that he escaped and went to live in obscurity on the continent.

Nowadays warlike leaders are not looked on as kindly as they were in the Middle Ages, and historians might judge Edward II more sympathetically than they do his belligerent father. However, by the measures of the time Edward II failed in the two most important functions of a king, since he neither defended his people nor upheld royal justice, and Furness was one of the victims of his failure. Robert the Bruce and the Scots certainly behaved no worse in England than Edward I and his armies had done in Scotland, yet the Scottish raids, following on the heels of famine, must have been a terrible shock to people living in Furness. They had enjoyed nearly two centuries of relative peace and economic development, and whatever the injustices of a system whereby the majority of people were tied to landlords who demanded all manner of rents and services, for generations they had had a measure of security. It is very difficult for us to imagine how people coped with losing everything in an age where there were no aid agencies or insurance companies, and when they could not put in a claim and go to the shops to replace stolen food, clothes, tools and blankets. In 1324, two years after the Great Raid, Ingram de Gynes died, and records for Kendal note that the burgage plots and other property he held through his wife, Christiana, were all worth much less than previously, or even nothing, because of the 'destruction of the Scots'. In 1341, long after Edward II had been got rid of, an enquiry into the Wapentake of Lonsdale looked at how the scale of taxation was revised downwards as a result of the Scots' incursions. The churches at Dalton, Ulverston, Aldingham and Urswick, which had been taxed at £8, £35 6s 8d, £53 6s 8d and £5 6s 8d respectively were now taxed at £2, £5, £10 and £2, while Pennington Church's taxable value was now precisely zero. Worse was to come. A determined pessimist couldn't have foreseen that just as famine and defeat were becoming unpleasant memories, pestilence would change England for ever.

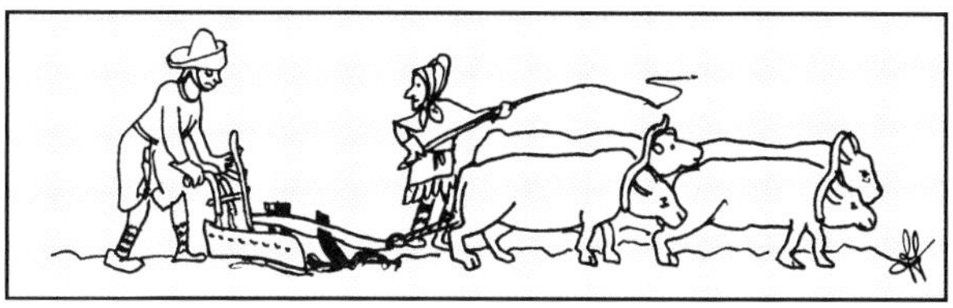

• VI •

From the Black Death until the Wars of the Roses.

The pandemic usually known as the Black Death entered southern England in 1348 after rampaging through Asia, the Middle East and the rest of Europe. The accepted view that this disease was bubonic plague, spread by infected fleas hopping from their black rat hosts on to humans, has been questioned, but the fact remains that in terms of mortality it was the single biggest disaster to hit the human race between the end of the Ice Ages and the Second World War. It has been estimated that between 1348 and 1350, and in outbreaks in the following decades, up to half of England's population died. Some studies suggest that the mortality rate was highest among adults who had been small children or in the womb during the famine earlier in the century, when, to say the least, their health didn't get off to a good start. The aristocracy escaped comparatively lightly, maybe losing around a quarter of their number, which could reflect more hygienic living conditions and better nutrition throughout their lives. This demographic collapse was the driver behind economic, social and political changes which carried on into the early modern era, changes from which there is no reason to assume the borough of Ulverston was immune, although we have far less information about what happened there in the century

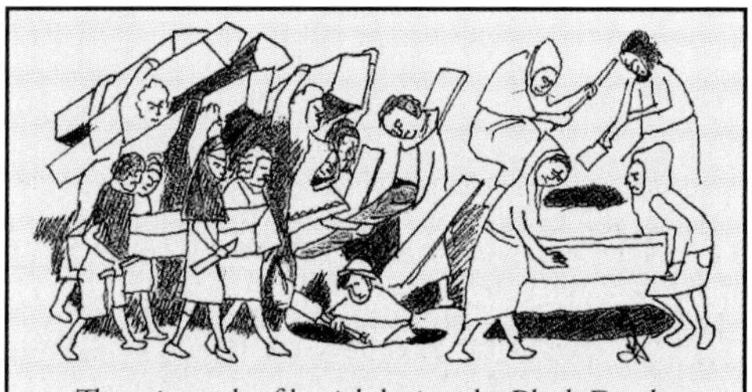

The grim task of burial during the Black Death.

after the Black Death than in the preceding century and a half.

The horror of this seemingly unstoppable disease must have been magnified for the English since it came at a time when everything seemed to be going swimmingly after the troubles of the early fourteenth century. Edward III (1327 – 1377) is often described in terms which make him sound like the ideal head boy in a ripping yarn. In contrast to his scandalous parents, he was chivalrous, courageous, a successful leader of men and co-operative with the nobles and parliament. Once he had got rid of his mother's lover, Mortimer, who had engineered a humiliating peace treaty with Robert the Bruce in 1328, he began to move against the Scots, and in 1333 won the victory at Halidon Hill which made his reputation. By this time Robert the Bruce's son, David, had become David II, and although Edward III tried to install John Balliol's son as king in Scotland, David II's forces eventually gained control over most of the country, and the two sides made a truce in 1338. The sting had definitely been drawn from the Scots, and Edward turned his attention to France, Scotland's ally, starting the long conflict known as the Hundred Years' War. As a grandson of Philip IV of France he claimed the French crown, and in 1346 was the architect of the English victory at Crecy where English longbows wreaked havoc among the French nobility. The cherry on the top of the cake came in the same year when an English force captured David II of Scotland at the battle of Neville's Cross, and the unfortunate man spent the next eleven years in custody.

With the threat of Scottish raids receding and the general tendency of people after the famine to marry earlier and have more children, we can perhaps assume that in the 1330's and 1340's Ulverston began to recover from its traumas. An 'inquisition' or inquiry in about 1346 into the Ulverston possessions of Christiana de Lyndsey's grandson, William de Coucy, (Christiana's son, also William, had taken Ingram de Gynes' family name of de Coucy), mentions that he held 'newly measured land in Newland', which we could take to mean that waste land had been brought into cultivation to sustain a growing population. The dye-house is also mentioned in this inquiry, so it was still in business, and the

Victoria County History has an interesting footnote on trade names which pop up in Ulverston in the fourteenth century. These include tailors, slaters and colliers (charcoal makers) and, at the luxury end of the spectrum, a goldsmith and a glasswright. Maybe these men worked on beautifying Furness Abbey and Conishead Priory, or maybe the good burgesses of Ulverston had plenty of money to spend on glass windows and bling.

It is in these years before the Black Death that the direct heirs of the de Lancastre family ceased to hold land in Ulverston and two different families, the de Nevills (or Nevilles) and the de Haringtons (or Harringtons) made their appearance. The estate originally given to the de Cornwall family came into the possession of Sir Edmund de Nevill in around 1332, although no-one seems to know why or how, and it remained with the de Nevills right until the reign of Elizabeth I. The de Nevills were a prominent northern family, one branch of which later came to hold the earldom of Westmorland. They successfully fought off various law suits, brought by people claiming to be the heirs of the de Cornwalls, to hold on to their manor in Ulverston. The de Harington family originally came from north-west Cumbria, and through a sequence of marriages and unfortunate drownings of male heirs had come into possession of the Muchland manor, originally granted to Michael le Fleming back in the early twelfth century. In around 1334, Sir John de Lancastre gave over his part of Ulverston to Sir John de Harington. It isn't clear if he did this because he had no heirs or because the de Lancastre family had fallen on hard times.

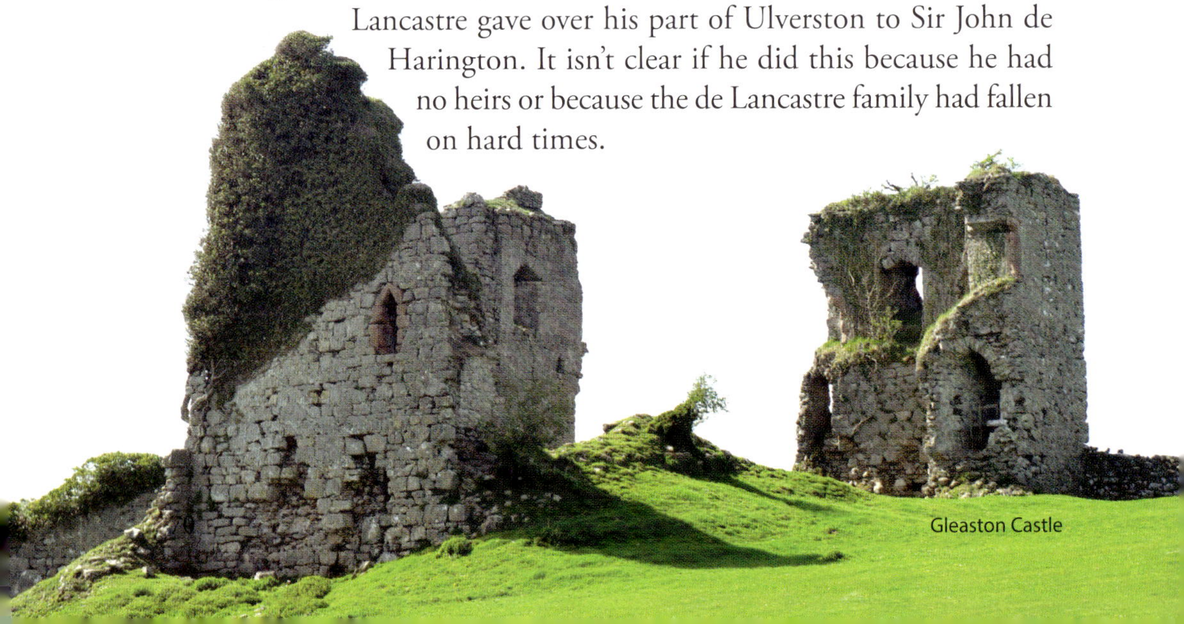

Gleaston Castle

Sir John de Harington, whose memorial can be seen in Cartmel Priory church, was a pretty substantial fellow, actively involved in national politics, having been knighted in 1306 and summoned to Parliament in 1326 when he was created the first Baron of Aldingham. Like many barons he found life precarious at times particularly when he was found complicit in the murder of Piers Gaveston although he was lucky enough to be pardoned twice. In 1323 he was outlawed as a follower of the unfortunate Sir Andrew Harclay, yet bounced back after another pardon, becoming a custodian of Edward II's truce with the Scots. It was Sir John de Harington who built Gleaston Castle and held manors at Witherslack, Hutton Roof, Austwick and Harrington, while the de Harington family in general came to have land from Cornwall to Ireland. The division of Ulverston is difficult to work out, since both Sir Edmund de Nevill and Sir John de Harington are named as free tenants of William de Coucy. Eventually after many twists and turns and legal battles the de Coucy part of Ulverston reverted to Furness Abbey. The de Coucy family fell out of favour because some of them, being French, took the French side in Edward III's wars in France, and the de Coucy share in Ulverston was granted to John de Coupland, the man credited with capturing David II of Scotland. This was only a grant for life, and the de Coucy family came back into favour with Edward III, so much so that he married off his daughter, Philippa, to Ingeram (or Inguerrand) de Coucy. In spite of this, it seems that the Abbey took possession of the de Coupland/de Coucy holding in Ulverston.

According to West, Sir Edmund de Nevill built Neville Hall, practically the only medieval building in Ulverston, apart from the Parish Church, whose site we can be sure of. We don't know if the de Lancastres, from William de Lancastre I down to the de Coucys, had any kind of hall in Ulverston for occasional visits, or where Roger de Lancastre and his son, John, lived, and it is noticeable that there is no hint that Ulverston at any time had even the smallest castle for defence. However, it is believed that Neville Hall had a tower, and since many towers were built across the north of England in the fourteenth century we might guess that

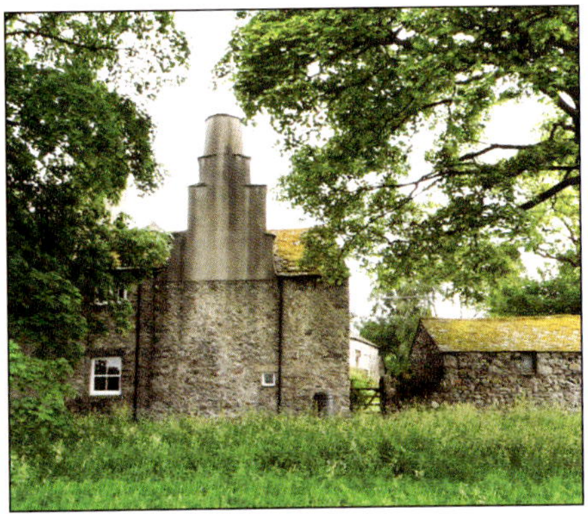

A view of the oldest part of Plumpton Hall, possibly built around an existing 14th Century small tower.

Edmund de Nevill built one here in case the Scots ever came back. Sir John de Harington's castle at Gleaston was in a pretty poor position defensively, which seems strange when one sees the still formidable remains of Wraysholme Tower, also built by the de Haringtons, on the shore near Cark in Cartmel. Possibly the oldest domestic building close to Ulverston still standing is Plumpton Hall, also on the shore, and the oldest part of the hall might conceivably have been a similar fourteenth century small tower.

It is a testimony to the strength of medieval English society and institutions that in spite of the despair engendered by the Black Death, the country didn't descend into anarchy. The justice system in the north certainly ground on, and between 1352 and 1354 we find the Abbot of Furness relentlessly pursuing his claim for the de Coucy part of Ulverston manor, granted to John de Coupland. At the same time, in its wake the pandemic brought a gradual breakdown of the old order in which landholders could keep the mass of people as serfs, tied to their land and subject to all kinds of dues and restrictions. Half of this compliant and submissive workforce had disappeared, leaving fields untilled and the nobility with no rents to collect. Survivors realised that their labour now had much more value, and began to wonder why they should toil away for the same measly rewards on some noble's estate when they could vote with their feet and move to another landlord willing to give them a better deal. This was anathema to Edward III and the nobility, and laws were passed to force people stay in their posts and to keep wages artificially low. These laws were frequently broken, and the records of Kendal note a case in 1378 when a Thomas Baker complained that his servant had left without reasonable cause in defiance of Edward III's laws. If we read between the lines, we can perhaps see evidence of a new mood of assertiveness among survivors of the plague in Ulverston.

We know that plague hit Ulverston: it had a starring role in a court case which, as the warring parties all had the same two names, is difficult to unravel. The gist of it is that when an Ulverston man, Thomas del Bouth, was dying of the plague, he bequeathed a 'messuage' to his daughter, Alice, wife of a Thomas del Bate, even though she also had the plague. Miraculously, she recovered, only to be successfully sued for this property by her niece, Thomas del Bouth's son's daughter, also called Alice. It is in another post-plague dispute involving Alice del Bouth's husband, Thomas del Bate, where change can be discerned. The prior of Conishead Priory complained that Thomas and many other men had fished in the prior's fishery at Ulverston, making off with salmon, bream, flukes, eels and flounders. Surprisingly, the jury agreed with the defendants' claim that holding tenements in Ulverston as free tenants gave them the accustomed right to fish in the prior's fishery in the Leven with nets called 'hanes' and to take fish from the sand and streams when the tide was ebbing. Only salmon were judged out of bounds, and fines were levied for any salmon taken, a verdict which came down more on the side of the 'common man' than of the landlord. A violent dispute of 1357 could also be interpreted as part of a general disgruntlement with landlords who refused to acknowledge a changing world. A Thomas Bardsey seized and beat up Roger Bell, the Abbot's bailiff, while he was out and about probably collecting money. In retaliation, Roger Bell assembled a posse which included the Abbot himself and which descended on Thomas's father's house in Ulverston where Thomas was holed up with the doors and windows barred. The Abbot's men forced their way in and hauled Thomas off to jail in Dalton.

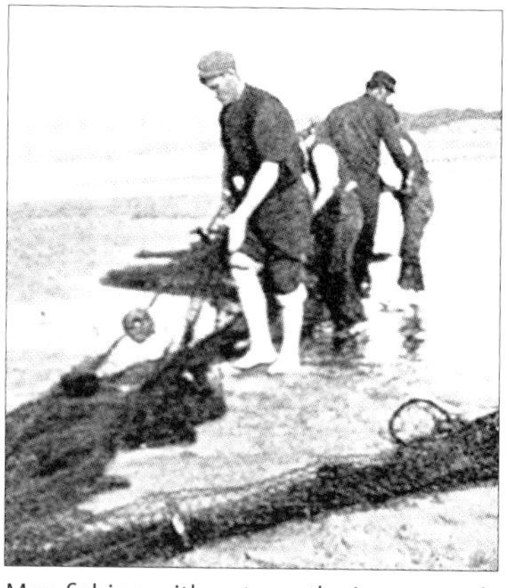

Men fishing with nets on the Leven sands in 1898, just as their ancestors did in the 14th century. Furness Year Book

The tension between the nobility's attempt to enforce the old order and ordinary people's efforts to break free came to a head in England in 1381 in the movement known as the Peasants' Revolt. By this time, not only had Edward III died, but so had his eldest son and heir, Edward the Black Prince, and the Black Prince's eldest son, yet another Edward. The Black Prince's younger son, Richard, had been crowned as Richard II (1377 -1399) when he was only ten years old, with Edward III's other sons, in particular John of Gaunt, the Duke of Lancaster, hovering in the background. With his vast estates, John of Gaunt was hugely wealthy and, like a banker taking bonuses, was widely regarded as a symbol of all that was wrong, especially when the infamous poll tax was brought in and raised until every adult, rich or poor, had to pay one shilling. Revolt broke out, mainly in Essex and Kent, and the rebels marched on London. Many were respectable yeomen and craftsmen fighting against restrictions on their ability to make a decent living. Under their leader, Wat Tyler, they called for the abolition of serfdom, rent on land to be limited, the right to sell goods in any city, borough or market and the sentence of outlawry to be rescinded for labourers who had not turned up in court to be charged for demanding higher wages. In addition, they demanded an end to the aristocracy's ancient grip on hunting in warrens, parks and woods and on fishing rights, which is a neat connection to Thomas del Bate and his friends in Ulverston. Once in London they caused scenes which have been repeated in riots down the centuries, setting buildings on fire and looting. They burnt John of Gaunt's London palace, the Savoy, to the ground, and John of Gaunt hightailed it off to Scotland. In the end, the revolt failed and its leaders were hunted down and executed, yet the

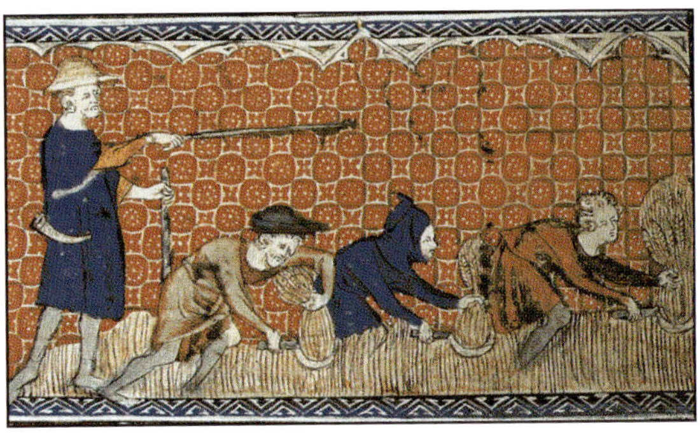

Reeve supervising serfs. From the Queen Mary's Psalter

nobility couldn't turn the clock back and re-populate England with downtrodden peasants, and to all intents and purposes serfdom disappeared. In a case of better late than never, in 1484 the inhabitants of Kendal were released from a whole list of traditional feudal dues, hinting at an acceptance of the social order envisaged by the revolt.

Ulverston is far from Essex and Kent and, apart from the disputes mentioned earlier, we have no way of knowing if revolutionary notions spread by the Peasants' Revolt reached Furness in the fourteenth century. In 1373, John de Nevill complained that one Thomas atte Bote had broken his mill dam. This might have been an accident on Thomas's part or part of an ongoing argument between John de Nevill and Sir Robert de Harington over the manor of Ulverston, rather than an attack on landlords' control of mills. Neither do we know how badly the Black Death hit Ulverston's population. Clearly, the borough survived the fate of many settlements which were simply deserted and never inhabited again as plague survivors moved away in search of a better life elsewhere. From references in the Victoria County History we can see that the mills were still operating, and in 1387 Sir Robert de Harington obtained a confirmation of Edward I's charter granting Ulverston a market and a fair. He may well have been trying to kick start the local economy, an economy which now more than ever depended on the undoubted winners of the population collapse, namely sheep.

The woollen industry, important before the Black Death, took off in the late fourteenth and fifteenth centuries when woollen cloth, as opposed to raw fleeces, became a huge export commodity. For reasons which were not entirely altruistic this trade was encouraged by Edward III and subsequent kings. The crown, perennially short of money, was constrained by the understanding that it could only tax people's income through parliament which, in turn, would normally only grant such taxes for wars. However, the crown could slap export taxes on wool and

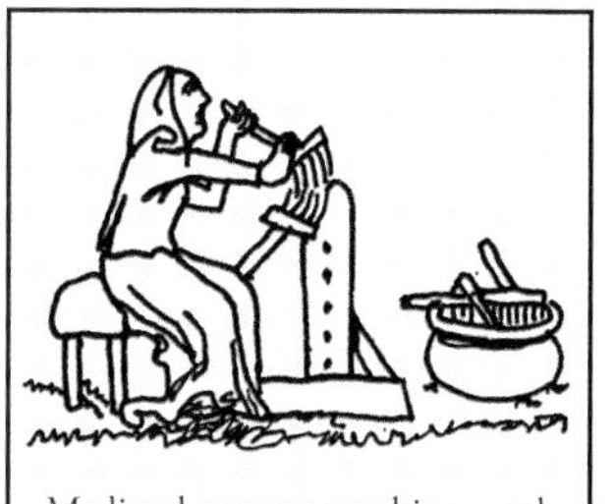

Medieval woman combing wool

'subsidies' on woollen cloth, giving it a vested interest in the health of the wool trade. Since there were fewer people to feed in the country, more land could be given over to raising sheep. This was not always a benign process: some landlords enclosed vast tracts of land and booted out peasant farmers to make way for sheep, a trend which caused a great deal of suffering. Kendal grew as a centre of woollen cloth manufacture, giving its name to 'kendilcloths' or 'kendils' which were a cheaper and coarser type of cloth, also made in Furness. In 1399 Henry IV granted exemption from subsidy for 'kendale' cloth and any other specified cloth which did not exceed the value of 13sh 4d the dozen, and parliament asked for this to be confirmed in 1402 and again in 1407. As always, where there is tax there is tax avoidance, and in 1423 the merchants of the Staple at Calais, which had the monopoly of buying English wool, accused Furness Abbey of trying to evade customs duty by shipping a load of wool for Flanders from Piel Castle. This was doubly cheeky, given that Piel Castle was meant to have been built to provide security not to assist in smuggling. Still, the evidence suggests that by the mid-fifteenth century wool and cloth merchants from Kendal and Furness were dealing with their counterparts in Manchester, and there is a reference to cloth from Kendal being sold in Bristol and its suburbs in 1443. We can see Ulverston after the Black Death as a smaller community quietly getting back on its feet by developing its woollen trade until it emerged to take advantage of the more eye-catching changes in the sixteenth century.

The Wars of the Roses

Having survived the Black Death and the Peasant's Revolt, in the second half of the fifteenth century England's ruling classes began to tear themselves apart in civil wars. Many people are aware that there was a connection between Ulverston and the unfortunate nine-day queen, Lady Jane Grey, and it was towards the end of these wars that this connection was made. Like everything else to do with these wars, from their causes down to whether it really was Richard III who murdered the princes in the Tower, even the name, 'The Wars of the Roses', has provoked heated debate, with some arguing that this name was an invention of later centuries. Certainly the idea of a struggle between the white rose of Yorkshire and the red rose of Lancashire sounds a lot more romantic than the gritty reality of a saga which would give the mafia a run for its money in terms of vicious infighting and hits on former allies as various descendants of Edward III squabbled over the crown. Unlike the civil wars of the seventeenth century this was not a clash of ideologies, neither was it a fight between the counties of Lancashire and Yorkshire. Its immediate cause may lie no deeper than the lack of a cast iron law about how the crown should be handed down. In theory real property was handed down to the eldest son, but in practice, if there was no suitable male heir, property could go to daughters or nephews and it could be divided. Of course, the crown could not be divided, and while primogeniture is straightforward on the surface, it was by no means clear what should happen if a king had no son or if his eldest son was unfit to rule. The ideal was for a king to have an heir and a spare, and perhaps Edward III took this too far by having five sons who grew up to have their own families, or, in the case of John of Gaunt Duke of Lancaster with his chequered marital history, his own two families. This meant lots of potential claimants to the throne.

Although Edward III's eldest son's child succeeded as Richard II with no serious conflict, as he grew up he fell into the bad old ways of over-spending, indulging favourites and trying to be an autocrat. To cut a long story short, Richard II faced opposition from his cousin, Henry Bolingbroke, son of John of Gaunt the Duke of Lancaster. Bolingbroke was forced into exile, and while he was abroad John of Gaunt died, upon which Richard seized all of Bolingbroke's rich Lancastrian inheritance for himself. This was seen as a threat to the whole system of inheritance, and Henry Bolingbroke returned, ostensibly only to wrest his lands and title back from Richard II. He ended up capturing Richard II and crowning himself Henry IV in 1399, letting Richard die in Pontefract Castle. This usurpation opened a whole can of worms, setting a precedent which was eagerly followed in the next century. Henry IV's grip on the crown was not secure, and the prestige of the monarchy only recovered briefly under his son, Henry V (1413 -1422), the last successful medieval king. Henry V died in 1422, whereupon his infant son was crowned Henry VI, and it was in his reign that things began to fall apart.

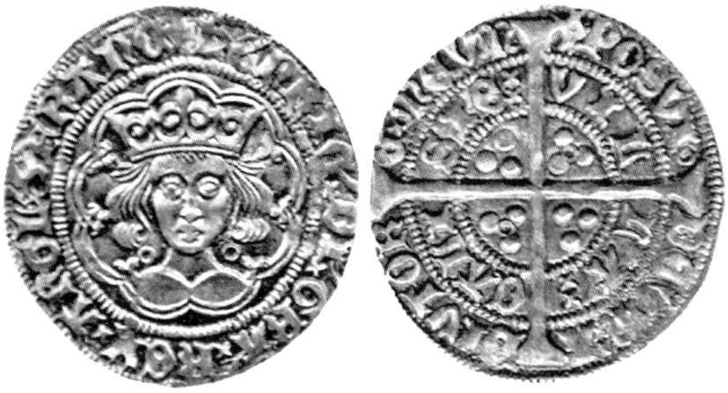

Groat with portrait of King Henry VI

Henry VI (1422 – 1461) would probably have been much happier as a monk or a priest in the chapel he built at Eton College than as a king of England with a feisty French wife, Margaret of Anjou. Religious, peace-loving and mentally fragile, he just wasn't up to fighting in France, where the English gradually lost most of their territories. Nor could he deal with the poisonous feud which developed between Edward Duke of Somerset who was also descended from John of Gaunt, Duke of Lancaster, and Richard Duke of York who had two of Edward III's other sons as his ancestors. This feud was compounded when it became entwined with a feud in the north between the Nevilles, led by the Earl of Warwick (the 'Kingmaker'), who came down on York's side, and the Percys, led by the Earl of Northumberland, who came down on Somerset and Henry VI's Lancastrian side. Posturing led to skirmishes, violence bred violence and the years between 1455 and 1485 read like an endless sequence of bloody battles and revenge killings in which first one side and then the other gained ascendancy. Although the Duke of York was killed in the Lancastrian victory at Wakefield in 1460, his son, Edward, succeeded in becoming crowned Edward IV in 1461 and in popping Henry VI into the Tower. Edward IV then reigned until 1470, at which point the former Yorkist mainstay, the Earl of Warwick, switched sides. Henry VI was dusted down and put back on the throne, and Edward fled.

In the following year, Edward IV came back, killed Warwick at the Battle of Barnet, wiped out every Lancastrian of note, including Henry VI's son, at the Battle of Tewkesbury and had the by now thoroughly confused Henry VI done to death. Then Edward IV turned on his own brother, the Duke of Clarence. He was allegedly drowned in a butt of malmsey for, among other things, spreading the rumour that Edward IV's marriage to Elizabeth Woodville was bigamous, and Edward's sons, soon to be the doomed princes in the Tower, illegitimate. Edward IV was no worse than his contemporaries and had a more attractive side. Intelligent, cultured and a snappy dresser, he began a long overdue organisation of the crown's finances, so much so that when he was felled by a seizure in 1483 he died rich, one of the few medieval monarchs to do so. On his death, the cycle of violence started again. His eldest son was only twelve and this was too good an opportunity for his other brother, Richard, to miss. Richard revived the bigamous marriage rumour, and Edward's two sons ended up in the Tower, never to be seen again. Richard became the much maligned Richard III (1483 – 1485) until two years later he was ousted by the only Lancastrian heir left standing, the obscure Henry Tudor.

These violent dynastic struggles might have debased the monarchy and proved fatal to many of the aristocracy and their armed retainers, yet unlike the wars in France they did not cause widespread destruction in the towns and countryside, and there is no record of armed conflict in Ulverston. There is a disappointingly brief note in the Victoria County History which states that 'Roland Kirkby of Ulverston was denounced among traitors in 1464, having adhered to the deposed king Henry VI after having sworn allegiance to Edward IV'. 1464 was the year of the Lancastrians' last stand in the north at Hexham, and this Roland may have been caught up in this skirmish. Lancastrian sympathies are certainly not true of Ulverston's absentee landlords, as is demonstrated by a look at the remarkable life of Cecily Bonville, heiress to the Harrington part of Ulverston.

By the time of the civil wars, through the marriage of Elizabeth, daughter of the 5th Baron Harrington, to William Bonville, the Harrington possessions in Ulverston and the title of Baron Harrington of Aldingham had passed to the rich Bonville family who, like the Harringtons, had estates in the west country. Elizabeth and William's son, another William, married Katherine Neville, sister of the Earl of Warwick (the Kingmaker), and Cecily was their only child. The Bonvilles were firmly in the Yorkist camp, and disaster struck the male line after the Lancastrian victory at the Battle of Wakefield in 1460. Cecily's father and grandfather were both executed after the battle, as was her maternal grandfather, Richard Neville the 5th Earl of Salisbury. In a display of vindictiveness, after another Lancastrian victory early in 1461 at St Albans, the vengeful Margaret of Anjou, Henry VI's wife, had Cecily's great-grandfather, the first Baron Bonville, killed as well. Only a few months old, Cecily was now the sole heiress to the vast Bonville and Harrington fortune, and, strange as it may seem after all this bloodshed, her inheritance remained intact. The reversal of fortunes which led to the Yorkist Edward IV gaining the crown must have helped, and Cecily's mother married again, this time to the first Baron Hastings, one of Edward IV's chief advisors. Her family's ties with Edward IV were reinforced in 1474 when Cecily, now of age, was married to Thomas Grey, the first Marquis of Dorset.

The rise of the Greys shows that although the upper aristocracy was being killed off left, right and centre, their numbers were always replenished by new arrivals. Edward IV, a dreadful womaniser, had been captivated by Elizabeth Woodville, the widow of a Lancastrian knight, Sir John Grey. He married her secretly, causing shock and consternation among his council who wanted him to make a prestigious foreign match, and he showered titles on her relatives, including her two sons by Sir John Grey. Queen Elizabeth Woodville, always with her eye on the main chance, arranged for Thomas Grey, her eldest son, to marry Cecily, the young heiress with the grand titles of 7th Baroness Harrington of Aldingham and 2nd Baroness Bonville. This is how the Grey family came to hold land in Ulverston, and it was Cecily's great-granddaughter who was the ill-fated Lady Jane Grey. Unlike her descendant, Cecily lost neither her fortune nor her head, and survived the dangers of Richard III's brief reign, when her new family secretly plotted to support Henry Tudor as long as he married the daughter of Elizabeth Woodville and Edward IV, another Elizabeth. The Greys remained in favour under Henry VII, and at the baptism of Prince Arthur, the eldest son of Henry VII and Elizabeth of York, Cecily carried the baby's train. If they wanted to survive, aristocrats had to trim their sails to suit the wind, but how deep this accommodation with the Tudors was in Furness is another matter.

• VII •

Dissolution and Dissent

Ulverston under the Tudors

Henry Tudor's victory at Bosworth in 1485 is regarded as one of the key turning points in English history, marking the end of the Middle Ages with its connotations of barbarism and the start of the early modern era. Pin-pointing 1485 as the beginning of a new age is fairly arbitrary, since the conflict between the houses of York and Lancaster was by no means played out, with relatives of Edward IV still getting their heads chopped off well into Henry VIII's time. On the other hand, it can't be denied that if Ulverstonians from 1485 time-travelled forward to 1585 they would see far more changes than if they went back a hundred years to 1385. They would see the once mighty Furness Abbey and Conishead Priory in ruins, the old familiar forms of worship replaced by a new bible in English and new services, churches stripped of their altars and decorations, and no Greys or Nevilles as absentee landlords. Whether these changes improved life for the inhabitants of Furness is debatable, given that in 1588, the year of the Spanish Armada, a commentator rather nastily remarked that 'the country is so rude, waste and unprovided of gentlemen'. We have to face the fact that Furness now had the reputation as a nest of potential traitors perfectly capable of letting the Spaniards in by the back door. This probably undeserved slur came from the obstinate survival of Roman Catholicism in the peninsula at a time when Protestantism had become conflated with 'English' patriotism. It might well be that the perception of Furness as somehow being backward originates in the sixteenth century, and this image wasn't helped by memories of Lambert Simnel's rebellion against Henry VII (1485 – 1509).

Henry Tudor's accession to the English throne was rather like a previously unknown wild card winning Wimbledon with everyone looking on in bemusement. His tenuous claim to the crown came from his mother, Margaret Beaufort, who was a descendant of John of Gaunt through his third wife, Katherine Swynford, whom he had married after the births of their children. Henry's father, Edmund Tudor, was the son of Owen Tudor, a Welsh gentleman who had somehow managed to marry Henry V's widow. After Richard III had helped himself to the crown, the unlikely co-conspirators of Margaret Beaufort and Queen Elizabeth Woodville, Edward IV's widow, hatched a cunning plan to try and put Henry Tudor on the throne on the condition that he married Elizabeth of York, Elizabeth Woodville's daughter by Edward IV. Surprisingly the plan succeeded. Plain Henry Tudor became Henry VII, reversed Richard III's ruling that Elizabeth of York was illegitimate, married her and by the end of 1486 had produced an heir, Arthur. Not everyone was convinced either that Henry VII had any claim to the throne other than by winning Bosworth or that he would last any longer than Richard III, and there were various Yorkist attempts to dislodge him. A prime mover in these was Richard III's nephew, the Earl of Lincoln, who had to flee to Burgundy where Edward IV's sister, Margaret, married to the Duke of Burgundy, nursed a particular hatred for Henry VII. Even though these two probably knew he was a fake, they put their weight behind a young unknown, Lambert Simnel, who had been coached to claim that he was the Earl of Warwick, the eldest son of Edward IV's brother, the Duke of Clarence (of butt of malmsey fame).

Lambert Simnel was taken to Dublin, a hotbed of Yorkist sympathisers, where he was crowned as Edward VI and was joined by Lincoln with a force of Swiss and German mercenaries, paid for by Margaret of Burgundy and led by a Colonel Martin Schwarz. This motley crew sailed to Piel Island where they landed and marched inland. It is unlikely that this was a chance destination: they would have known that no-one in Furness would offer any resistance and they may well have hoped that the locals would join a Yorkist claimant. It has to be remembered that before he seized the crown for himself the much-maligned Richard III had been a very popular deputy for Edward IV in the north, and gentlemen like Sir Thomas Broughton of Broughton Tower and Sir John Huddleston of Millom were pretty much die-hard Yorkists. In the event, local support in Furness did not materialise in any strength, and Lambert Simnel's cause suffered a setback when Henry VII had the real Earl of Warwick paraded in London. The rebels were defeated near Nottingham, the Earl of Lincoln was killed and Lambert Simnel survived to work in the palace kitchens where his head was a lot safer on his shoulders than that of the genuine Earl of Warwick who was eventually executed after another unsuccessful rebellion. The significance of Lambert Simnel's rebellion for Furness was not whether or not Martin Schwarz gave his name to Swarthmoor outside Ulverston, where his mercenaries camped, but in how the ease with which he landed at Piel Island was used to impugn the loyalty of the peninsula much later in Elizabeth I's reign. We can guess that there was already an undercurrent of indifference, if not outright hostility, to the Tudors in Furness before Henry VIII started dissolving the religious houses, and from comments made at the time of the dissolution we can see that these first Tudors had only a precarious legitimacy in many people's eyes.

In spite of all this, Henry VII did not make a bad fist of being king considering that he had had none of the training usually given to a potential heir. He has a reputation for being a terrible miser, and with some enthusiasm he carried on Edward IV's efforts to make the crown financially independent of parliament by accumulating its estates and running them efficiently. These money-grabbing tendencies got worse after the deaths of Arthur, his eldest son, in 1502, and of his wife,

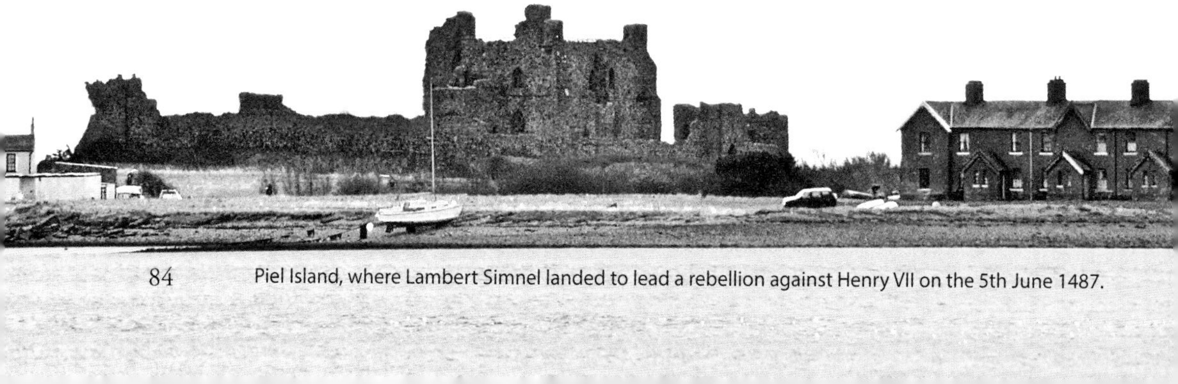

Piel Island, where Lambert Simnel landed to lead a rebellion against Henry VII on the 5th June 1487.

Elizabeth of York, in 1504, when he resorted to selling justice and fining the nobility for feuding or keeping private armies, so he was not the most popular man among the upper classes. This doesn't mean that Ulverston suffered under his rule and for most ordinary people this was a time of relative peace and well-being. For a start, Henry VII disliked expensive wars, and married off his eldest daughter, Margaret, to James IV of Scotland to ensure peace with England's traditional enemy in the north. This period is seen as a bit of a golden age for artisans, craftsmen and yeomen farmers. With the population still low after the Black Death there was enough food to go round and, although there were regional variations, living standards rose, especially in areas involved with the woollen industry.

Henry VII followed previous kings in encouraging the wool trade, and in 1509 we hear of Thomas Pennington of Furness who was a 'yeoman, kendilman, clothier or carrier'. He may have been typical of independent men who were part time farmers and part time dealers in woollen cloth, making a decent living in a world where serfdom had disappeared. Since the Victoria County History notes that the market and fair in Ulverston were the subjects of inquiries in 1498 and 1500, we can assume that trade was carrying on in the borough. An interesting feature of Ulverston Parish Church is an inscribed stone, found in the tower, which requests prayers for the soul of William Dobson who 'gave unto this work' and who was a gentleman usher to Queen Elizabeth. If, as some historians believe, this refers to Henry VII's queen, Elizabeth of York, rather than Elizabeth I, then the people of Ulverston may have done some improving building work on their church during Henry VII's reign, as did the inhabitants of many other communities across England in these more settled and prosperous times. Henry VII died in 1509, and although there were various

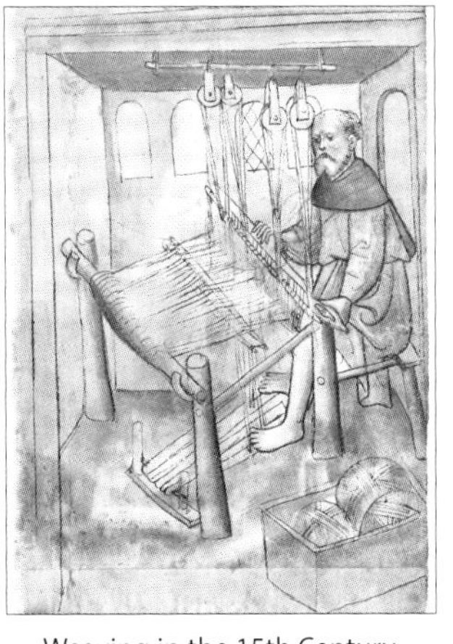

Weaving in the 15th Century.

Yorkist claimants floating around, for the first time in nearly a century a son followed his father to the throne, and the seventeen year old Henry VIII was crowned to the kind of rejoicing which, with the benefit of hindsight, we might think slightly misplaced.

Henry VIII and the Dissolution of the Monasteries

Henry VIII (1509 -1547) wrought huge changes in England. In less than three years from 1536, Furness lost Conishead Priory, Furness Abbey and a whole social system which, whatever its shortcomings, had provided some sort of welfare support, education and health care. The Furness religious houses provided guides across the sands and courts to settle disputes, functions which were vital for the local economy, and although at times they may have been annoying landlords, at least they were always there, and people knew where they were with them. After the dissolution of the monasteries these institutions underpinning communal religious life with its processions and feast days and power to bind the community together were gone, causing the kind of anger and confusion we might feel if it was suddenly announced that the monarchy and Houses of Parliament were to be abolished and we were to be ruled directly from Brussels. It is easy to portray Henry VIII as a monster, riding roughshod over anyone who dared stand in his way and beheading the unwanted wives he could not divorce in his obsessive quest for riches and a legitimate male heir. A more balanced view would be that he was a king whose ambition often exceeded his grasp and income, and that the clash between his wishes and events over which he had no control conspired to form a perfect storm which changed England forever.

Henry may have yearned to be like a great medieval English king, be crowned king of France and found a dynasty, but times had moved on. His adventures in France achieved little apart from wasting money, after which Parliament put its foot down and refused to fund any more wars. As the only surviving son of Henry VII he was the last man standing of the Tudor line, and if he died without a male heir there were still several candidates from the house of York who had good claims to the throne, the thought of which probably gave him sleepless nights.

At the same time, the reforming ideas of Luther and his contemporaries were gaining momentum on the continent, ideas which Henry at first vehemently opposed, so much so that the Pope gave him the 'Defender of the Faith' title which English monarchs, with no apparent sense of irony, still use today. However, his 'great matter' or striving to get out of his marriage to Katherine of Aragon, his brother Arthur's widow, who had not provided him with a son, led him to follow the reformers and open the Pandora's Box of turning to the Bible, rather than to the church and the Pope, for authority. It's possible that the blessing of the church on an annulment of his marriage might have been a formality if the Pope hadn't been under the thumb of Katherine's nephew, the Holy Roman Emperor Charles. Henry's advisors finally helped him cut the Gordian knot and solve the problem by declaring that as an emperor, he, not the Pope, was the supreme head of the church in England. The Act of Supremacy overturned an arrangement which had existed since the Anglo-Saxon kings converted to Christianity, and contravened the clause of Magna Carta declaring that the English church should be free from royal interference. The clergy in England were forced to agree to the Act, and Henry got his divorce. More pertinently, the English church's vast wealth was now at his disposal. This wealth was totalled up in the 'Valor Ecclesiasticus' of 1535, and in 1536 all religious houses worth less than £200 a year were ordered to surrender to Henry's agents to be dissolved. Conishead Priory fell into this category, and its attempted closure in 1536 led to an outcry.

Henry VIII didn't invent dissolving monasteries; he took an occasional policy to its logical conclusion. Previous rulers had dissolved religious houses and used the money to endow colleges at the universities of Cambridge and Oxford which were taking over the monasteries' educational role, and there is general agreement that by the sixteenth century monastic life had gone into a decline. In the 1520's Cardinal Wolsey, Henry's right-hand man, until he botched up the divorce from Katherine of Aragon, had tried to dissolve Conishead Priory, and had

had permission from the Pope himself to close 29 religious houses to fund a college at Oxford. One way of looking at Henry's swoop on the monasteries is as an extension of his father's and Edward IV's efforts to consolidate and make profitable the royal estates, which, since the Act of Supremacy, now included everything owned by the English Church. Although Conishead Priory, together with Cartmel Priory across the Bay, was technically dissolved in 1536, the locals were so incensed that, in one of the first examples we have of people in Furness involved in an ideological struggle, the 'armed commons' put the canons back in the priory. It also appears that a number of men from Furness joined the Pilgrimage of Grace, the uprisings in the north against Henry's recent policies and especially against their chief architect, Thomas Cromwell. The rebels, who included members of the gentry, had a wide range of national and localised political, economic and religious grievances, from opposition to Henry's Statue of Uses, which would make it harder for the gentry to pass on land, through the assault on religious houses to fears that even baptism was about to be taxed. Henry's deputies employed the well-tried strategy, which rebels fell for every time, of making promises to negotiate and then rounding up the ringleaders when their cause had lost momentum. In early 1537, all the canons from Cartmel were indicted for treason, and four were executed together with ten local men. Luckily for them, the canons from Conishead escaped with their lives through lack of evidence against them.

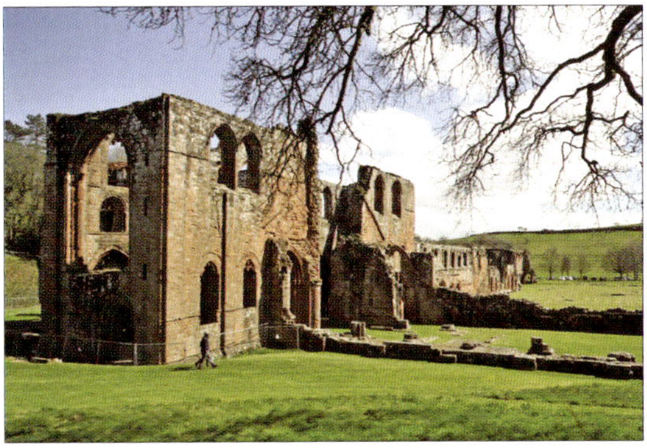

The ruins of Furness Abbey dissolved by Henry VIII in 1537.

The uprising in the north made Henry more obdurate, and in April 1537 the monks at Furness Abbey were forced to sign a deed of surrender, making the abbey the first of the great monastic houses to be dissolved.

The lead was then stripped from the roofs and melted down, making the surrender irreversible. Before the surrender, in a febrile atmosphere of spying and accusations of treason the monks surprisingly let rip with incriminating statements such as 'no secular knave' should be head of the church, and that Henry wasn't even a proper heir to the throne since his father had only gained it by violence. Such sentiments suggest that the Tudors were far from being universally accepted as the ruling dynasty in Furness, and that the Wars of the Roses were still being fought in people's heads. Nevertheless, they were fought in vain. Henry's ruthlessness prevailed and with the end of the abbey and the introduction of instruments of state control such as parish registers, Furness underwent an administrative shake-up comparable with the coming of the Normans.

There is an argument that the deleterious effects of the Dissolution of the Monasteries on local communities and on clerics themselves have been exaggerated. By the sixteenth century, most monastic land was already rented out to tenant farmers who in effect merely swapped one landlord for another. After the Dissolution the majority of monks were pensioned off or became parish priests; the Abbot of Furness for example ended up as the vicar at Dalton church. Callous though it sounds, just as some survivors eventually benefited from the Black Death, winners began to emerge from the bitterness and turmoil of the Dissolution in Furness, as the end of monastic control enabled local families to continue their climb from the ranks of tenant farmers to the gentry. One such family was the Sandys family, originally from the Solway, who seem to have been tenants of Furness Abbey in the area between Windermere and Coniston. Probably through the offices of an influential uncle, William Sandys was appointed Henry VIII's Receiver in Furness, and was able to accumulate tracts of land and an interest in the Abbey's three iron furnaces in this area. One of his sons, Edwin, became a Protestant Archbishop, and another son, William, eventually bought the site of Conishead Priory.

For the mercenary another silver lining of the Dissolution was the sudden availability of great quantities of quality building stone, and this

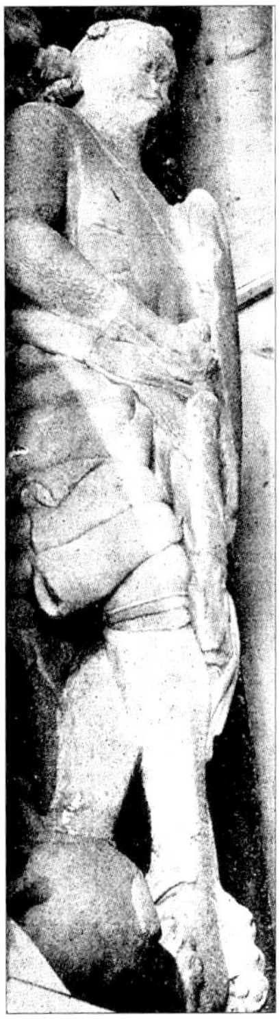
Effigy recovered from Furness Abbey. North Lonsdale Magazine

came in handy for the people of Ulverston when the parish church collapsed in the winter of 1540-1541. According to one account in the Victoria County History, the 'steepil standing in the middle thereof which was false in the foundation, unknown to anybody, which suddenly fell down carrying with it the whole church', and it has usually been assumed that the tower we can see today was the offending unsafe structure now rebuilt. However, some local historians believe that the tower is still the Norman construction, and the steeple in the middle of the church a feature which has disappeared. Whatever the truth of this, when Henry VIII was petitioned for help, he ordered the locals to take stone from Furness Abbey and Conishead Priory to rebuild the church, which they most likely did. It is often said that Ulverston's market became established after Furness Abbey disappeared and could no longer jealously guard its own market at Dalton. There seems enough evidence that Ulverston had had a market at least since its charter was granted in the thirteenth century, although by 1646 it was described as a 'great market town', so there may be some truth in the idea of Ulverston rising as Dalton declined, and this in part might have something to do with the rise of local business-minded families.

Henry VIII's successors

The next traditional landowners in Ulverston to disappear were the Grey family, whose fortunes became entangled with the religious and political upheavals following Henry VIII's death. One of the many contradictory aspects of Henry VIII's character is that although he wrought the most radical change in the English church for centuries, he was conservative when it came to religious doctrine, and was unwilling to let Protestant reformers challenge official beliefs or question established rituals. This all changed when he died in 1547. Protestant ideas established among some of the nobility and upper clergy were unleashed on the public at large after the accession of Edward VI, Henry's nine year old son. Edward VI (1547 – 1553), by all accounts a serious-minded if not priggish child, was brought up as a Protestant, and under the Protectorship of his maternal uncle, Edward Seymour the Duke of Somerset, an assault began on all traditional Catholic practices, now condemned as superstitious idolatry. Churches were stripped of statues, crucifixes and rood screens, medieval wall-paintings were whitewashed over, and stained glass windows were smashed, while congregations were made to use a new prayer book with religious processions and mystery plays banned. This iconoclasm spread to Furness, where there is evidence in the church at Great Urswick of the whitewashing of medieval paintings and the destruction of statues, perhaps as a result of the preaching of the few Protestant priests recorded in the area. Even so, from events later on it seems that many people in the area were reluctant to embrace Protestantism, unlike the Grey family who came a cropper by nailing their colours to a rather wobbly Protestant mast.

From a distance of more than four and a half centuries, the sad story of Lady Jane Grey has the power to rouse our sympathy. Her father was Henry Grey, the Marquis of Dorset and grandson of Cecily Bonville, the heiress whose possessions included the former Harrington part of the manor of Ulverston, and who survived the vicissitudes of the Wars of the Roses. Henry Grey did very well for himself, ending up married to Henry VIII's niece, Frances Brandon, the daughter of Henry's sister Mary and Charles Brandon the Duke of Suffolk. When Charles Brandon's sons by another marriage died, the title of Duke of Suffolk came through Frances Brandon to Henry Grey, and he and Frances had three daughters, Lady Jane being the eldest. Jane was a prototype bluestocking. Intelligent, studious and determinedly Protestant, she seems to have been fonder of her books than her pushy parents, and if Edward VI hadn't been such a sickly youth, she might have been left in peace. As it was, by 1553 it became clear that Edward VI wasn't long for this world, and John Dudley, the ambitious Duke of Northumberland, who had replaced the Duke of Somerset as Edward's chief adviser in a ruthless coup, became afraid of what would happen when the inevitable happened. Henry VIII's will, confirmed by an Act of Parliament, stated that if Edward died childless he should be succeeded by Mary, Henry's daughter by Katherine of Aragon, and that if she in turn died without an heir, the crown should go to Elizabeth, Ann Boleyn's daughter. All through Edward VI's reign Mary had remained defiantly Catholic, and she was probably the last person the Protestant Duke of Northumberland wanted to see on the throne.

Northumberland and the Greys cooked up a scheme whereby Jane Grey would marry Northumberland's son, and Edward VI persuaded to

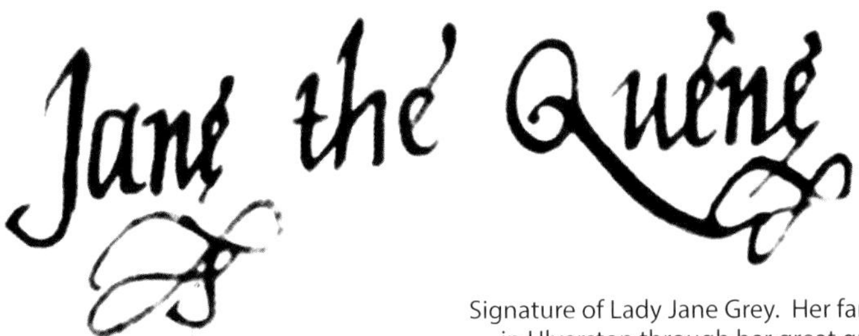

Signature of Lady Jane Grey. Her family inherited land in Ulverston through her great grandmother Cecily, 7th Baroness Harrington of Aldingham

change the line of succession to this line of Henry VIII's family. This Edward duly did as he was dying, and after his death in 1553, Northumberland and the Greys proclaimed that Jane Grey was now the new queen, an announcement which did not go down a storm. For all the reservations people might have had about Mary's Catholicism, she was Henry VIII's eldest child and the legal successor, and very few could stomach the notion of a son of John Dudley, born a commoner, being married to a queen of England or even, heaven forbid, becoming a king. Support fell away from Northumberland, and Mary was able to take control of London and the crown. Belying her image of an embittered persecutor of heretics, Mary refused to execute Lady Jane or her father until, with what looks like wilful stupidity, he joined in a rebellion against her. Jane went to the scaffold and the Grey estates, including their part of the manor of Ulverston, went to the crown.

Tragic though Jane Grey's fate may have been, the Greys' demise was another opportunity for local families around Ulverston to go up in the world. It's not entirely clear exactly what the Greys owned in Ulverston, but they held at least part of Plumpton, roughly the area along the shore between Arrad Foot and what is now Canal Foot. In 1557 this land, together with Plumpton Hall, was bought by John Sawrey. This purchase might have been connected with the sale three years earlier of the site of Conishead Priory to William Sandys, son of the William Sandys who had been Henry VIII's receiver in Furness. The Sawreys and Sandys were neighbours at Greythwaite, the Sawrey family holding Low Hall and the Sandys family Upper Hall, and both families were involved in the iron industry. After the Dissolution, another John Sawrey had been William Sandys senior's partner in the three bloomsmithies previously owned by Furness Abbey. This John Sawrey died in 1547, and William Sandys had to pass on one of the bloomsmithies to his widow who had remarried into the Rawlinsons, another family long associated with the iron industry in Furness. Plumpton had an iron ore mine to which the canons of Conishead Priory had been granted access by William de Lancastre III all those centuries earlier, a fact which, given that people in those days had extraordinarily long memories for rights and customs, wouldn't have been lost on William Sandys junior, the buyer of Conishead Priory, and owner of two bloomsmithies. The John Sawrey who bought Plumpton may have done it to steal a march on William Sandys junior by gaining ownership of the mine,

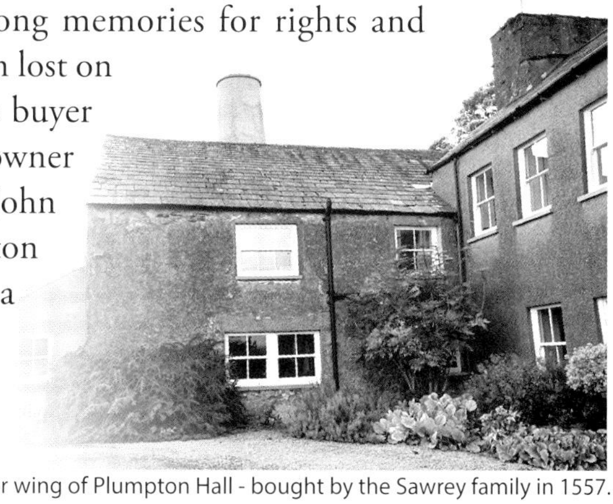

Tudor wing of Plumpton Hall - bought by the Sawrey family in 1557.

or the two men may have been business partners, both now owning land on the shore with easy access for trading boats and close to Ulverston's market.

The Sawreys of Plumpton certainly prospered, recording a pedigree, or becoming counted as gentry in the next century, as did William Sandys junior's descendants at Conishead, the Dodding family, even though William Sandys junior himself was murdered in an unsavoury dispute over tithes later on in Elizabeth I's reign. The somewhat sniffy comment quoted earlier that there were no gentry in Furness and that the place was a nest of Catholic traitors ignores the rise around Ulverston of families like the Sandys, Sawreys and Rawlinsons who were busy bettering themselves and who, as far as we can tell, by Elizabeth I's reign were Protestant either by conviction or in self-preservation.

Between 1547 and the 1560's the official religion of England changed three times, causing a fair amount of bewilderment and division in Furness as elsewhere in the country. Henry VIII was a sort of Catholic when he died in 1547 and Edward VI enforced Protestantism. Mary, who reigned from 1553 until 1563, restored Roman Catholicism and Elizabeth I (1563 – 1603) switched the English church back once more back to being Protestant. In spite of its hold over ordinary people, the appeal of the traditional Catholic religion with its long-established communal rituals diminished under Mary. Initially reasonably tolerant of private beliefs, Mary became increasingly repressive in the face of sullen opposition to her very unpopular marriage to King Philip of Spain, and she is mostly remembered, perhaps unfairly, for burning Protestants at the stake. Elizabeth I succeeded to the throne with the surprisingly modern idea that people could believe what they liked as long as they remained loyal to her: she did not, in her famous phrase, want to 'make windows into men's souls'. All the same, the Catholic mass was forbidden, papal power was abolished and a revised Book of Common Prayer was issued for use in all churches.

These switches and the way they divided communities are neatly illustrated in the mirror image careers of two Furness clergymen, Edwin Sandys, a son of William Sandys senior, and a John Christopherson of Ulverston. Edwin Sandys, who must have shown intellectual promise as a youth, was packed off to Cambridge and became a Protestant cleric. Perhaps unwisely he supported Lady Jane Grey's claim to the throne, and was imprisoned by Mary when she became queen. He managed to escape and fled abroad, returning after Elizabeth I's accession when he became Bishop of Winchester and then of London before being made Archbishop of York. John Christopherson's career was less happy. He remained a Roman Catholic and did his fleeing abroad in Edward VI's reign, returning only after Edward's death. He was chaplain to Queen Mary, and by the end of her reign was the Bishop of Chichester. Not the kind of man to keep his head down, he preached against Protestantism soon after Elizabeth I became queen, and was put into prison where he died. There must have been many people in Furness who wanted a quiet life and were willing to adjust to these switches in state religion, but some remained firmly Catholic. They carried on attending secret masses held by underground priests, a practice which became much riskier after the unsuccessful rebellion of the northern earls in 1569, the failure of which saw off Sir John Neville, the last of Nevilles who had held land in Ulverston since the fourteenth century.

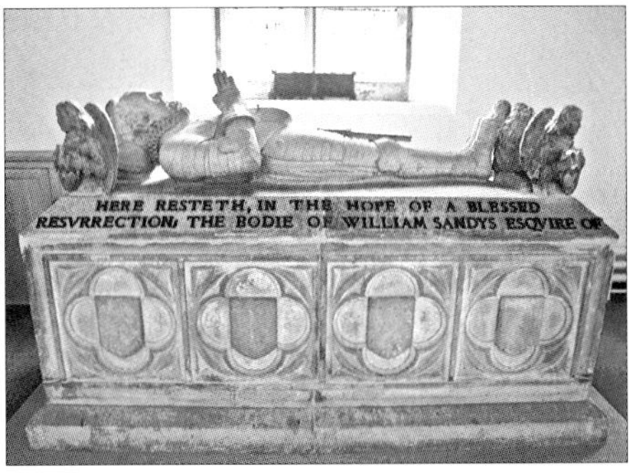

Memorial to William Sandys, owner of Conishead Priory after the dissolution.
St Mary's Church, Ulverston

The extensive Neville family, who held the earldom of Westmorland in the north, joined forces with their rivals the Percys, the traditional holders of the Earl of Northumberland title, in this sole major rebellion against Elizabeth I. Queen Mary had restored the Percys to the earldom of Northumberland after the fall of John Dudley, and the current Percy

Earl of Northumberland, perhaps not the brightest bulb in the box, had a number of grievances against Elizabeth I. By 1569, Mary Queen of Scots had been forced out of Scotland by the Scottish nobility exasperated by her scandalous private life, and she was in a polite form of custody in England, a nasty thorn in Elizabeth I's side. Mary Queen of Scots was the grand-daughter of Henry VIII's sister Margaret who had been married off to James IV of Scotland. She was a Catholic who had probably been complicit in the murder of her second husband Lord Darnley, and was about the only descendant of Henry VII left to whom the crown of England could go unless Elizabeth suddenly married and miraculously produced an heir. As someone who had a good claim to the throne, she was a magnet for Catholic plots, and the Earls of Westmorland and Northumberland planned to spring her from custody, make her queen and restore Catholicism. Their plan foundered when Mary was moved beyond their reach, the rebellion failed and as punishment the Neville lands in Ulverston were taken by the crown to be sold off in parcels. In response to the rebellion, more repressive anti-Catholic laws were passed, and this legislation, coupled with threats from Spain, encouraged the notion that to be a Catholic was equivalent to being a traitor. This was probably unfair on those in Furness who remained Roman Catholic, served by priests who periodically had to escape to the Isle of Man or Scotland in a boat kept at Piel Island specifically for this purpose.

Although its story is tangential to the history of Ulverston, the activities of the Company of Mines Royal in Furness should be mentioned. The Company of Mines Royal was a joint venture between representatives of Elizabeth I and expert German miners from the Tyrol set up to mine and smelt ores, especially copper, in the Lake District north of Keswick and on the Coniston Fells. The Germans, who had far more technical knowledge than the English at this time, were successful in mining copper ore and in establishing a smelter near Keswick, much to the annoyance of the Earl of Northumberland, the major landowner in the area, who claimed that the mines were his and who kept disrupting their work. It took a court to decide that he didn't have a case, and this was probably one of the grievances behind his rebellion. Men from the Mines Royal are the main source of damning comments about Elizabethan Furness, one going so far as to tell Elizabeth I that the country people were 'void, both of the fear of God and of your Majesty's laws'. This unimpressed representative visited Furness on a couple of occasions on one of which he met up with William Sandys. The purpose of his visits was to find new sources of charcoal for the Company's smelter. Without charcoal there could be no copper or iron, and it is clear that who owned the woods and what was done with them were already vexed questions by Elizabeth I's reign. In his book *The Early Iron Industry of Furness*, Fell makes a great deal of a decree of Elizabeth I in 1564, before the Mines Royal was established, which banned the use of wood to make iron for sale within the manor of Hawkshead. He states that this decree effectively abolished the bloomsmithies, and that the reason behind it was that wood was running out. On the other hand, in 1570 William Fleming of Coniston sold 2,000 pack horse loads of charcoal, made in Satterthwaite, Coniston and Grizedale, to the Mines Royal for their smelter, which suggests that there was plenty of woodland if it was managed properly. The Mines Royal had frequent complaints about woodland being made waste by cattle instead of being systematically cut and regrown. Whatever the reasons behind the decree of 1564, after Elizabeth's death in 1603 it was obviously quietly forgotten, the bloomsmithies were revived and the woodlands of Furness and the iron industry they supported were to play a major role in Ulverston's later prosperity.

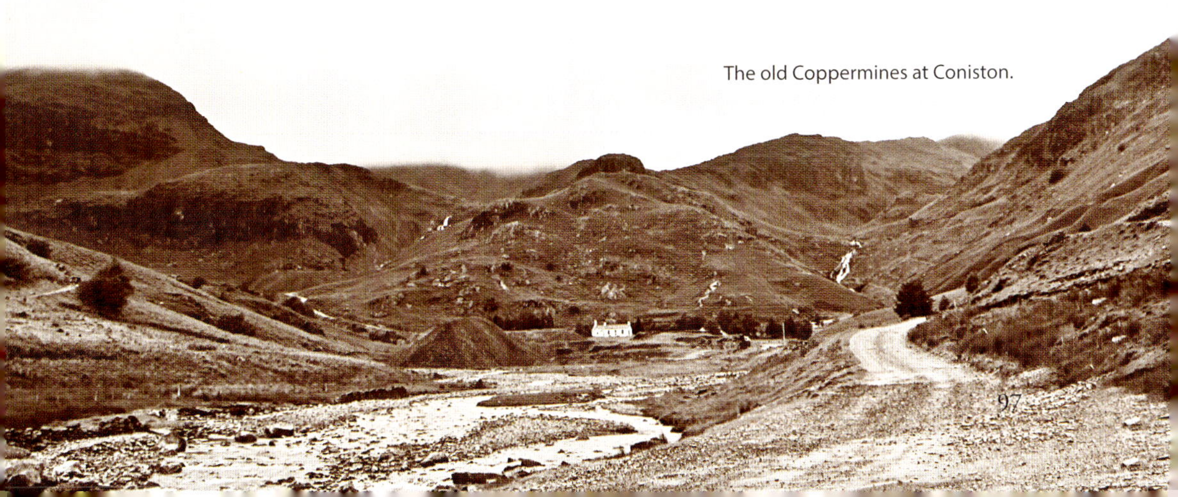

The old Coppermines at Coniston.

• VIII •

Civil War
Commonwealth and Restoration

Ulverston in the Seventeenth Century

Towards the end of her reign, Elizabeth I made a last barn-storming speech to fractious members of a parliament convulsed with opposition to her lavish granting of 'monopolies', royal permissions to be sole providers of anything from salt to starch. Proclaiming that they would never have a prince who loved them better, she pressed all the right buttons, and the Commons departed happy. Just as the dissolution of the monasteries and the creation of a Protestant Church of England would have been inconceivable at the start of the sixteenth century, so none of these MP's would have predicted that in less than fifty years' time, after bitter civil wars, a Parliamentary army would have captured and executed their king and made England a republic, the Commonwealth. Neither could they have anticipated the accompanying explosion of revolutionary ideas which have inspired generations of reformers and political theorists down to the present day. These ideas did not pass Furness by, rough and godless though the area might have appeared to the cosmopolitan employees of the Mines Royal, nor did people there escape the nastiness of civil war when neighbour fought neighbour and those who wanted to avoid conflict were squeezed by

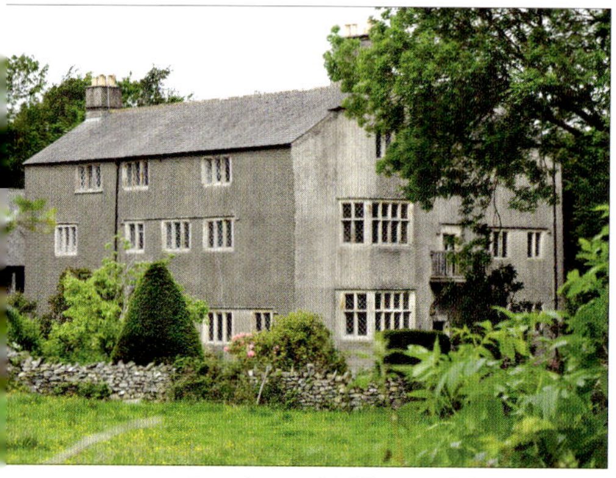

Swarthmoor Hall home of the Fell family from the reign of James I.

both sides. Moverover, it was in the Commonwealth era, through the Fell family of Swarthmoor Hall, that Ulverston became the centre for a new religious movement, Quakerism, which emerged from the religious and intellectual turmoil of the time. As it evolved, Quakerism was to punch above its weight in contributing to industrial and economic development not only in Furness but the whole of the country.

Well before armed conflict broke out, the economic and religious fault lines in English society which led to civil war were evident in Furness. A feature of the Tudor period was rapid population growth in England, and although this might be seen as a sign of success, more people meant increasing numbers of landless labourers who needed to buy food, so prices went up, causing poverty among those who had few resources. The Mines Royal were quick to point out that they were bringing employment and better wages to impoverished labourers in the Coniston area, implying that this was an endemic problem. While the poor struggled, rising food prices benefited farmers with secure tenures and fixed rents, and manufacturers with money to invest; people like the Sawreys at Plumpton and the heirs of William Sandys, the Dodding family, at Conishead. These families represented the 'middling sort' who were on the rise and whose income from agriculture and trade or industry was keeping well ahead of their outgoings, unlike some traditional great land-owning families whose income from rents was not keeping pace with inflation. With the survival of Roman Catholicism in Furness, this new gentry found itself divided by religion. In spite of the fines levied on 'recusants', or people who refused to attend Protestant churches, the Preston family who

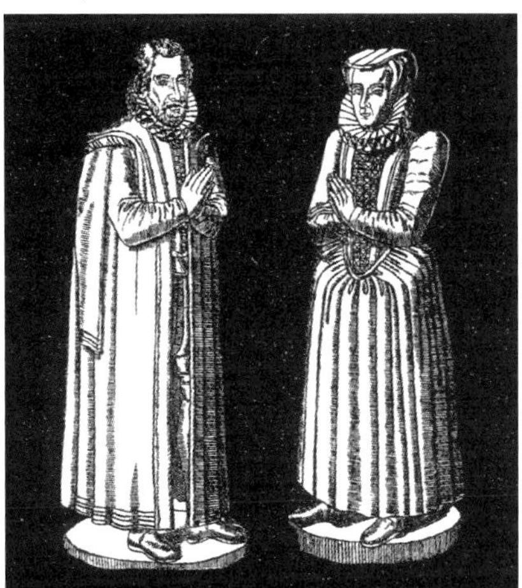

HERE BEFORE LYETH BVRIED THE BODIES OF MYLES DODDING ESQ: & MARGARET HIS WIFE WHO DIED IN THE YEARE OF O LORD 1606 AFTER THEY HAD LIVED MARIED 43 YEARES & HAD ISSVE TENNE CHILDREN OF WHOME THERE ONLY SVRVIVED THEM MYLES DODDING & HENRYE.

now held Furness Abbey manor and Holker Hall were Catholics, as were the Kirkby family from Kirkby Ireleth. To get round these anti-Catholic laws, families like the Kirkbys were 'church Papists': the men in the family went to church to avoid fines while the women took charge of practising Catholicism in secret and teaching it to their children. Neither Roman Catholics, like these Furness families, nor the more radical Protestants, the Puritans, were particularly enthused by Elizabeth I's successor, James Stuart I and VI.

James I and the rise of the Fells at Swarthmoor Hall

The reign of James I (1603 – 1625) is sometimes overlooked, and James never comes across as a particularly attractive man. All the same, unlike his son and successor, Charles I, he was clever enough to keep an uneasy peace between competing interests. As Mary Queen of Scots' son he had been king of Scotland since he was a few months old, and was widely accepted in England as the only possible heir to Elizabeth. The one great advantage in the north of his accession to the English crown was that it laid to rest any residual fear of Scottish raids and brought an end to the lawless era of the reivers in the borders. James wanted to take this one step further and unite England and Scotland into one country, Britain. This notion was strenuously opposed by the English parliament as its members feared, with some justification given James's belief in the divine right of kings, that if the king created a new country it might result in the loss of English law, customs and 'liberties' painstakingly acquired over the centuries. Thus the union of the two countries would have to wait until the early eighteenth century when the powers of the monarch were more circumscribed.

James's religious settlement, in which he tried to steer a middle course between Catholics and radical Protestants, pleased neither side. He made peace with Catholic Spain, which annoyed the Protestants who believed Englishmen should support their co-religionists on the continent, and after the Gunpowder Plot of 1605 he enforced the anti-Catholic laws he had previously relaxed. He also made little headway in resolving the recurring problem of the crown's finances, a fundamental issue behind the later civil war. Not only was he saddled with the legacy of Elizabeth I's debts, he also wanted to spend money on his family and inner circle of Scottish favourites about whom salacious rumours floated. Since Parliament refused to subsidise his extravagance, James tried to raise money by indirect taxes using his royal prerogative. This led the Commons, again with some justification, to fear that a financially independent monarch with no need to go cap in hand to Parliament could soon become a tyrant.

James's efforts to raise money can be seen in Furness where titles to manors which had previously reverted to the crown were sold to local gentry. In 1609 he sold Neville Hall manor and the part of Ulverston manor which had been held by Furness Abbey. After changing hands several times this latter title ended up with the Catholic Kirkbys of Kirkby Ireleth. Later on in 1613 he sold off the Ulverston manor portion which had belonged to the Greys, and this was acquired by the Fells of Swarthmoor Hall, whose family came from Hawkeswell near Broughton Beck. These Swarthmoor Fells certainly seemed to have thrived under James I despite national political problems. Iron-making was revived in Furness at this time, and Alfred Fell recounts that a new forge was built at Cunsey while Force Forge, later bought by the Fells of Swarthmoor and managed by the Rawlinsons, was built on Sawrey land in the Rusland valley. This was also a time of home improvements amongst the gentry. While it is a brave person who steps into the minefield of exactly when Swarthmoor Hall was built, it was

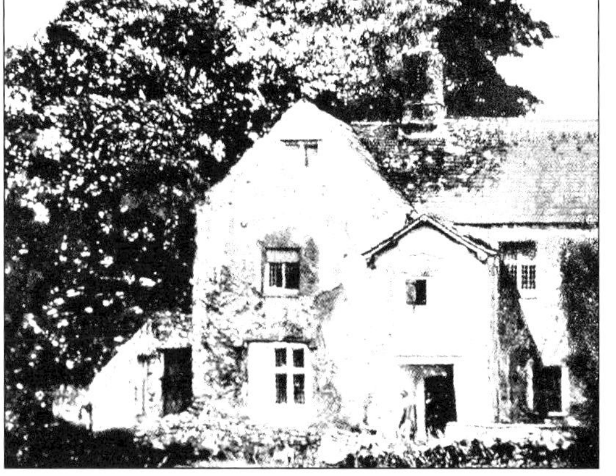
The only surviving picture of Neville Hall which may have been rebuilt or extended during the reign of James I.
Picture North Lonsdale Magazine

probably in James I's reign that it was extended and gained its distinctive main staircase. Neville Hall, as seen in a surviving photograph, may also have been built or extended in this period. Circled by confident gentry families and aided by its position on the coast, Ulverston was beginning to replace Dalton as the main market in Furness, and this can only have been helped by a localised outbreak of the plague which seems to have killed half of Dalton's population in 1631. Backward though Furness may have seemed to people from the south of England, there is no reason to assume leading families like the Fells were politically ignorant and, when civil war came in the 1640's, different families quickly formed their own opinions on which side to support.

The Civil War in Furness

In 1659, just before the restoration of the monarchy, Parliament debated how England had descended into a civil war which no-one had anticipated or wanted. Boiled down, their discussions pin-pointed three main factors behind the conflict: the constitutional crisis between King and Parliament regarding the extent of their legal powers; the religious divide between Protestants and Catholics; and economic changes, particularly inflation, which had left the Crown short of income.

Like Henry VIII, Charles I was a second son who came to the throne following the death of his elder brother with an inflated view of his position in the world. There the resemblance between the two kings ended. Whereas Henry VIII combined ruthlessness with the sense to keep those who mattered onside, Charles I was not very bright when it came to political realities. Besides his admirable qualities as a connoisseur of the arts and devoted husband and father, he possessed an unshakeable belief that as king, appointed by God, he was set apart from other men and could rule as he saw fit, ignoring any whingeing from his inferiors. Money, as always, was at the root of his problems with Parliament. Since Parliament was as obstructive as ever in writing the monarch a blank cheque, Charles decided to dismiss it and raise income from his prerogatives. In some quarters these indirect taxes were considered unconstitutional and a threat to English 'liberties', which at this time did not relate to personal freedom but to historic rights to the enjoyment of land and private possessions.

The king's dubious money-making methods are highlighted in a little note in the Victoria County History about George Fell senior and George Fell who in 1631 were 'compounded' or fined for refusing a knighthood. Mining obscure laws, Charles had found that men of a certain level of wealth were obliged to present themselves for knighthood, and he caught out many members of the gentry besides the Fells for failing to do this. The sense that Charles I was flouting accepted custom grew when he hit upon a wizard wheeze to collect 'ship money' throughout the country. Although it was accepted that this tax could be levied in ports during wartime, Charles's prosecution of inland landowners who refused to pay it alienated those who felt he was overstepping his authority.

Charles's religious policy made matters worse. His marriage to a French Catholic, and the appointment of Laud, his Archbishop of Canterbury, who was definitely what we would call a 'High' Anglican, fond of vestments, candles, gold plate and smells and bells, led Protestants to fear that the country was drifting back to 'popery'. Matters came to a head in Scotland where Presbyterian Protestantism, which dispensed with bishops, had become deeply rooted. Charles saw no reason why, as king of Scotland, he should not order the Scots to use his new English prayer book and to reinstate the authority of the bishops. The Scots saw every reason not to accept this, and most of their leaders signed the Covenant of 1637 pledging to oppose Charles. In 1640 a Scottish army invaded England and camped outside Newcastle, forcing Charles to recall Parliament to grant him money to resist them. Things went from bad to worse amid conspiracy theories of a Catholic plot to return England to the Church of Rome with Charles planning to bring over an Irish Catholic army to achieve this. The final straw came when Charles broke all protocol and marched with a band of armed men into Parliament to arrest five MP's whom he accused of treason. Although he failed, most Londoners, who by now formed nearly a tenth of England's population, turned against him. Parliament gained control of the London militia, and Charles was forced to leave the capital. In August 1642 he raised his standard at Nottingham, and civil war had begun.

The apocryphal tale of the Huntingdon squire who had no idea there was a war on until he chanced upon the king's army gearing itself up for its first major battle at Edgehill gives the impression that people outside the south-east of England were pretty much in the dark over this crisis in national politics. This isn't borne out by events in Furness, where the rumour that an Irish army was set to invade must have been widespread, since a petition was delivered to Parliament requesting a fleet to guard the coast. The leading families quickly divided into two camps, and it is difficult to work out if they were driven by deeply held beliefs or by local friendships and rivalries. The Catholic Kirkbys of Kirkby Ireleth and Prestons of Furness Abbey manor and Holker came out on the king's side, as did the Flemings of Coniston, the Penningtons of Pennington and Muncaster and Sir William Huddleston of Millom. Among those who supported Parliament were Thomas Fell of Swarthmoor, the Doddings at Conishead, Sawrey at Plumpton, the Sandys from Bouth and William Rawlinson of Graythwaite. These Parliamentarians belonged to families who had prospered since the dissolution of the monasteries and whose main connection may have been through the iron industry. They were also bound by at least one marriage after William Rawlinson married a daughter of Anthony Sawrey of Plumpton. Although people may have wanted to stick with their friends and relatives, conviction sometimes overcame family bonds. The Rawlinson family were divided by faith, with the branch at Cark being Catholic, and this branch came out for the king.

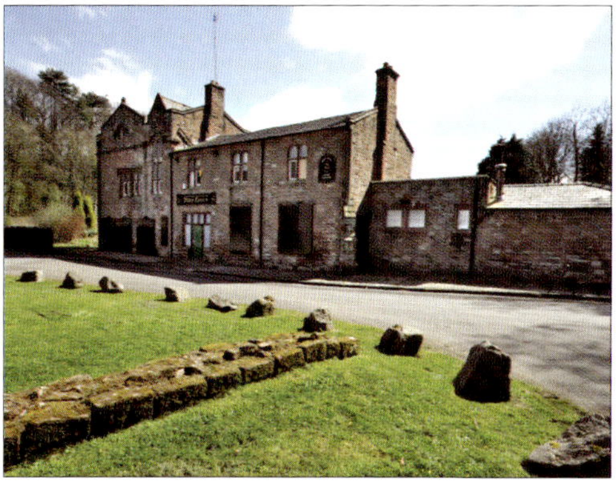

Abbey Tavern, the site of Furness Abbey Manor House, home to the Royalist Preston family in the civil war

The civil wars were a disaster for England, devastating the economy and, in proportion to the population, killing as many people as the First World War. Ulverston escaped relatively lightly. There were a couple of nasty skirmishes in Furness, but the area's main problem seems to have come from Royalist forccs, always short of money and provisions, sweeping in to loot anything they could lay their hands on. In February 1643, Parliamentary forces took Lancaster from the Royalists. Among the early casualties was Roger Kirkby who fled to Ireland where he died. Presumably to consolidate their hold in the north, Parliament sent a ship laden with ammunition to Piel, with George Dodding of Conishead on board. Unluckily for George, the voyage was a disaster and his ship had to be towed ignominiously into Wyre harbour where it was emptied of its cargo and blown up, and George was taken prisoner. While the Royalists were trying to recapture Lancaster, their commander, Lord Molyneux, led a plundering party into Furness, only desisting and retreating into Westmorland when more Parliamentary troops moved north. In September of the same year, the king's supporters in Furness bounced back under Sir William Huddleston of Millom. He crossed the Duddon sands and, together with Royalists from Muncaster and Kirkby Ireleth, occupied Dalton and popped all the Parliamentarians he could find under lock and key in Dalton Castle. Down but not out, some escaped and asked for help from a Colonel Rigby who was besieging Thurland Castle near Kirkby Lonsdale. Dropping everything, the colonel dashed to Furness, spent a night in Ulverston and the next day, October 1st, advanced to Lindal after morning prayers. Following exchanges of

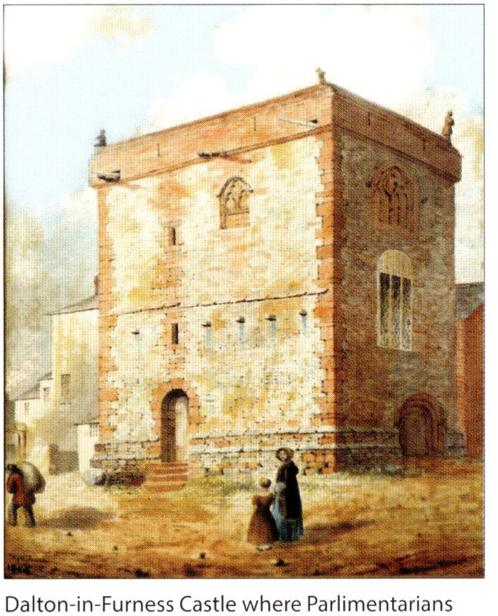

Dalton-in-Furness Castle where Parlimentarians were briefly imprisoned by Royalists in the civil war. Painting by W.P. Richards, courtesy of Sheila Atkinson.

verbal abuse, there was a scrappy fight and the Royalists broke and fled.

Following the skirmish at Lindal, Furness seems to have remained under loose Parliamentary control, with a fleet calling in at Piel at intervals, until after the Royalist defeat at Marston Moor in July 1644 when a retreating Royalist, Sir John Maney, arrived to collect the king's manorial rents. By this time, William Rawlinson of Graythwaite had raised a cavalry troop and gone off to fight for Parliament elsewhere, as had Colonel Dodding. In a vicious encounter at Piel, Maney suppressed opposition from locals and Parliamentary sailors, leaving him free to extort 'rents' as he pleased. He was halted by the approach of Colonel Dodding and a Scottish army and disappeared in the direction of Oxford, where Charles had his court during the war. This was the last action of the civil war in Furness, and when Charles I surrendered to the Scots in 1646, Royalists like Thomas Preston of Holker, Robert Rawlinson of Cark and John Kirkby of Kirkby Ireleth made their peace with Parliament. Whereas William Rawlinson and Colonel Dodding supported Parliament with some zeal, and the Royalist gentry were committed to the crown, one doesn't get the impression that the people of Ulverston were raring to lay down their lives for either side. On his rent-collecting trip, Maney listed tenants in Ulverston to guard the town for the king, but they made it clear that they were unwilling to leave Furness and fight elsewhere. In common with many other Englishmen, they probably hoped that both sides would go away and leave them in peace. When we look at Ulverston in the Commonwealth period we find the scars of war healing fast, and some people doing very nicely for themselves.

Oliver Cromwell and the Commonwealth

The complex politics of the Commonwealth are dominated by the figure of Oliver Cromwell, who presided over the attempt to govern England without a king. After Charles I's first surrender in 1646 the majority of Parliament was in favour of a negotiated settlement, in spite of Charles's stubbornness and duplicity. The stand-off was complicated by a new force in England, the New Model Army, created by Parliament and usually described as the first professional army in the country. Many of its junior officers and men had developed radical political beliefs, including extending the franchise to every adult male, ending compulsory tithes and, still a step too far for us in the twenty-first century, disestablishing the Church of England. Unlike the majority of MP's, these men wanted Charles brought to account and tried. Charles made things worse for himself by escaping custody and, in an unlikely alliance with the Scots, re-igniting the civil war. This second civil war ended when Cromwell and the New Model Army defeated Charles outside Preston. After more dithering by Parliament, the army lost patience and in December 1648 sprang what was in effect a military coup. Parliament was purged, leaving the so-called 'Rump' and Cromwell set up a court to try Charles for treason. Charles's execution in January 1649 left a crown-shaped hole at the top of government, and shrunken Parliaments and the army tussled over what the new political order should look like. In 1653, following his successful military occupation of Scotland and bloody conquest of Ireland, Cromwell succeeded where Charles I had failed, and marched into Parliament to dismiss it. By the end of the year he had been proclaimed Lord Protector and until his death in 1658 ruled to all intents and purposes as a military dictator, appointing major-generals as governors of the English regions. Cromwell was sincere in his belief that government should make people 'good', and so introduced the unpopular Puritan measures associated with him, such as banning Christmas, the theatre, horse races, casinos and brothels. These constitutional experiments rather fell apart after Cromwell's death in 1658, and government gradually ground to a halt. From his exile in the Netherlands, Charles II cunningly offered his help to the Speaker of the Commons, promising that he would not rule as his father had done, and that there would be no reprisals. With the army now under the command of General Monck, a former Royalist, it seems that people accepted this offer with relief, and when Parliament declared in May 1660 that government should be by king, lords and commons, England's flirtation with republicanism was over.

The turbulence of the Commonwealth and the growth of new political ideas went hand in hand with a flourishing of new and alternative religious beliefs. Puritans had always emphasised salvation through individual faith, rather than through the intercession of a priest. For them, communion was less important in a church service than the sermon. The practice of sponsoring lecturers to preach in different churches was common, a practice which had spread to Furness by the 1650's. Some puritan sects rejected the established church altogether, and with the collapse of censorship in the civil war they were able to publish their views in widely read pamphlets. Among these was the belief that any man or woman could receive divine inspiration, interpret the Bible in their own way and preach to a congregation. Some people, influenced by current prophesies, also believed that the civil war represented a struggle against the anti-Christ, that these were the latter days of the world and that the Second Coming was at hand. It is against this background of heightened religious sensibility that Quakerism, in which Ulverston was to play such an important part, was born and mushroomed into a serious challenge to the established Protestant church.

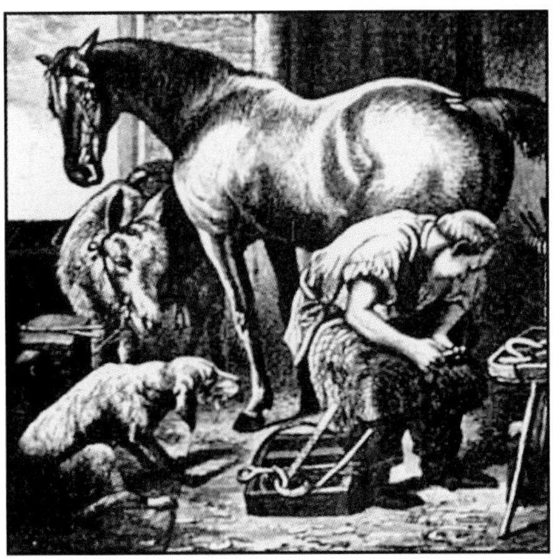

The town blacksmith, an indispensable part of life in Ulverston in the 17th Century.

The Ulverston to which George Fox, the founder of Quakerism (or The Society of Friends) came in 1652 was not suffering unduly under the Commonwealth. In a record of 1646 it was described as a great market town, and trade seems to have been flourishing. Because it was not obligatory for marriages to take place in churches until 1753, occupations do not regularly appear in parish records until 1754. Nevertheless, there are scattered references to occupations in the years 1653 and 1655. These include a miller, a husbandman and a blacksmith, and a series of occupations to do with the wool and clothing trade, including a dyer, a webster (weaver), a mercer (or dealer in cloth), a clothier, a hatter and a tailor. There are also whitesmiths, who worked in tin and mended metal goods, a mariner (probably involved in the coastal trade) and a piper, whose prospects of work under the Puritans might not have been so bright. Some families were prospering: Andrew Fell, from a branch related to the Fells of Swarthmoor, was able to build a new house on Daltongate when he married in 1654, and this is also the year on a date stone on the building in Market Street next to the Rose and Crown, suggesting re-building in the town centre. What is now Murray's chemists, one of Ulverston's oldest surviving buildings, may have been built around this time, if not earlier, by the Fells of Swarthmoor as a manorial court house. With no pictures of Ulverston until the eighteenth century, we can only guess the stages by which the town changed from a medieval settlement, perhaps with the gable ends of its houses facing the road, to the more modern layout of the eighteenth and nineteenth centuries. William Rollinson, the eminent historian of the Lake Counties, sees the years around 1650 as the time when the 'Great Rebuilding', during which medieval farmhouses and cottages were torn down and rebuilt, reached the north of England. With an end to problems in the Borders and a revival of the wool trade, people could afford to build houses with load-bearing masonry walls and slate roofs in the place of simpler dwellings based on an oak cruck frame, and this may have been happening in Ulverston.

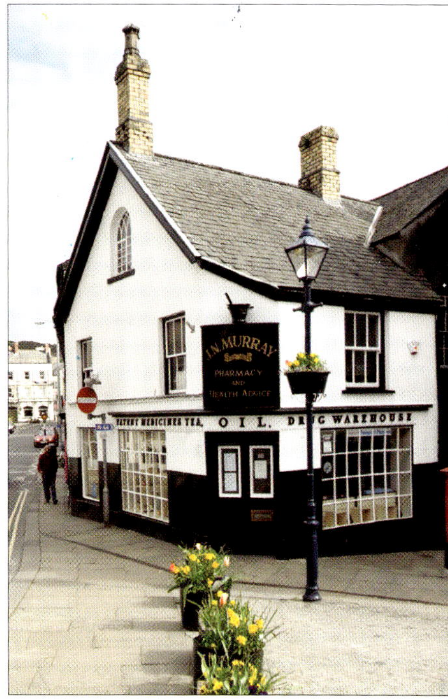

One of the oldest surviving buildings in Ulverston, perhaps built as a manorial court house and market building.

George Fox and Quakerism in Furness

Just as Furness had been divided by civil war, the arrival of George Fox shows people in and around Ulverston torn between clinging to stability and engaging in new ideas. George Fox's father was a Leicestershire weaver while his mother came from the gentry. Like many of his contemporaries he thought deeply about religion and sought out new religious experiences. Eventually he took to the road, preaching the belief that Christ could be found in everyone and attracting large audiences in the north, especially around Sedbergh. Arriving at Swarthmoor Hall, whose hospitality to preachers was well-known, he was persuaded by Margaret Fell to speak to the congregation in Ulverston parish church. Listening to him there, she had a road to Damascus moment, and from then on tirelessly supported Fox and his movement despite persecution and imprisonment, eventually marrying him eleven years after Thomas Fell's death.

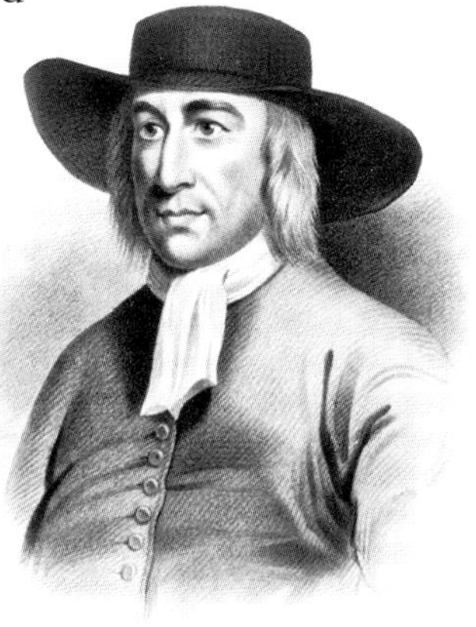

George Fox

Even the normally non-committal Victoria County History describes Margaret Fell as a 'woman of heroic type', and she would have been a force to reckon with in any age, let alone one in which dissenting women could face acute hostility. She was born Margaret Askew at Marsh Grange near Dalton, and there are claims that she was the great-granddaughter of Anne Askew, one of the first Protestant 'martyrs' in Henry VIII's reign. This is not the case, although she seems to have been an educated and intelligent Puritan. Married to Thomas Fell of Swarthmoor Hall when she was nineteen, she had one son and seven daughters who grew to adulthood. By 1652 Thomas Fell, a former MP, had been appointed a circuit judge and when George Fox turned up in Ulverston he was away on judicial business. On his return, local men, including the parish priest and Sawrey of Plumpton, outraged by Fox, asked him to show this interloper the door. Fell, who comes across as amazingly reasonable for a time when religious tolerance was not in the national mind-set, gave his wife and Fox a hearing. Although he never became a Quaker, he allowed Margaret and other converts, including his seven daughters, to hold their meetings in Swarthmoor Hall. It was this secure base, the home of eight committed women with an estate to support them, which ensured the long-term survival of Fox's movement.

By 1657 the numbers of Fox's followers nationwide had grown to around 50,000 men and women. Among them in Furness were people connected to the Fell family, like their land steward, Thomas Salthouse, and Thomas Rawlinson, their manager at Force Forge. These followers faced brutal persecution, being the victims of the first anti-dissenter laws, and Fox was regularly beaten up and imprisoned. This hostility to Quakerism was founded on the ingrained assumption that social cohesion and national survival depended on everyone having the same religious beliefs. The Quakers posed a threat, demanding social reforms as well as religious freedom. They refused to pay tithes, disrupted church services, challenged local magistrates and, believing that everyone was equal in the sight of God, objected to taking their hats off to authority figures. While they appealed to people who wanted real change to come from the civil wars, to others they were an anti-social menace and potential rebels. In spite of Margaret Fell's personal entreaties, Cromwell began to clamp down on the Quakers by attempting to impose compulsory attendance at the established churches, and many were imprisoned.

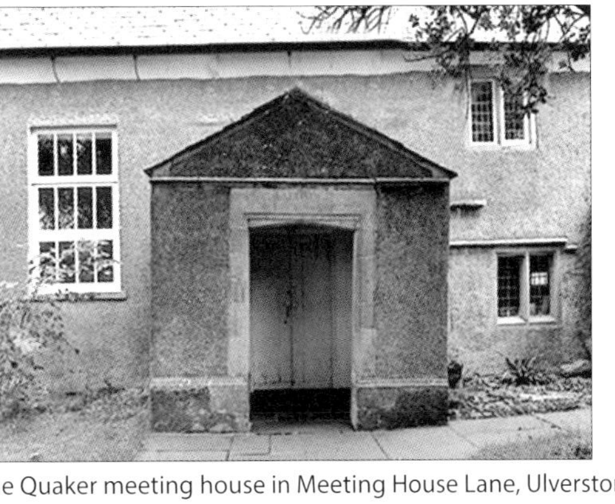

The Quaker meeting house in Meeting House Lane, Ulverston.

Following the restoration of the monarchy in 1660, Margaret Fell persuaded Charles II to release 4,000 Quakers from prison. This did not put an end to their persecution. During the reigns of Charles II (1660 – 1685) and his brother, James II (1685 – 1688), the fortunes of the Quakers like the Fells and other dissenting groups like the Catholics depended on the vagaries of national politics rather than on high-minded ideas of tolerance. At least Charles II, who was fairly cynical and much preferred spending time with his mistresses, horses and dogs to micro-managing his kingdom, didn't insist on a vengeful bloodbath, and only those who had signed his father's death warrant were hunted down. Disputes over land were cleared up, and Thomas Fell's heir, George, was granted a general pardon, even though his late father had been described as a 'grand malignant'. People were keen to put the trauma of civil war behind them, and in Furness, the Parliamentary George Dodding's son, Myles, married Margaret Kirkby, daughter of the Royalist Roger Kirkby. However, it would be fair to say that England remained mired in the problems which had caused the civil war. Many people were violently anti-Catholic, a prejudice which regularly rose to hysteria at the slightest rumour of international plots to reconvert the country back to Rome. This popular sentiment fed into the debate over the monarch's powers. In 1662 Parliament passed a series of acts, among them the Act of Uniformity and the Test Act, to suppress Catholics and Protestant dissenters like the Quakers. Among other measures, they required all clergymen, university dons, teachers and members of town and city corporations to swear an oath to conform to the Church of England. Because Quakers refused to swear oaths, all these positions were closed to them. Whether Charles II had any sincere religious beliefs at all is open to question, but his natural inclination was towards tolerance, especially since his mother was a Catholic. He therefore sought discretionary power to suspend these Acts, but Parliament declared he could not do this. If this wasn't enough to tie everyone in knots, there were international issues to complicate things even further.

One of Charles II's sisters had married William of Orange, the leader of the Dutch Republic, and had produced a son, also William. Hygienic, go-ahead and tolerant, the Dutch Republic had grown into an economic powerhouse, threatening England's trade, and Cromwell had already fought one war against them. In the opposite corner was Catholic France, with its absolute monarch, Louis XIV, whose brother was married to Charles's younger, and more favourite, sister, Henrietta. Although most Englishmen saw France as their natural enemy, Charles would have preferred to ally with France against the Protestant Dutch, and he fought the Republic with varying degrees of success. To introduce another twist, Charles with his brood of illegitimate offspring had no legitimate child, so his heir was his brother James, who, to make things worse, decided to convert to Catholicism. At this, constitutional experts went into a tailspin. If obedience to the monarch was an overriding duty, and principles of heredity were to be followed to the letter, they would have to pledge allegiance to a king whom Parliamentary Acts barred from so much as teaching in a school. Some MP's thought they had a get-out clause, since James's two daughters, Mary and Anne, were Protestants. In a moment of rapprochement with the Dutch, Mary had been married off to her cousin, William of Orange. There was a movement in favour of excluding James from the succession and naming Mary as Charles's heir. Charles refused to do this, or to collude with the fiction that his grown-up son, the Protestant Duke of Monmouth, was legitimate and therefore his rightful heir. Supported by a healthy subsidy from France, Charles II was managed to rule during his final years without Parliament, and when he died in 1685, James succeeded in coming to the throne.

The rebellion mounted by the Duke of Monmouth against James II in 1685 was a dismal failure. However, within three years James managed to alienate just about everyone in the establishment including the normally conservative bishops. Like a terrier with a bone he clung on to his insistence that he could abrogate anti-Catholic and anti-Dissenter Acts. Although his motive was to keep Catholic officers in his army, this was beneficial for Quakers like the Fells. His persistence succeeded in

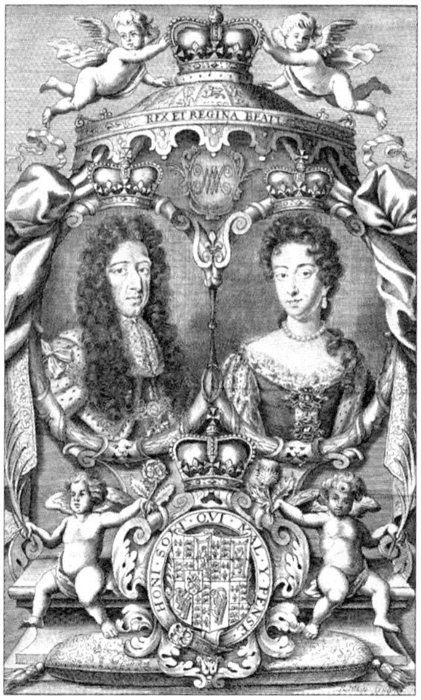

A 1703 engraving of King William III and Queen Mary II. R White, engraver

fuelling simmering opposition to an absolute monarch and in stoking the paranoia that he intended reconverting England by force, an idea given weight by his ally Louis XIV's persecution of Protestants in France. The stakes were raised when James's second wife had a son, dashing everyone's hopes that he would soon die leaving his Protestant daughter Mary to succeed. Mary's husband, William of Orange, had assumed that the English crown would one day belong to his wife, and he would be able to unite the Dutch Republic and England to fight the French. Joining the voices claiming that James's son was a changeling smuggled in a warming pan, and egged on by leading English politicians, he gathered an army and invaded England in November 1688. Support quickly fell away from James. William entered London and James was encouraged to slip away into exile. In 1689 William and Mary were crowned as joint monarchs, a novel constitutional arrangement, and England at last began to break free from the outmoded conflicts of the past.

We have an amazing window into life in Ulverston during the reign of Charles II in the Household Account Book of Sarah Fell, one of Margaret Fell's daughters, which runs from 1673 until 1678. This is a mine of information on the day to day finances of a seventeenth century estate in the time of the early Quakers. In spite of the persecution of Dissenters, the Fell family had held on to their house and land. In 1665 George Fell was granted the estate after it was forfeited when Margaret, his mother, was convicted at Lancaster Assizes. He had tried to persuade her to conform to the Parliamentary Acts, and it is possible that his public conformity was a subterfuge to prevent his family's ruination. George died in 1670 and most of the estate passed to one of his sisters, Rachel, who had married Daniel Abraham, a Quaker from a Manchester family. In the 1670's Sarah continued to live at Swarthmoor Hall and the Account book shows Ulverston to have been a busy community with its shops, thriving market and professional tailors and shoemakers. Foreign goods came to the town by way of Lancaster and Kendal while iron from the Fells' forge was sent as far away as Cornwall. The Fells also acted as informal bankers for their neighbours. At the same time imprisonment of Quakers remained a threat, with Daniel Abraham being sent to Lancaster jail in 1684. It was only after the national changes of 1688 and 1689, when the relative powers of the monarch and Parliament were settled and some religious toleration was introduced, that this threat ended and conditions allowing the next stage in Ulverston's growth began to emerge.

• IX •

THE BOOM YEARS

ULVERSTON IN THE EIGHTEENTH CENTURY

Prints from the mid to late eighteenth century afford us our first views of historic Ulverston. Some of the buildings they show were later demolished and rebuilt in the next century, but others, like the 'new' market building whose down pipe is marked 1736 have survived until today. These pictures of streets and shops with slate roofs suggest that by now Ulverston was more than a village. Occupations in the marriage registers for the decade between 1754 and 1764 reveal that while Ulverston was still important as an agricultural community, it was also an established port and a centre for shopkeepers and skilled craftsmen. 'Husbandman' or agricultural worker was by several times the most common occupation, with nearly fifty getting married in these years, and this was followed by mariners, with sixteen appearing before the altar. Then there were tanners, shoemakers, blacksmiths, masons,

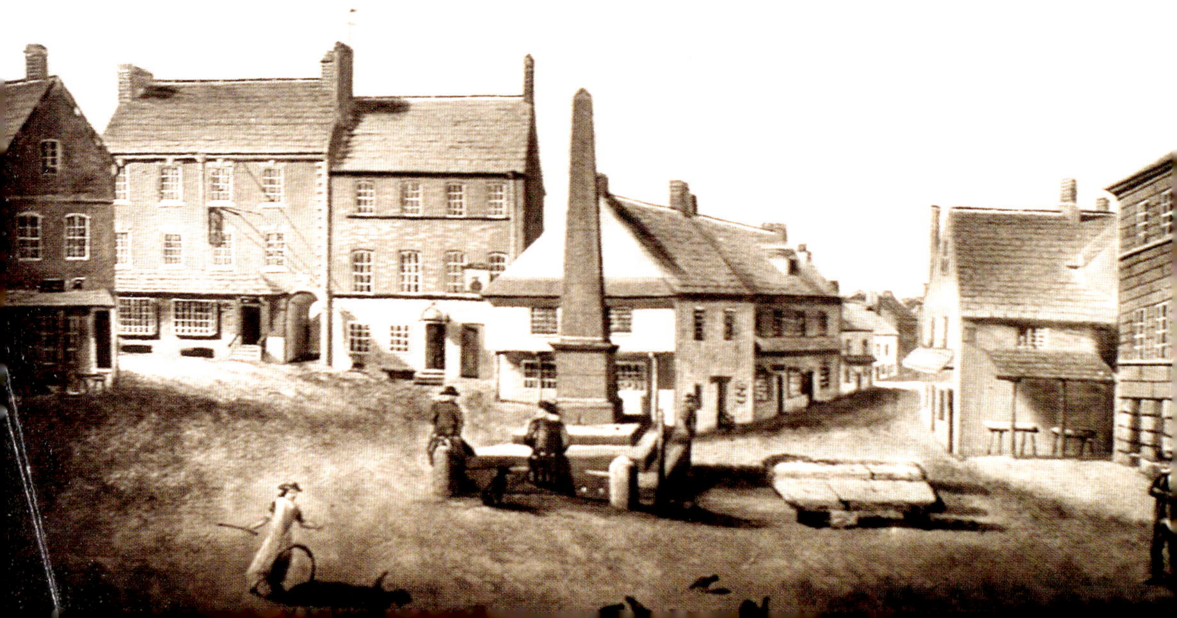

carpenters and cabinet makers, as well as workers in the cloth trade such as weavers, flaxmen, a dyer and a bleacher. The people of Ulverston could be fashionably dressed by a hatter, a breeches-maker, a stay-maker and a glover; buy ribbons and fancy goods from milliners and indulge in a visit to a tobacconist who, one hopes, didn't dodge the excise officer. At one end of the social scale seven husbands-to-be identified themselves as gentlemen, who didn't need to work, and at the other just three men were classed as labourers with no specific trade or skill. There is no doubt that Ulverston was growing and participating in the boom of the eighteenth century when Great Britain emerged as the dominant European mercantile power and the foundations were laid for rapid industrialisation in the nineteenth century. This phase of the town's growth culminated at the end of the eighteenth century with the building of Ulverston Canal, a project which was emblematic of changes taking place all over the country.

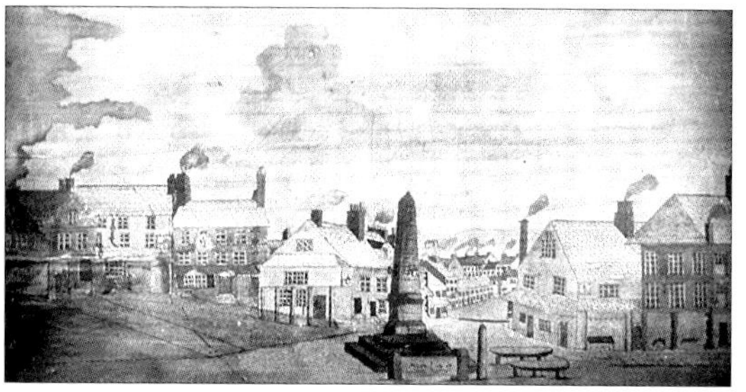

(and opposite) 18th Century prints of Ulverston. Our first pictorial images of the town. Chronicles of Ulverston

The reasons for this boom can be traced back to the political and religious settlement under William and Mary. With admirable spin, historians, eager to see the positives arising from the constitutionally awkward deposition of James II, turned what was in reality a Dutch invasion into the 'Glorious Revolution'. By this time, politicians were grouping into the forerunners of modern political parties: the Tories who, roughly speaking, placed more emphasis on the semi-divine nature of monarchy and who had supported the Stuarts; and the Whigs, who wished to curb the monarch's powers. The Tories were not particularly enamoured of William of Orange since his arrival on the scene had broken strict hereditary principles, and the Whigs were determined to place limits on the crown. Between them they drove a hard bargain with

William who wanted English money to fight France. A Bill or Declaration of Rights altered for ever the balance between Parliament and the crown. From now on the monarch could no longer suspend laws made in Parliament, or raise money or have an army except through Parliament, and Parliaments were to have free and frequent elections. Most importantly, the Bank of England, modelled on the Dutch Bank of Amsterdam, was established in 1694. Instead of having to borrow money at high interest rates from whoever was willing to risk lending it, the government could now borrow against the security of a steady stream of parliamentary income from taxation. Interest rates paid by the government fell, freeing money to be poured into building the navy and army which ultimately enabled England to become an imperial power.

The settlement under William and Mary was better news for dissenting groups like the Quakers. By the end of the seventeenth century most people realised that England was unlikely to return to the days of uniformity of worship, and that a measure of tolerance was needed to achieve peace and prosperity. The Toleration Act of 1689 gave dissenters freedom of conscience and ended their persecution as long as they recognised William and Mary as monarchs and rejected the authority of the Pope. Toleration only went so far. Dissenters were still denied civil rights and were prevented from going to university and from joining the professions. The result was that many Quakers, who had been in supportive networks from the time of persecution turned to business, where their trustworthiness earned them respect. All the same, Parliament put its foot down and declared that neither the monarch nor their spouse could ever be Roman Catholics. This was all very well when William died in 1702 and was succeeded by his sister-in-law Anne, the younger daughter of James II. Whereas the Dutch William had never been particularly liked, in spite of the far-reaching reforms of his reign, Queen Anne (1702 – 1714) was a lucky and popular combination of genuine Stuart and English protestant. The spadework having been done under William, she presided over success against the French in the War of the Spanish Succession and the bludgeoning of the Scots into union with

England to create Great Britain, fulfilling the dream of her great grandfather James I and VI.

The determination to end Scottish independence was tied in with the problem of the succession to Anne. All of Anne's many children died young, while James II's son, the 'warming pan baby', had grown up and been recognised as James III and VIII by France, becoming a magnet for Tories who secretly hankered after the old days. The English Parliament decreed that as a Catholic, James (the Old Pretender) could not be considered Anne's heir, and, after searching for a suitable Protestant of royal blood, settled the succession on Sophia, a granddaughter of James I and now the Electress dowager of Hanover, a minor north German principality. For its part, the Scottish Parliament announced that the successor to the Scottish crown might not necessarily be the same person as the successor to the English crown. The English threatened the Scots with an export ban unless progress was made towards union, and after a series of negotiations, the Act of Union was signed on 1 May 1707. Scotland lost her parliament and separate crown in return for freedom of trade within Great Britain and with the 'plantations', or colonies, especially those in North America.

The 1713 Treaty of Utrecht which ended the war between England and France over the Spanish succession was the final piece in the jigsaw of English dominance in Europe. This granted England exclusive commercial concessions in the Spanish Empire, and paved the way for the expansion of British trade, especially the slave trade. In what seems to us as barbarism, most people saw very little wrong in buying Africans from slave-traders and shipping them in appalling conditions across the Atlantic so that those who survived died of overwork or cruelty on sugar, tobacco and cotton plantations in the West Indies and North America. Neither can we pin the blame on a few heartless slavers and believe that this terrible triangular trade only benefited a handful of merchants in major ports like Bristol and Liverpool. The slave trade stimulated the entire English economy, with direct or indirect profits going to many people, including individuals from Ulverston who made fortunes in the

West Indies trade, and the farmers in Furness who grew beans for slaves on the plantations.

Following Queen Anne's death in 1714, the Electress Sophia's son, George Ludwig of Hanover was crowned George I (1714 – 1727) and saw off the Old Pretender's attempt to seize the throne in 1715. Barely speaking a word of English and far more interested in his beloved Hanover than in Great Britain, George I was the kind of absentee king the Parliamentarians in the Civil War would have longed for. From his reign onwards, monarchs might have reigned but real power lay more and more with Parliament and with a new figure, the Prime Minister. Politics became less about kings throwing their weight around and threatening to behead their opponents and more about politicians making speeches in parliament and deals in smoky back rooms. The dying gasp of the old way of doing things came in 1745 when the Old Pretender's son, Charles Stuart (Bonnie Prince Charlie), backed by French money and troops, made a bid for the crown and was defeated at Culloden by George II's son, the Duke of Cumberland, marking the last time the succession was decided by force.

During this domestic peace, Ulverston's population more than doubled. According to JD Marshall in *Furness and the Industrial Revolution*, in 1710 the town had 1168 inhabitants and by 1801 the number had grown to 2937. He believes that the greater part of this increase took place before 1760. A major factor in Ulverston's growth was the expansion of the local iron industry after 1711 when blast furnaces were introduced in Furness, a development in which Quakers played an important part. As we have seen, local families like the Fells of Swarthmoor and the Rawlinsons of Graythwaite had long been involved in making iron. Although the simple medieval bloomeries had been developed by adding bellows powered by waterwheels, and waterwheels drove mechanical forge hammers to bang at the wrought iron 'blooms', all this was on a relatively small scale. Elsewhere in England iron-making had moved on following the introduction of the first blast furnaces at the end of the fifteenth century, probably copying furnaces in Liege.

Used by the Chinese for hundreds if not thousands of years, the blast furnace was a huge leap in technology for Europe, and was a structure not unlike a tall very broad chimney or kiln. Iron ore, charcoal and a flux, limestone, were poured in at the top and a great bellows, driven by a waterwheel, kept the fire inside burning continuously. With impurities taken away by the flux, which melted and could be run off as slag, the result was molten iron which could be 'tapped' from the bottom of the furnace and made to run into channels in a bed of sand, where it cooled and solidified. This was 'pig' iron, which was weak in tension and had to be further refined in a finery to make wrought iron. However, the molten iron could also be poured into shaped moulds to make cast iron products like cannon and, later on, anything from cooking pots and fire grates to industrial components. Blast furnaces, which could keep going day and night for months at a time and could produce far more iron than the simple bloomeries, were voracious consumers of charcoal.

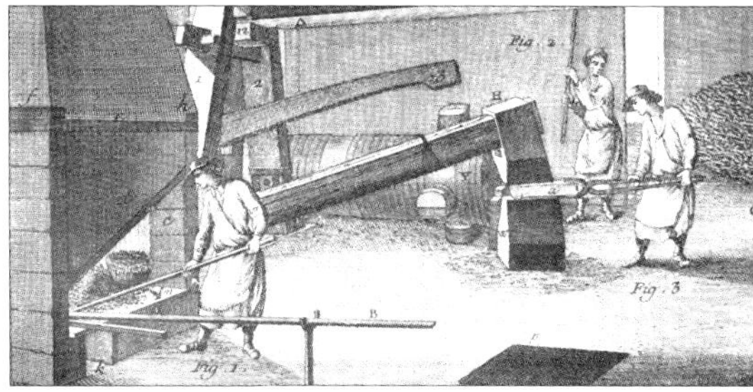

A finery forge showing a pile of charcoal in the background.

Blast furnaces came to Furness when a group of Cheshire ironmasters arrived in the area in search of new sources of charcoal and decided to build a blast furnace at Cunsey in 1711. In response, local ironmasters William Rawlinson of Graythwaite and John Machell of Hollow Oak, Haverthwaite, took partners, formed a new company, which became the Backbarrow Company, and built a blast furnace at Backbarrow. Building a blast furnace was a venture requiring capital and confidence, and this is where the Quaker business networks came in. All over England Quakers, having been driven into trade, had formed complex webs of interconnections through marriage and shared business interests. William Rawlinson's father had been one of George Fox's original converts in Furness, William himself had married into a family of affluent Quaker West Indies merchants based in Bristol, and two of his three partners in the Backbarrow Company were also Quakers. Before 1712 William Rawlinson had been selling iron to a Quaker merchant in Lancaster, and the Quaker network gave the Backbarrow company access to other iron merchants in Bristol, Warrington and Whitehaven, ensuring a market for their iron. Moreover, William was friendly with the great Quaker ironmaster Abraham Darby who, at his furnaces in Coalbrookdale in Shropshire, discovered that iron could be smelted with coke (coal with the sulphur burned off), so ending the iron industry's reliance on vast amounts of charcoal. However, the blast furnaces in Furness continued to use charcoal, the significance of which is touched on below.

These connections would have given Furness ironmasters the confidence to expand, and they were also given a boost by events far away in northern Europe. Britain had been able to import iron from Sweden until the early part of the eighteenth century when a conflict largely forgotten by us, the Great Northern War, broke out. This was an attempt by Russia and a whole collection of Baltic and north European statelets to clip the Swedish Empire's wings. Hanover and therefore Britain by extension joined in on the Russian side and in 1717 there was a trade embargo with Sweden. The price of iron rose, making it worthwhile to increase iron production in Furness. Stimulated by the triangular slave trade between Britain, Africa and the Americas, demand for Furness iron products increased throughout the first half of the eighteenth century, with pots and pans being sent to the West Indies and Furness bar iron being shipped to Liverpool to make anchors and chains. In 1747 another Cheshire man, Richard Ford, built a blast furnace at Newland just outside Ulverston and the town acquired its first large-scale industrial plant.

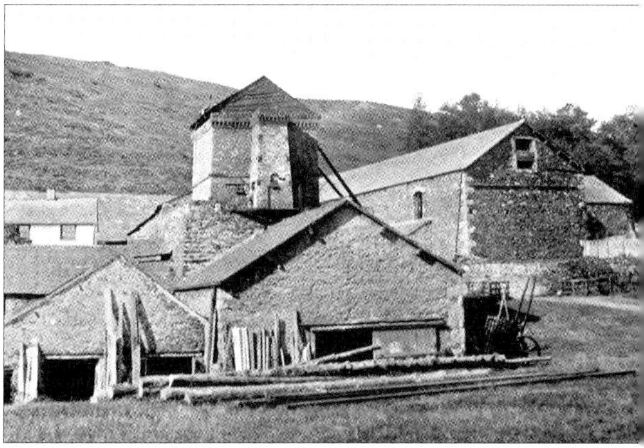

The iron works at Newland, the first blast furnace at Ulverston.
North Lonsdale Magazine

Like BAE Systems in Barrow today, the blast furnaces and refining forges of eighteenth century Furness generated economic activity way beyond providing direct employment for a discrete group of workers. The industry needed miners to raise the ore and carriers, maybe farmers working part-time, to cart ore and charcoal one way to the furnaces and iron the other way to ships waiting on the shores of Morecambe Bay. More ships visiting meant more trade in other goods, more sailors about the place and shipwrights building more small ships locally. The furnaces needed tanners to make the leather bellows, basket makers to make swills, and saddlers to make saddle trees for pack horses. Central to all this activity were the woods of Furness. The furnaces consumed huge quantities of charcoal so finding enough at a suitable price was always a problem, and as early as 1712 the rival Cunsey and Backbarrow companies combined to fix the price of charcoal from local suppliers. The upside for local landowners was that woodland increased in value, bringing with it the incentive to manage it effectively, cutting and re-growing wood on a coppice cycle. After 1731 more tenant farmers gained the right to profit from woodland. The potential to boost their income rose, since they could earn up to three times their rent if their woods were used for charcoal. This was by no means the only way to make money from woodland. Iron mines needed props, finery forges needed hammer beams, ship and house carpenters needed timber, tanners needed oak bark and swillers needed oak poles so, as one commentator said, 'The tree was as much a universal provider as the sheep'. Tenant farmers enclosed agricultural land to plant trees, and by 1748 there were at least two hundred yeomen wood owners in Furness. This is not irrelevant to Ulverston's fortunes: if the farmers in the area were getting richer from their woods, then they had more money to spend in the town's shops,

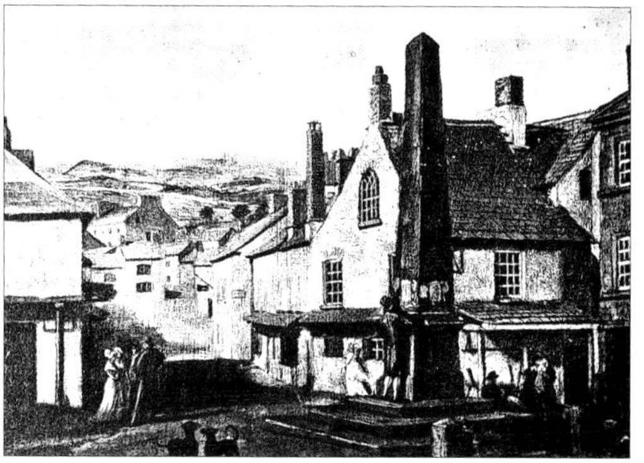

An 18th Century social scene in Ulverston.
The Chronicles of Ulverston

and could splash out on sugar and tobacco imported from the West Indies and North America and fancy clothes and hats.

If money could be made from trade, it could also be lost, and one formerly influential local family suffered a complete reversal of fortune. Swarthmoor Hall had passed to Thomas Fell's daughter, Rachel, who had married Daniel Abraham of Manchester, and in turn to their son, John Abraham. John's son, Thomas, moved to Whitehaven where he became a merchant and in 1749 he married a wealthy heiress from Warrington. Only two months after their marriage the entire Swarthmoor Hall estate, together with its three mills and a shop in Ulverston, was up for sale and when it failed to find a buyer it went for auction in 1752. Worse was to come. In the following year Thomas Abraham was declared bankrupt. It is thought that his trading in tobacco, perhaps with his brother in Virginia, was a failure, a cautionary tale for fellow Ulverston businessmen.

Individual casualties aside, developments in the iron industry meant that Ulverston was flourishing, and in the latter part of the eighteenth century the effects of the Industrial Revolution began to be felt in the town. This was the time when the factory system was born, new machines invented, agriculture was revolutionised and inland transport improved. The construction of Ulverston canal, which opened delayed and over budget in December 1796, encapsulated the changes affecting Britain. It has been argued that the canal, running from the edge of town to Morecambe Bay, was a white elephant, born from the prevailing canal mania and doomed both by the shifting of the River Leven away from its opening into the bay and by the coming of steam locomotion on the railways in the next century. This is probably unfair. Those who pressed for its construction didn't have a crystal ball, and their enthusiasm has to be seen in the context of national industrial growth, when manufacturers and businessmen wanted to move with the times and not let old ways hold them back.

Industrial growth was inseparable from the expansion of British trade. Rather than supporting Hanoverian monarchs in their European quarrels, Parliament wanted Britain's foreign policy to concentrate on using the navy to protect merchant shipping and overseas colonies. Profits on goods like tobacco and sugar produced by slave plantations flowed into the pockets of merchants and investors, and this money was then available to provide capital for industrial innovation. Britain's expansion was not inevitable: after the glorious victories in the Seven Years War (1756 – 63), failure in the American War of Independence (1775 – 1783) came as a terrible shock. There was a feeling that Britain had overstretched herself, and in the 1770's exports fell. Nevertheless, trade picked up again in the 1780's, especially with the newly independent United States of America which exported its raw cotton in exchange for ironware and manufactured goods. At home the drive to find more efficient ways of doing things knew no bounds.

The introduction of mass production techniques which revolutionised manufacturing is usually attributed to Josiah Wedgewood, who in 1759 took over a workshop in the pottery producing area of Staffordshire. He broke down the pottery manufacturing process into stages, each of which could be performed repetitively by production workers. The result was a huge leap in output, a leap which hit the buffers of shortcomings in England's inland transport system. Until the eighteenth century parishes had been responsible for roads, whose condition seems to have ranged from the passable to the lamentable. The sea and navigable rivers were still the best way to transport raw materials and finished goods, while strings of packhorses braved the potholes to reach inland destinations. For Wedgewood with his workshop in the land-locked Midlands, the expense of bringing in Cornish clay and the risk that a load of fashionable chinaware might reach a customer in pieces put a damper on his plans to dominate the world of pottery. He was therefore an enthusiastic backer of turnpikes, roads built and maintained by trusts formed of local businessmen who then charged a toll for their use. An Act of Parliament had first provided for turnpikes in 1706, and by 1741 a few major turnpikes linked London with towns like Oxford and Birmingham, which was already a centre for skilled metalwork. Between 1741 and 1770 the number of turnpikes increased dramatically with over 11,000 miles of road being built. Better roads meant that carriers' wagons could now be used to transport goods, and improvements in passenger coach design led to reduced journey times for travellers. This in turn sparked a great increase in the number of stagecoach services linking different towns and the rise of the coaching inns.

Advances in road transport spread north, and an Act of 1763 allowed for a turnpike between Kirkby Ireleth and Kendal, passing through Lindal, Ulverston, Penny Bridge, Bouth and Newby Bridge. This road must have been an improvement, since Marshall writes that in February 1775 the vicar of Colton was able to ride to Kendal one evening after several days of heavy rain without too much trouble. With other roads in the Lake counties also being turnpiked, carriers began to advertise their services carrying goods between towns like Ulverston, Kendal and Whitehaven. Stagecoaches started to appear, including in 1781 the first public coach service to run across the sands between Ulverston and Lancaster. The service left Ulverston's Sun Inn on Sundays, Tuesdays and Thursdays, and returned on Mondays, Wednesdays and Fridays. It is

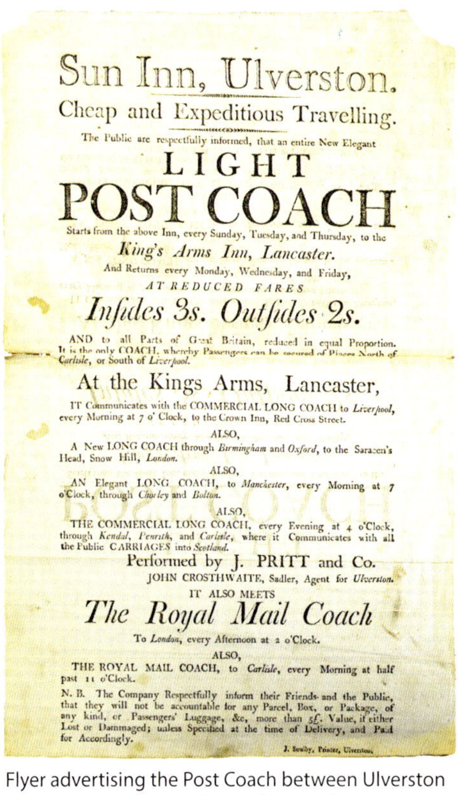

Flyer advertising the Post Coach between Ulverston and Lancaster and beyond.

Courtesy of Cumbria Archive and Local Studies Centre, Barrow-in-Furness.

often assumed that this route was extremely dangerous, with its risk of fog and quicksand, and there were indeed occasions when coaches were lost. However, stagecoaches frequently crashed on roads, and even before the public service started, Thomas West was sanguine about the risks of the journey across the bay, saying that it was less dangerous than formerly and that there were comparatively few accidents.

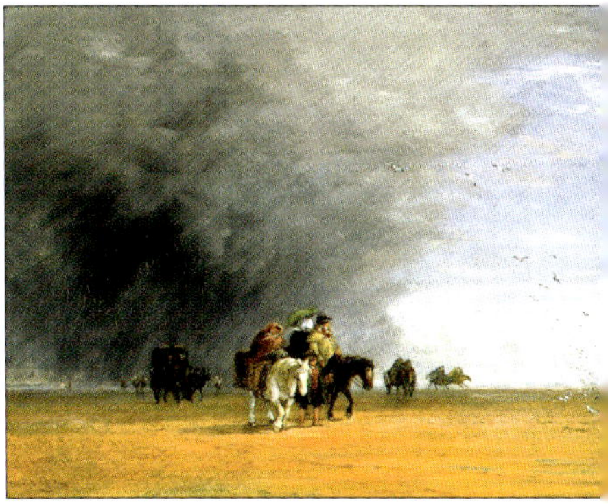
Crossing the sands 1848. David Cox

In spite of improved roads, the limitations of horse power hampered the efficient transport of ever-increasing quantities of heavy raw materials inland, and the second half of the eighteenth century saw the next revolution in transport, the building of canals. As early as 1720 an Act of Parliament enabled the Mersey and the Irwell, the rivers linking Manchester and Liverpool, to be made navigable along their length, but it was the Earl of Bridgewater who really kick-started the canal era. He constructed a canal from his coal mines in Worseley to Manchester, halving his coal's price in the growing textile town. Wedgewood persuaded Bridgewater's engineer to supervise building a much longer canal from the Trent to the Mersey, and when he moved his workshops to its banks his costs plummeted and his profits rose. The mathematics weren't complicated. While a horse could carry two or three hundredweight on its back, it could pull a barge weighing up to fifty tons on a smooth canal, so canal schemes popped up everywhere.

If the pottery industry took off in the Midlands after 1760, in Lancashire it was the cotton industry which made its own quantum leap. Cotton had been imported from the Middle East since at least the sixteenth century when fustians, or cloth with a linen warp and a cotton weft, were woven in the Blackburn and Bolton areas. By the end of the seventeenth century merchants from Liverpool were competing to control the import of cotton, especially from North America, and these imports increased rapidly after the 1730's. Cotton cloth was popular, being lighter and easier to wash than the old linens, and as weaving became more efficient it wasn't long before the spinners who spun cotton yarn at home couldn't keep up with demand. Cometh the hour cometh the inventor, and in 1764 James Hargreaves produced the first successful multi-spindle spinning machine, the Spinning Jenny. This was developed by Richard Arkwright into the 'water frame' spinning machine, which he patented before going on to create what is generally considered to be England's first modern textile factory, a water-powered spinning mill at Cromford in Derbyshire in 1771. Not to be outdone, Samuel Crompton improved on Arkwright's machine with his unpatented spinning mule. These machines spread like wildfire, since cotton spinning was very profitable and any mill with a water wheel could be converted into a cotton-spinning factory. Meanwhile, in Matthew Boulton's engineering workshop in Soho, Birmingham, the next big thing was taking shape. The power of steam was no mystery, and Newcomen's steam-powered beam engines had been draining mines for decades, but at the Soho works James Watt designed and built a much more sophisticated steam engine which could turn wheels. The first cotton mill to be powered by steam appeared in Manchester in the very early 1780's, a portent for the next century when, after Boulton and Watt's patent expired, steam-powered cotton mills sprang up all over Lancashire.

Mechanisation, like the turnpikes, didn't pass Furness and Ulverston by. Textile workers carrying out their trade at home or in small workshops had been part of Ulverston's economy for centuries, and after 1780 there was a marked increase in the number of weavers appearing in the Ulverston marriage registers. In 1793 Thomas Stephenson a cotton spinner from Manchester

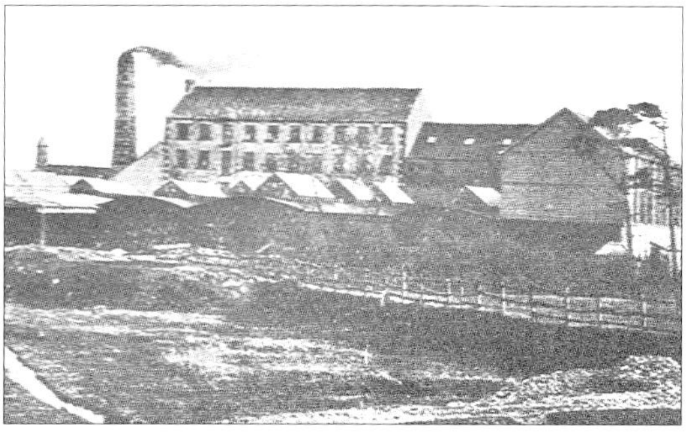

The former cotton mill at Lund Beck after it had been converted to a tannery. North Lonsdale Magazine

married in the Parish Church, and in 1797 two cotton spinners of Ulverston appear in the records. Marshall thinks that by 1790 Ulverston may have had four water-powered cotton spinning mills, at least two of which had previously been used for grinding corn or leather manufacture. By the early years of the next century Ulverston's largest cotton mill was Low Mill, sometimes called Lundbeck Cotton Works, at Lund Beck, while there were two small mills on the Ellers.

It is likely that there was money for investment in Ulverston from the West Indies trade since several individuals from the town were involved in this trade, mainly through links with merchants in Lancaster and Liverpool. These individuals were largely from humble backgrounds, the sons of yeomen, mariners and small traders, who had the good fortune to be apprenticed to West Indies merchants in one of these two cities. These positions were a springboard from which they were able to go into business on their own account. One such person was William Lindow, a mariner's son, who worked for the Rawlinson firm in Lancaster. He progressed from being the Rawlinson resident agent in Grenada to taking shares in slave-trading ships and buying up plantations, making substantial sums which enabled him to buy both a smart house in Lancaster and Swarthmoor Hall, and to build a new house, 22/24 Soutergate, in Ulverston. The most notorious slaver was John Bolton, born to an apothecary in what became the Hare and Hounds (now demolished) in King Street, Ulverston. Starting as an apprentice in the Liverpool firm of Rawlinson and Chorley, he returned from the West Indies with a small fortune to establish himself as a Liverpool merchant, owning ships which carried slaves and cotton and influential enough to bribe voters in the Tory political machine in Liverpool. In 1807 he bought the ultimate status symbol, Storrs Hall on the shores of Windermere and, it is widely believed, defied the ban on trading in slaves after 1807 by bringing slaves in by boat at night to the hall's cellars.

The connection between fortunes made from the slave economy and investment in new industry can be seen across the estuary at Cark where James Stockdale, a Lancashire merchant who had made his money from plantations in the West Indies, built a large cotton spinning mill in 1784. Imitating mill owners further south, he installed one of Boulton and Watt's steam engines to power it, a startling innovation which led to the village pub being renamed 'The Engine'. Another large water-powered mill was built upstream from the ironworks at Backbarrow, a mill which gained an ugly reputation in the next century for exploitation of child labour. With an engineer appearing in the Ulverston marriage register for 1788, and a mill-wright in 1791, it seems that new skills were coming into the town as manufacturing became more complex. Indeed, in the second half of the eighteenth century as a whole, the Ulverston marriage registers record approximately a hundred separate occupations or trades, with new trades appearing nearly every year, and small industrial businesses flourishing on the outskirts of town. Among these were two ship-building businesses at Saltcoats, a brick works at Sandhall and a tannery at Dragley Beck.

The Jesuit priest Thomas West, author of *The Antiquities of Furness*, gives many handy snippets of information about the Furness he lived in in the mid 1770's, although his claim that people in Ulverston were unusually sober and virtuous should perhaps be taken with a pinch of salt. When William Wilberforce visited in 1779 he noted that the inn was 'crowded brim full of people'. An economic historian will delight in West's meticulous list of the prices of food, from oatmeal to salmon, available in Ulverston market. He comments that there were 70 ships registered in Ulverston, most of them involved in the coastal trade, and that Ulverston was known as the 'London' of Furness. One Furness industry which caught his eye was the slate industry, with its great quarries at Coniston from where slate was taken by boat down to Nibthwaite then carried to Penny Bridge before being shipped to Bristol, Chepstow and London. There were also the quarries on Kirkby Moor overlooking the Duddon. As the demand for slate for new mills and housing grew, slate almost rivalled iron and high grade iron ore for furnaces elsewhere as a Furness export.

An aspect of the Furness economy which concerned West was the 'unimproved' state of its agriculture. The medieval farming system, especially in arable areas, had been based on large open fields, in which each farmer had a number of 'strips', and common land which was shared by everyone for grazing animals and producing fuel. By the end of the eighteenth century this system had practically disappeared as Enclosure Acts enabled richer farmers to enclose land, creating separate farms of smaller fields bounded by hedges and walls. Better crop rotation, the use of manure, the introduction of new crops such as turnips and better animal husbandry resulted in increased agricultural yields, and meant that Britain was more able to feed a growing population. West's enthusiasm for these improvements was not shared by husbandmen who hadn't been rich enough to buy land under the Enclosure Acts. Denied the use of common land, they either became paid agricultural labourers or drifted away from the countryside to work in the new factories, make roads and dig canals. In the first edition of *Antiquities of Furness* West grouched about the old system of shared fields and common pasture prevalent in Furness which he thought prevented the improvement of every acre. By 1805 the editor of the second edition was able to add a satisfied footnote, *'since the above was written, all the large Town fields have been divided and the parcels enclosed'*. In Ulverston it was the building of the canal which led to the enclosure of common land through which it passed, and thus to the ending of centuries of common rights.

We are lucky that in 1849 William Salmon wrote *A History of Ulverston Canal and the Commerce of the Port*, an account which Jack Layfield included in *Ulverston Canal and The Construction of Collins Weir* (2007). This book, and the original 1793 Act of Parliament authorising its construction, reveal the purpose for which the canal was intended, and the reason it became the 'shortest, deepest and widest' canal in England. The preamble to the Act says that although ships came and went from Ulverston, the town had no 'basin, dock, wharf or pier', so everything had to be taken to and from the sea beach, which made the 'carriage, delivery and exportation of goods and merchandise… expensive and incommodious'. We can imagine that hauling loads of pig iron over what was common land, and basically a bog, to ships lying aground at low tide or in the channel at Conishead Bank was a difficult job, and we can only guess how many cases of tea and sugar and bales of cotton coming the other way were dropped in the mud. The preamble calls for a navigable cut or canal to be made from Hammerside Hill to the edge of town, with a dock or basin wherever it was convenient. It is clear that what the backers of the scheme wanted wasn't a typical long narrow canal where long narrow barges could transport heavy goods across the country, but something more like a dock, where several sea-going vessels could come in at the same time to be unloaded and loaded, and where inward and outward goods could be kept safe in warehouses. Some of these backers were Liverpool merchants, involved in the West Indies, who perhaps wanted an easier way of sending cotton into Furness and of bringing out the iron products vital to their trade.

A first meeting to discuss building a canal was held at the Braddyll Arms public house (now sadly closed) in August 1791, and the Ulverston Canal Navigation Company was soon formed. The company's solicitor, William Burnthwaite, drew up the necessary Act of Parliament, and a bank, Fell, Burton and Co, handled the issuing of shares to raise money for the project. Before the establishment of a more formal banking system in the next century, businesses such as iron firms, the ship-building business of Petty and Postlethwaite and weaving manufacturers like the Fell family could act as bankers, lending money to their fellow businessmen. Among the first shareholders in the Canal Company were the influential, wealthy and well-connected Wilson Braddyll of Conishead Priory and his wife Jane. However, in what appears to have been an early attack of nimbyism they opposed the original plan for the canal to cross their land to Conishead Bank, insisting that it go to Hammerside

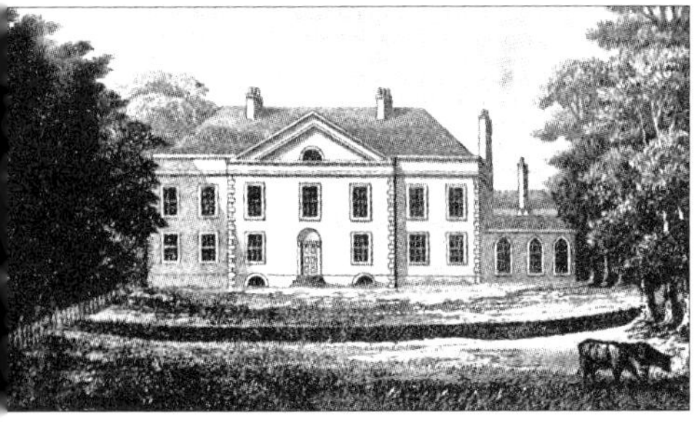

Little Croft, home of Thomas Sunderland, built on the site of the present Coronation Hall.
North Lonsdale Magazine

instead. Having achieved this concession, Wilson Braddyll was instrumental in getting the bill through Parliament. In contrast, the Duke of Buccleuch, who now held the manor of Ulverston, seems to have been quite relaxed about having a canal cut through his 'commons and waste'. A driving force behind the canal was undoubtedly the businessman and artist Thomas Sunderland, after whom the elegantly curving Sunderland Terrace in Ulverston is named. Thomas's father, originally from Yorkshire, had married into the ironmaster Rawlinson family. Thomas was heavily involved in the iron business, moving in the 1780's into Little Croft, a smart mansion built by another ironmaster, where the Post Office and Coronation Hall are today. A fellow ironmaster, John Machell, was also a shareholder in the canal, as were shipbuilders and men who wanted to build warehouses.

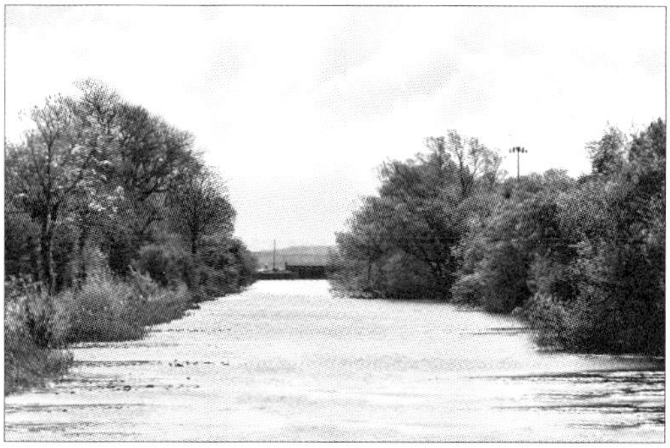

Ulverston Canal, the shortest and deepest canal in Britain.

As well as attracting support from Liverpool merchants, the Ulverston Canal Company had connections with the Lancaster Canal Company, maybe not surprising since Ulverston was classed as a creek of the port of Lancaster. The Ulverston Act of 1793 implies that there should be a reciprocal arrangement between the two companies, and that coal carried from the Lancaster side to Ulverston should not be liable to the duty imposed on coal carried by sea. The Ulverston Company employed the civil engineer John Rennie, who had already worked on the Lancaster canal, to survey the route and oversee the canal's construction. Rennie went on to work on other major canals, docks in London and also extensive drainage schemes in Lincolnshire and Norfolk, so it would be pleasing to think that the experience of constructing Ulverston canal through the mosses stood him in good stead in his later career. William

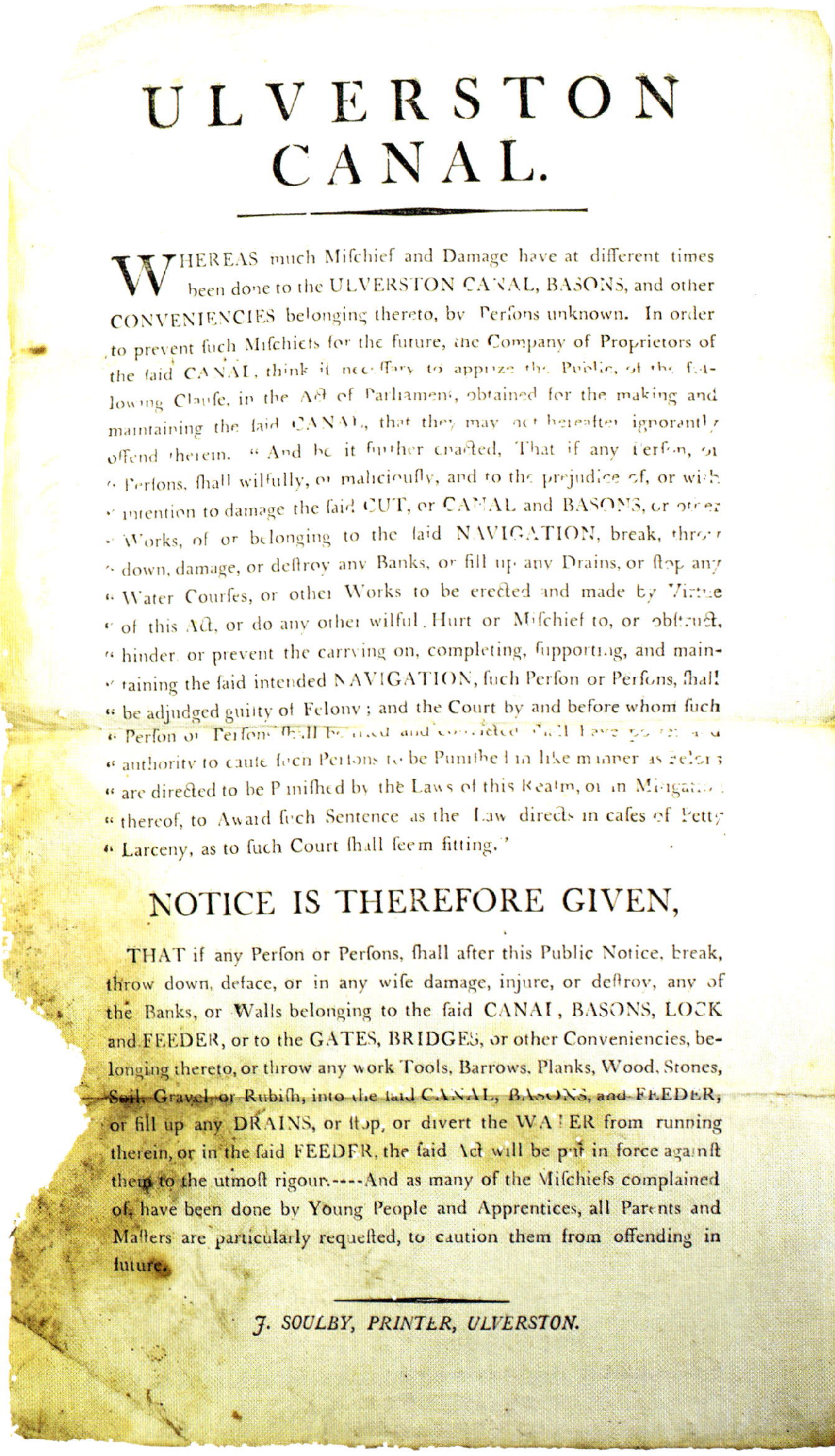

ULVERSTON CANAL.

WHEREAS much Miſchief and Damage have at different times been done to the ULVERSTON CANAL, BASONS, and other CONVENIENCIES belonging thereto, by Perſons unknown. In order to prevent ſuch Miſchiefs for the future, the Company of Proprietors of the ſaid CANAL, think it neceſſary to apprize the Public, of the following Clauſe, in the Act of Parliament, obtained for the making and maintaining the ſaid CANAL, that they may not hereafter ignorantly offend therein. "And be it further enacted, That if any Perſon, or "Perſons, ſhall wilfully, or maliciouſly, and to the prejudice of, or with "intention to damage the ſaid CUT, or CANAL and BASONS, or other "Works, of or belonging to the ſaid NAVIGATION, break, throw "down, damage, or deſtroy any Banks, or fill up any Drains, or ſtop any "Water Courſes, or other Works to be erected and made by Virtue "of this Act, or do any other wilful Hurt or Miſchief to, or obſtruct, "hinder or prevent the carrying on, completing, ſupporting, and main- "taining the ſaid intended NAVIGATION, ſuch Perſon or Perſons, ſhall "be adjudged guilty of Felony; and the Court by and before whom ſuch "Perſon or Perſons ſhall be tried and convicted ſhall have power and "authority to cauſe ſuch Perſons to be Puniſhed in like manner as Felons "are directed to be Puniſhed by the Laws of this Realm, or in Mitigation "thereof, to Award ſuch Sentence as the Law directs in caſes of Petty "Larceny, as to ſuch Court ſhall ſeem fitting."

NOTICE IS THEREFORE GIVEN,

THAT if any Perſon or Perſons, ſhall after this Public Notice, break, throw down, deface, or in any wiſe damage, injure, or deſtroy, any of the Banks, or Walls belonging to the ſaid CANAL, BASONS, LOCK and FEEDER, or to the GATES, BRIDGES, or other Conveniencies, belonging thereto, or throw any work Tools, Barrows, Planks, Wood, Stones, Soil, Gravel or Rubiſh, into the ſaid CANAL, BASONS, and FEEDER, or fill up any DRAINS, or ſtop, or divert the WATER from running therein, or in the ſaid FEEDER, the ſaid Act will be put in force againſt them to the utmoſt rigour.----And as many of the Miſchiefs complained of, have been done by Young People and Apprentices, all Parents and Maſters are particularly requeſted, to caution them from offending in future.

J. SOULBY, PRINTER, ULVERSTON.

Soulby's poster complaining of vandalism to the Ulverston canal works.

Courtesy of Cumbria Archive and Local Studies Centre, Barrow-in-Furness.

Salmon leaves us in no doubt that the canal was a massive deal for Ulverston, describing the public holiday and perhaps not very solemn procession on the day Thomas Sunderland cut the first sod. He tells us that the end of the day was marked by scenes of drunkenness in the Market Place, another nail in the coffin of West's claim that the townspeople were a sober lot.

Digging the canal did not go entirely to plan, not least because of an enormous rock in the way. Moreover, a poster complaining of vandalism to the canal works shows that such anti-social behaviour is not a modern phenomenon. The poster was printed in 1794 by John Soulby, who married the widow of the first printer in Ulverston, taking over the business and producing many handbills which entertain and inform readers today. The canal opened for business in December 1796 and on its first day four vessels, including two brigs from London and a sloop carrying coal, were dragged up the canal by enthusiastic crowds and triumphantly docked in the basin. During the next few years a warehouse and canal offices were built, and slate and coal wharfs, together with iron ore floors where ore could be stored before shipping, were erected. Before the turn of the century, the shipbuilders Hart and Ashburner had moved from Saltcoats to the canal and built a slip at the low yard.

Ulverston in the late eighteenth century was not all serious-minded businessmen focussed only on making money: it was a town which was developing a strong social and cultural life. The theatre was popular at this time, and people in Ulverston shared the current enthusiasm for long performances which could include at least one full play, songs, sketches and addresses.

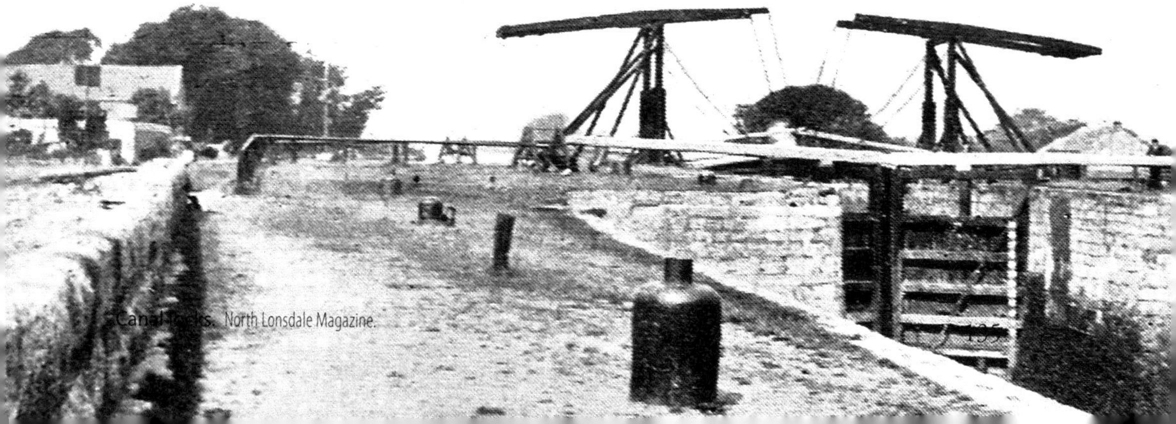

Canal locks. North Lonsdale Magazine.

At first these performances took place in makeshift buildings behind inns, like the barn behind the White Hart on Daltongate in which Harriet Mellon, who went on to star on the London stage, made her debut. These ramshackle structures were evidently not good enough for a better class of audience, and in 1796 a purpose-built theatre and Assembly Rooms were planned. This building, now the auctioneers' premises on Theatre Street, became known as the Theatre Royal, while another theatre on Stockbridge Lane became the New Theatre. The appearance of John Soulby's lending library, established in 1797, and the popularity of public lectures show people's appetite for engaging with new ideas and their urge to connect with the world outside their own community. By the end of the century Ulverston was a thriving port and social centre, but not everyone in Furness was prospering, and this was brought home with a vengeance in the first year of the next century.

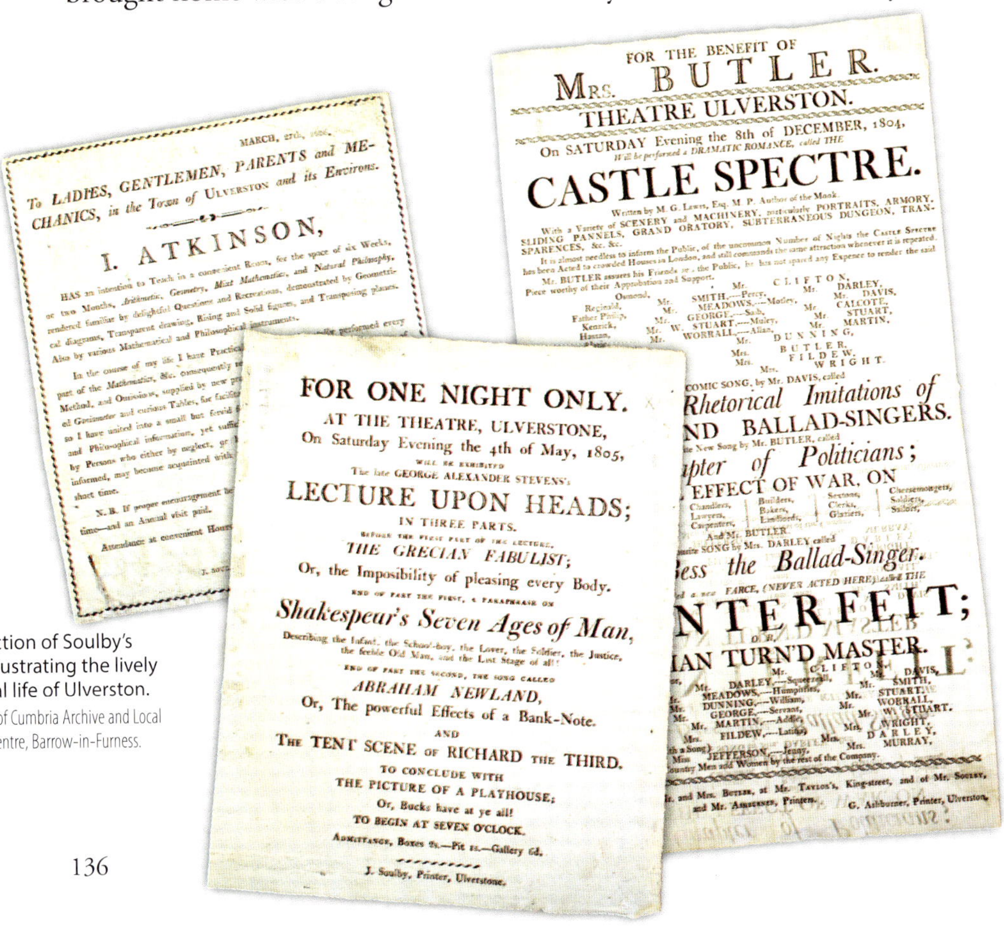

A selection of Soulby's bills, illustrating the lively cultural life of Ulverston.

Courtesy of Cumbria Archive and Local Studies Centre, Barrow-in-Furness.

• X •

Into the Industrial Age

Ulverston in the First Half of the 19th Century.

The decades between the start of the nineteenth century when Britain was at war with France and the Great Exhibition of Industry in 1851 saw England altered almost beyond recognition by a rapid industrialisation which had no precedent in history. Unlike many market towns further south in Lancashire, Ulverston did not expand to become a large industrial centre, yet it was not unaffected by the political and economic ferment of these decades. As early as 1800 a small army of slate quarrymen from Tilberthwaite, Coniston, Torver and Kirkby descended on the town, forced open warehouses and distributed flour to local women. Two years later magistrates were sitting in Ulverston to arrange who should be conscripted into the militia when they were rudely interrupted by a similar organised demonstration. The magistrates fled, although not before one unfortunate worthy had been hung upside down by his ankles out of a window.

The slate quarrymen had their specific local grievances and were also part of a swell of politicised dissent against the war with France and the government of Prime Minister Pitt the Younger, a dissent which had led rioters in 1795 to throw stones at the windows of No.10 Downing Street chanting 'No war, no famine, no Pitt, no King'. The many well-off Englishmen, like Wedgewood, who had hailed the French Revolution of 1789 as the 'dawn of universal liberty' must have wondered where it had all gone wrong.

While some of the English middle class initially welcomed the French Revolution as a sign that their bothersome neighbour and rival was moving from an absolute monarchy to a government with which it would be easier to do business, for many skilled and literate workers it was a wake-up call to improve their own lot. Inspired by Thomas Paine's 'The Rights of Man' they formed political societies, many with the ultimate aim of achieving the vote for all adult men. The French then threw a spanner into the works by invading the Netherlands in 1793. Pitt the Younger wasn't keen on war, yet faced with the French on the Dutch coastline where they could block British trade with Europe, he sent the navy off to attack French colonies. In the closing years of the eighteenth century his government was caught between a rock and a hard place. Napoleon's rise to power in France after a string of victories in Europe led to fears of a French invasion of England, while myriad taxes, including the novel income tax, to pay for the war, coupled with high prices led to hardship and the very real threat of revolution at home. It was one of these wartime taxes, a levy of 10 shillings on every ton of slate carried by sea, which hit the Furness quarrymen hard. In spite of representations to Pitt, the tax was levied, the slate trade stagnated and quarrymen were laid off to face either pauperism or conscription into a counter-revolutionary war. Fortunately for the quarrymen, the slate trade picked up again after the brief breathing space provided by the Peace of Amiens in 1802, and when war against Napoleon started up again in 1803 it was the patriotic 'establishment' in Ulverston who appear to have gained the upper hand.

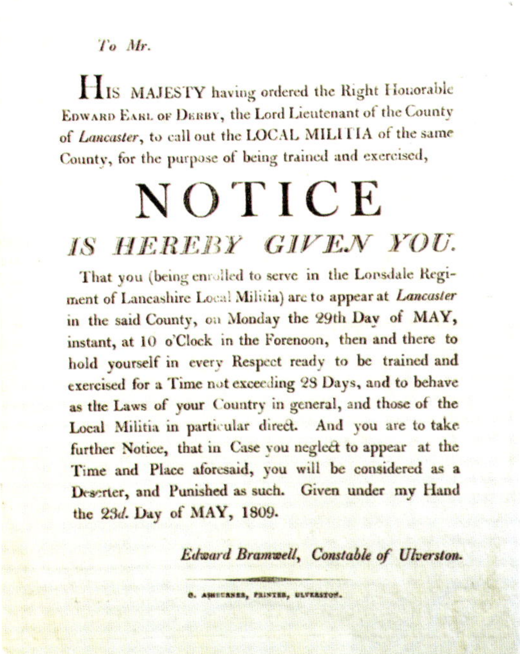

To Mr.

HIS MAJESTY having ordered the Right Honorable EDWARD EARL OF DERBY, the Lord Lieutenant of the County of *Lancaster*, to call out the LOCAL MILITIA of the same County, for the purpose of being trained and exercised,

NOTICE

IS HEREBY GIVEN YOU.

That you (being enrolled to serve in the Lonsdale Regiment of Lancashire Local Militia) are to appear at *Lancaster* in the said County, on Monday the 29th Day of MAY, instant, at 10 o'Clock in the Forenoon, then and there to hold yourself in every Respect ready to be trained and exercised for a Time not exceeding 28 Days, and to behave as the Laws of your Country in general, and those of the Local Militia in particular direct. And you are to take further Notice, that in Case you neglect to appear at the Time and Place aforesaid, you will be considered as a Deserter, and Punished as such. Given under my Hand the 23*d.* Day of MAY, 1809.

Edward Bramwell, Constable of Ulverston.

Call up papers for the Lancashire Local Militia, an army in reserve during the Napoleonic Wars.
Men were required to serve 5 years and train 4 times a year.
Courtesy of Cumbria Archive and Local Studies Centre, Barrow-in-Furness.

From 1803 until the Battle of Trafalgar in 1805 a French invasion of Britain was a distinct possibility, and in many places leading citizens formed volunteer battalions to resist any attempted landings. Ulverston was no exception. Wilson Braddyll came up with the funds and Thomas Sunderland was put in command, first as a major and then as a lieutenant colonel, of the Ulverston Volunteers, soon to become the Ulverston Volunteer Light Infantry. Undoubtedly the gentlemen industrialists and professionals of Ulverston, who overnight became officers in the Volunteers, were motivated by a genuine desire to defend their country, and Thomas Sunderland took the whole business of drilling his 320 recruits very seriously. He produced a training manual and invented an early horse-drawn troop-carrier. All the same, accounts of the Ulverston Volunteers bring Dad's Army irresistibly to mind. The officers clearly enjoyed dressing up in their splendid uniforms, and they must have relished the special ceremonies, dinners and balls, although the enormous hats they wore were impractical and various lengthy plumes had to be cut off. When it came to the nitty gritty, a plan to take the Volunteers away on permanent duty one January was shelved after many of them pointed out that it would be a 'serious inconvenience', which begs the question of how they would have described an invasion. It is probably not too far from the truth that this militarism was an opportunity for the influential classes to demonstrate their authority and to stifle any murmurs of anti-war dissent among the lower orders. One fierce notice, signed by leading ironmasters amongst others, instructed the locals to drive away their livestock and destroy food stores if the enemy invaded. Clearly optimistic that the French would be repulsed, the signatories promised compensation for everyone with the exception of able-bodied men who hadn't joined up. Such steps were unnecessary. The invasion scare died down after Trafalgar, and in 1806 the Ulverston Volunteer Light Infantry, now lacking financial support, was disbanded with kind words from the War Office.

During the Napoleonic Wars it seems that in many ways it was business as usual in Ulverston. The canal was built in the war years and although JD Marshall claims that the war and its aftermath badly affected the Furness iron trade, it remained a major industry in the area. Hostilities were an inconvenience for trade, however, as demonstrated by the fate of the 20 gun 'Argo', built by Hart and Ashburner at Canal Head for the West Indies trade and captured by a French privateer off Madeira. If the enemy didn't get you, your own country might. There is evidence that ironmasters complained about naval press-gangs taking sailors from the coastal vessels upon which their trade depended, and sought written protections against impressment. One of the saddest individual stories is that of the army veteran, Patrick Kearney, who endured the long terrible campaigns against Napoleon's armies in Portugal and Spain only to die many years later in Ulverston workhouse. Presumably the thanks of a grateful nation didn't extend to a pension. An image of Ulverston thriving in spite of the war is given in an 1807 report by John Britton and others, included by Rob McKeevor in his *'Ulverston Anthology'*.

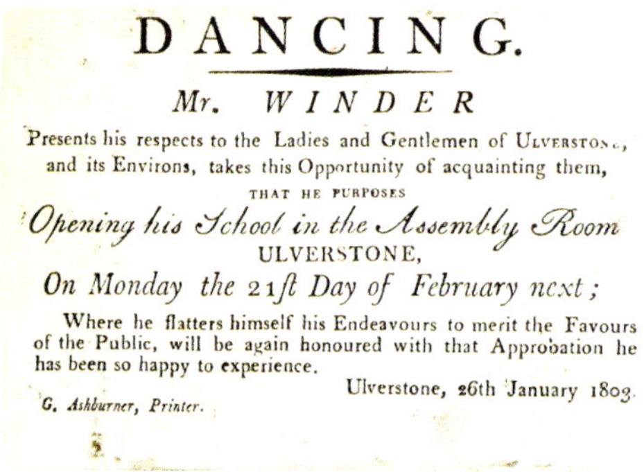
DANCING.

Mr. WINDER

Presents his respects to the Ladies and Gentlemen of ULVERSTONE, and its Environs, takes this Opportunity of acquainting them,

THAT HE PURPOSES

Opening his School in the Assembly Room

ULVERSTONE,

On Monday the 21st Day of February next;

Where he flatters himself his Endeavours to merit the Favours of the Public, will be again honoured with that Approbation he has been so happy to experience.

Ulverstone, 26th January 1803.

G. Ashburner, Printer.

An 1803 invitation to join a dancing school. There was still fun to be had in Ulverston despite wars abroad.

Courtesy of Cumbria Archive and Local Studies Centre, Barrow-in-Furness.

This complimentary little piece mentions features of Ulverston which crop up in other descriptions from the first half of the nineteenth century. They include its export of iron ore, pig and bar iron, limestone, slate, barley and beans for slaves, and its manufacture of cotton, check, canvas and hats. The authors noted that good quality houses were being built due to increasing trade in the town and they praised the 'spacious and clean' streets. Wartime seems to have made little impact. Indeed, most descriptions of Ulverston right up to around 1850 suggest a busy and improving town, even though the national economy and politics were going through all kinds of turmoil in the aftermath of the Napoleonic wars.

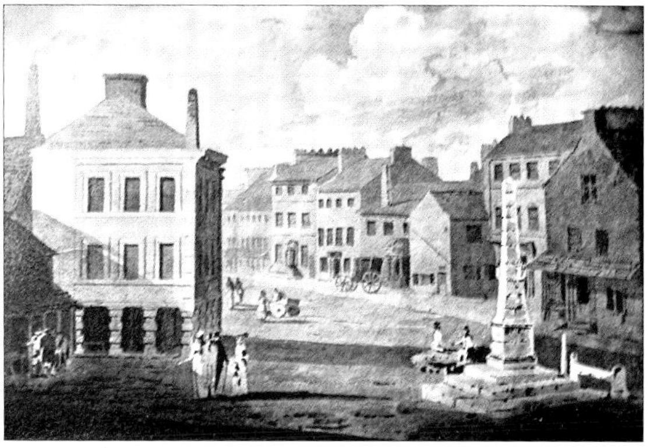
A view of Market Street in the 18th Century. Chronicles of Ulverston

A sense of the re-building which went on in the town centre in these years can be gained from comparing two pictures of Market Street. The first, a painting from around 1800 of the right hand side of the street looking down from the market cross, shows a jumble of buildings of different ages and styles presenting an uneven frontage to the street. Two of these buildings still have their gable ends facing the road, which suggests that they are on the footprint of medieval structures. The second, a photograph from around 1865, reveals a complete change. The sideways facing buildings have gone, and this side of the street now has a neat unbroken frontage. Ulverston's continuing improvement reflects the fact that until the completion of the Furness Railway in 1846 and the subsequent growth of Barrow from a tiny hamlet into a major town, the town remained the only market and port of any size in Furness, with Kendal and Whitehaven being its nearest commercial rivals.

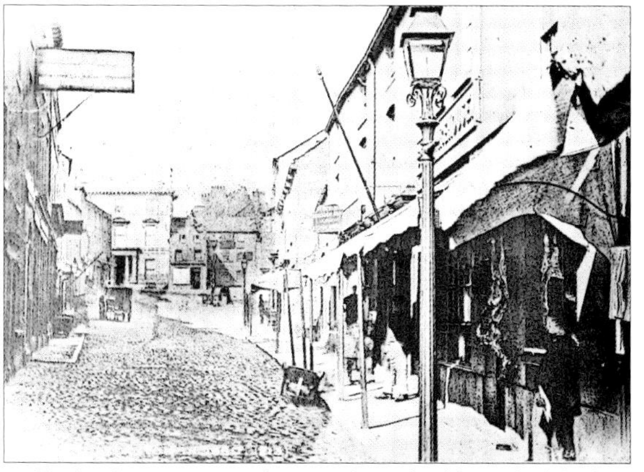
Market Street in 1865, showing the re-building which had taken place earlier in the century. Courtesy of Peter Lowe

The canal contributed greatly to Ulverston's 'advancement of trade', and its construction was also the impetus for a major change in its outskirts, the draining and enclosure of common land between the town and the shore, completed in 1812.

Before its enclosure, Ulverston's common land, which was mostly boggy mosses liable to extensive flooding, stretched from Greenodd Sands to Priory Point, with the western part between Sandhall and Priory Point being known separately as Oxenholme Common. In the context of the nationwide enclosures of the eighteenth century it might only have been a matter of time before local wealthy farmers made moves on the commons, and began hatching plans to reclaim land from Morecambe Bay, later to become something of an obsession. By 1799, when the Act of Parliament allowing the enclosure was passed, the canal had already been dug through common land, setting in train improved drainage of the mosses, and this would make completing the job more attractive. The procedure for enclosures began with the appointment of commissioners to divide up the land among those who could afford to buy out people with long-standing rights to it. This duly happened, with the addition of exhaustive instructions about who was going to be responsible for new walls, drains and roads. These enclosures increased the amount of agricultural land around Ulverston, but it was bad news for those who had had rights to the commons and who were too poor to buy any of the divided land. This may have contributed to the rise in the proportion of labourers, as opposed to husbandmen and tradesmen, in

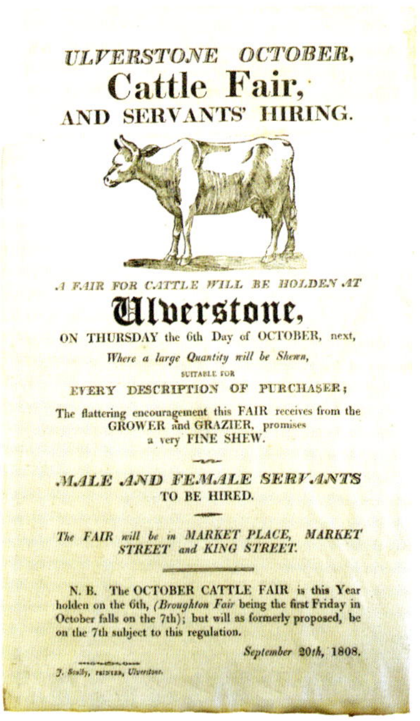
ULVERSTONE OCTOBER,
Cattle Fair,
AND SERVANTS' HIRING.

A FAIR FOR CATTLE WILL BE HOLDEN AT
Ulverstone,
ON THURSDAY the 6th Day of OCTOBER, next,
Where a large Quantity will be Shewn,
SUITABLE FOR
EVERY DESCRIPTION OF PURCHASER;
The flattering encouragement this FAIR receives from the GROWER and GRAZIER, promises a very FINE SHEW.

MALE AND FEMALE SERVANTS
TO BE HIRED.

The FAIR will be in MARKET PLACE, MARKET STREET and KING STREET.

N. B. The OCTOBER CATTLE FAIR is this Year holden on the 6th, (Broughton Fair being the first Friday in October falls on the 7th); but will as formerly proposed, be on the 7th subject to this regulation.

September 20th, 1808.

An 1808 poster advertising the forthcoming cattle and servants hiring fair.
Cumbria Archive and Local Studies Centre, Barrow-in-Furness.

Ulverston's population in the early nineteenth century.

Until the coming of the railways, the main challenge facing the Canal Company was to do with geography rather than the ambition of its builders. Left to its own devices, the channel of the River Leven tended to shift from one side of the estuary to the other and back again on an unpredictable cycle. When the canal opened in 1796 the channel was at Canal Foot and by 1802 it had moved away, fortunately returning in 1814 for a span of about thirty years before setting off again in 1844 or 1845. Figures given by William Salmon for the number of ships using the canal illustrate both the effect this had on shipping and the way trade increased after the 1820's. Between 1808 and 1814, when the channel had moved away, an average of 132 vessels a year used the canal, while in 1821, when the channel had moved back, this had nearly doubled to 259. The canal was leased between 1822 and 1827, and Salmon, obviously keen on numbers, bemoans the lack of statistics for these years. However, between 1829 and 1835 the yearly numbers were never less than 400 ships, and between 1836 and 1847 never less than 500 and often more than 600. It was only in 1848, with the double whammy of the moving channel and the completion of the Furness Railway line from the slate quarries and iron mines to Barrow that the number of vessels plummeted to 368, never to recover to the dizzy heights of the early 1840's. These little ships carried out tons of iron ore and slate as well as copper ore from the re-opened Coniston mines, vast quantities of woodland products like swills and hoops for making barrels, gunpowder from the works established at Low Wood in 1798, cotton yarn from the spinning mills, linen goods from the weaving sheds, leather from the tanneries and malt. In return they brought in coal, which was rapidly replacing peat as the domestic fuel of choice, raw cotton and consumer goods such as tea, sugar, alcohol and dried fruit.

All this activity benefited Ulverston's tradesmen, especially the growing number of inn-keepers, and encouraged the continuance of ship-building and ship repair. Between 1798 and 1829 twenty seven ships were launched at Ulverston, and in turn this industry stimulated other trades

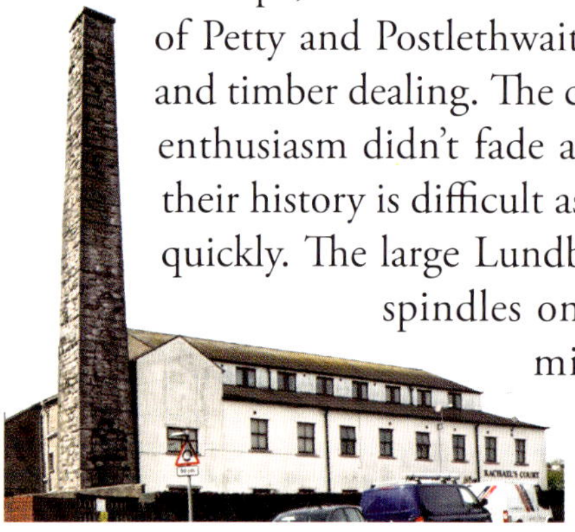
Rachel's Court, a former cotton mill.

like rope, sail and anchor making, while the ship-building firm of Petty and Postlethwaite eventually expanded into banking and timber dealing. The cotton mills set up in the first flush of enthusiasm didn't fade away without a trace, but unpicking their history is difficult as mills changed owners and use fairly quickly. The large Lundbeck Mill, which in 1806 had 4,700 spindles on 22 mules, remained as a spinning mill, enlarged and with an auxiliary steam engine, until around 1860, and at some point a steam-powered cotton mill, now the Rachel's Court flats, was built on the Ellers. Manufacturers like the Fell family with their weaving sheds at Stone Cross up Daltongate seem to have used both cotton and flax spun at different mills to make the linens, checks, ginghams and canvas mentioned in contemporary descriptions. The canal statistics show that although the Backbarrow and Newland iron furnaces were still in operation in the nineteenth century, the export of haematite ore, much in demand for its high quality, was by many times more important than the export of bar or pig iron. The only eighteenth century iron firm to survive through to the next century was the Newland Company, later Harrison, Ainslie and Company, which also acquired the Backbarrow furnace in 1818. They and other newer companies, like that of Charles Storr Kennedy, the son of an Ulverston customs officer, became rich through leasing ore mines from the Lords of the Manor in Furness and shipping the ore to furnaces in growing industrial areas like south Wales. In a portent of things to come, the Newland Company in particular objected to the canal tolls, and preferred to cart ore to the tiny port of Barrow where they built an ore quay.

A detailed plan of Ulverston made in 1832 by the Yorkshire surveyor, John Wood, for Colonel Braddyll of Conishead Priory shows a small town, clustering around the cross-roads at the Market Place, with gardens and fields where now there are streets and buildings. The only two areas

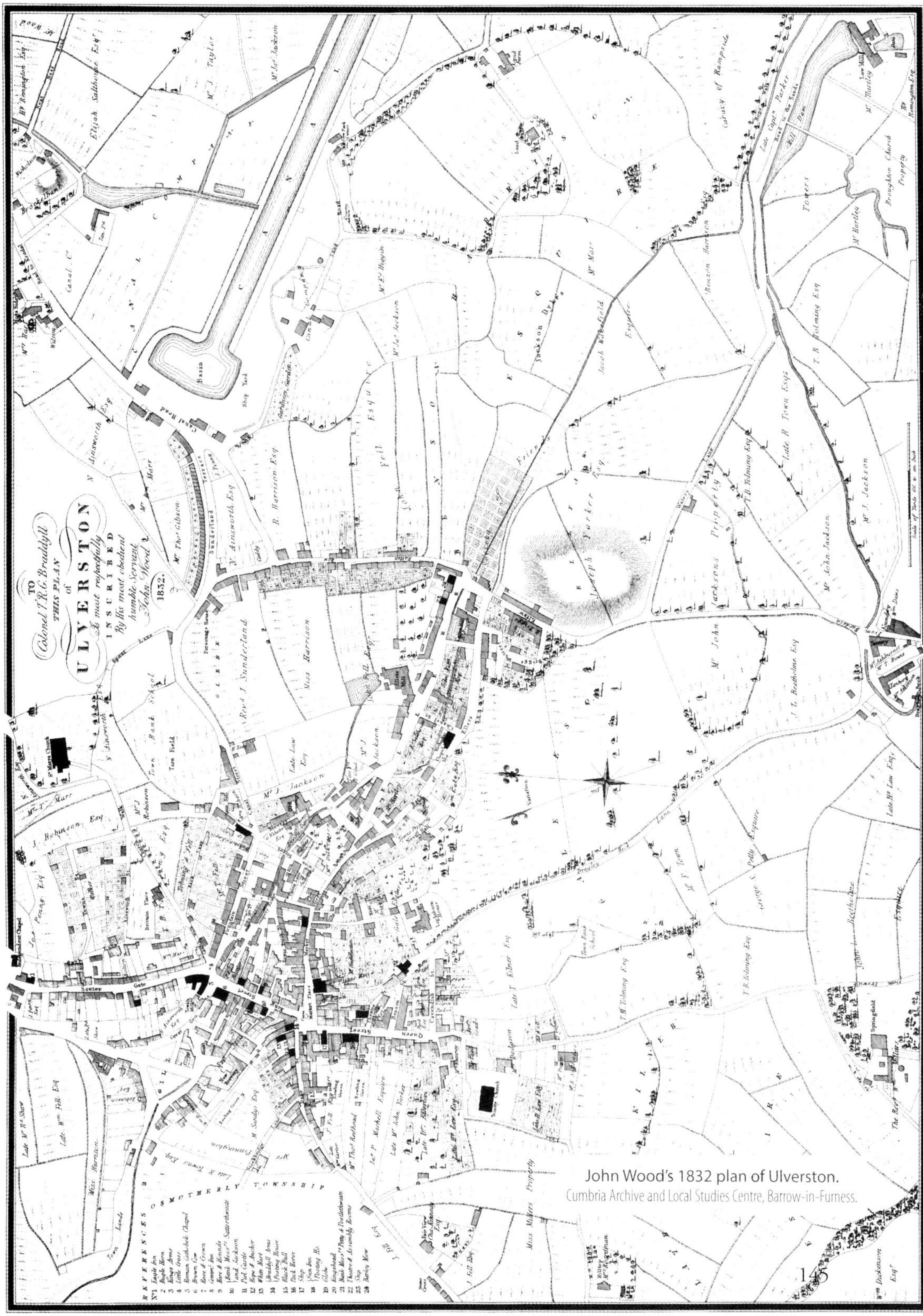

John Wood's 1832 plan of Ulverston.
Cumbria Archive and Local Studies Centre, Barrow-in-Furness.

with substantial in-filling were the block between King Street, Upper Brook Street, The Gill and Mill Street (then called Great George Street), and the block bound by King Street, Fountain Street, Union Street and Market Street. Two streets are apart from this central core, which probably corresponds to the medieval borough, with stretches of open ground between them and the town centre. One, Sunderland Terrace, was relatively new, and is usually said to have been built for ships' captains and other people who had business with the canal. The elegant curve in which it was built appears in the plan much as it does today, with empty space in front of most of its length. The other is Ratten Row, a much older street, running north to south from a junction with Sunderland Terrace to the bottom of the Ellers, and having an almost continuous row of houses with back gardens on one side. Ratten Row was later re-named Quebec Street, and the old houses were demolished in the 1930's, although long-standing residents still use this name when talking about the modern Quebec Street. There are 'Ratten Rows' all over the country, and nearly as many explanations of the name's origin, ranging from a place where soldiers were mustered to a roundabout burial route to a church avoiding a main road. Ulverston's Ratten Row is mentioned as early as 1421, and it might have been the part of town where people who were not burgesses lived.

Although Ulverston in 1832 was much smaller than it is today, the plan shows some of the industry and amenities which made it the commercial and social centre of Furness. In 1832 there were three mills in the town centre. The grain mill, Town Mill, now a public house, was on Great George Street, and there were two mills on the Ellers, both with mill dams. The plan doesn't specify what the larger mill, now demolished, produced, but the smaller mill still standing at the bottom of the street was then a cotton mill. There was a ship yard at the Canal Basin, and breweries at the 'Old Brewery' on part of the present day Robinsons site, and a 'New Brewery' on Upper Brook Street. To oil the wheels of commerce there were two banks: Satterthwaite and Jackson at what is now the Chippy Bank; and Petty and Postlethwaite on Theatre

Street. The town's social and cultural centre, the Theatre Royal and Assembly Rooms, is shown as are nineteen public houses. Several of these, notably the King's Arms, the Rose and Crown, the Piel Castle, the Hope and Anchor, the Sun, the Globe and the King's Head, still survive with the same names at the time of writing. Two inns, the Sun and the Braddyll Arms, are named as posting inns, where stage coaches could change their horses, showing that Ulverston was an established halt on the nationwide network of posting houses.

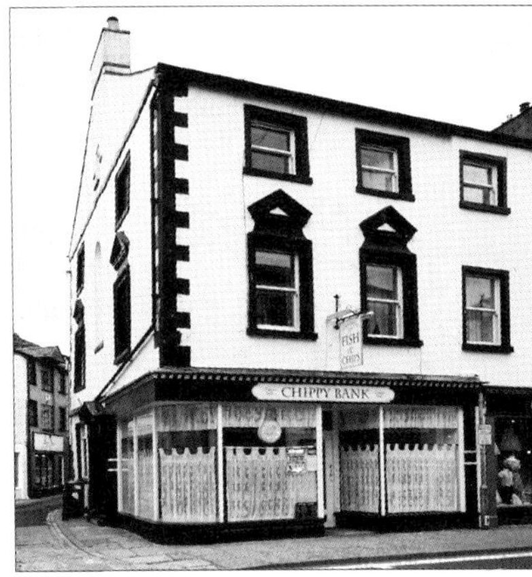

The former Satterthwaite and Jackson Bank on King Street, now a fish and chip shop known as the Chippy Bank.

From the different places of worship marked on the 1832 plan, we can see that by now Ulverston accommodated a wide range of religious affiliations. Growing tolerance towards Roman Catholics meant that penal laws against Catholicism had been repealed in the last quarter of the eighteenth century, and Thomas West noted that the number of Catholics, especially Irish immigrants coming to work as iron miners, was increasing in Furness. For a time he rented what was known as the 'First House' on Fountain Street, and one of his successors as Catholic priest to Furness, Dr Everard, bought and probably extended this fine house, which is now a terrace of four. In 1806 Dr Everard built a Catholic chapel, now an antiques salesroom, next to the house, and this is shown on the plan. Members of the Church of England could attend the parish church of St Mary's or a new Anglican church, Trinity Church. Built to accommodate Ulverston's rising population, this church, now flats, was designed by the London architect Anthony Salvin. The former slaver, John Bolton, eminently respectable despite having killed a fellow Ulverstonian in a duel, subscribed £500 towards the building and laid the foundation stone in October 1829. Those with a non-Conformist streak could attend the Independent Chapel at the top of Soutergate. Henry Birkett tells how such was the hostility to the Independents that during the building of the chapel, every day's work was torn down at night until a watch was mounted. Although John Wesley was not impressed with Ulverston when he visited, by 1811 there were enough of his Methodist followers to build a chapel on Back Ellers.

The course of the streams which ran through Ulverston providing power for the mills is less clear on the plan. Early accounts often mention the open streams at either end of King Street and the hazard they posed if they were swollen with rain. By 1832 it appears that the process of covering these waterways in the town centre was under way. Only the stream which runs from the Town Mill is shown, emerging in what is now Buxton Place car park and flowing under Union Street into a dam for the Old Brewery before dividing and making its way down to power the mills on either side of the Ellers. The stream from Upper Brook Street, which joined it in Buxton Place at Soapery Bridge where there was a small soap factory, is not shown. Park's detailed plan of Ulverston's streamlets is later than 1832, and although he gives a wonderful picture of all the water which flows under the feet of unsuspecting pedestrians nowadays, he did not distinguish between those which were covered and those which were still open.

When we compare this 1832 plan with the first Ordnance Survey map of 1851, drawn before the Furness Railway reached Ulverston, we can see that the town has hardly grown, even though its population is said to have increased by about 2,000. Lightburne House, formerly Little Croft and once the residence of Thomas Sunderland, was still on the edge of town, which is maybe difficult to imagine if we are outside the Coronation Hall which stands on its former site, and Brittain Place was still the only building on Church Walk. There were more houses between the bottom of Sunderland Terrace and the canal, and a few more buildings put up on the triangle of land bounded by Sunderland Terrace, Quay Street (which followed the line of the modern A590), and Ratten Row. The other side of Quay Street, the old route into town before Sunderland Terrace was built, was still empty.

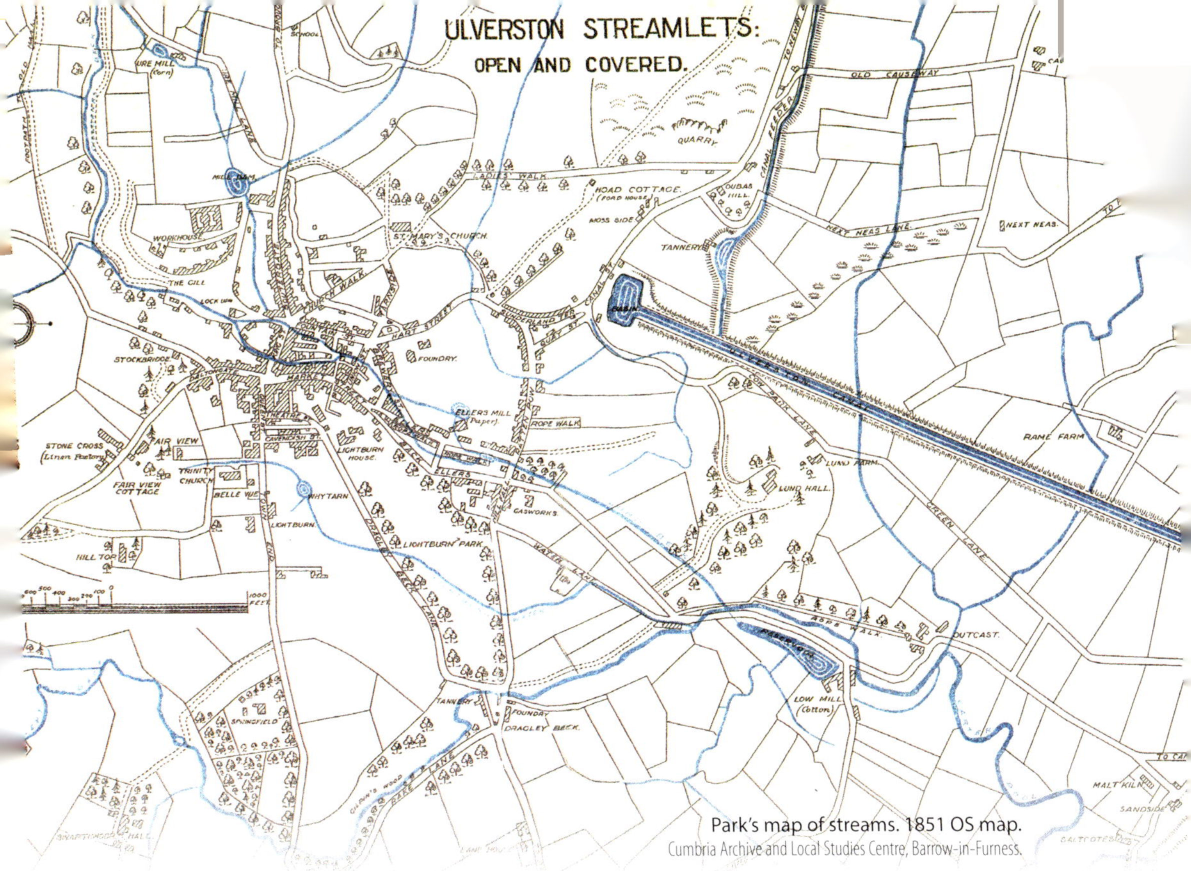

Park's map of streams. 1851 OS map.
Cumbria Archive and Local Studies Centre, Barrow-in-Furness.

Because the Ordnance Survey map covers a much wider area than the 1832 plan, we can see more of the small industrial sites on Ulverston's outskirts, such as the linen weaving factory at Stone Cross at the top of Daltongate (formerly Duke Street), the tan yard and iron foundry at Dragley Beck and the cotton mill at Low Mill. There was a rope walk off Ratten Row and another, which is now a footpath, at Outcast. At the canal basin was a slate and timber depot, and further down a timber yard, a smithy and an iron ore depot, while limestone quarries, a wharf and limekilns are marked along the shore between Canal Foot and Plumpton Hall. Even harder to picture if we go there today when land has been reclaimed is that the spring tide high water mark still lay only a few yards from Sandside, Saltcoats and Sandhall. However, two new features in the town let us know that Ulverston was not staying still. The first is the gas works on a new road, now Morecambe Road, leading off Hill Fall, the continuation of Ratten Row which in 1832 was rather more romantically named Elf Law. The gas works had been built in 1834, using coal imported from Wigan to manufacture gas for lighting the streets, a very smelly process which can't have been pleasant for the inhabitants of Ratten Row. The second is the Union Workhouse, by far the biggest building in Ulverston, built off Stanley Street where the medical centre is now. Before the railway reached Ulverston, more than any other new building the Workhouse was a symbol of the great social changes in Britain in the first half of the nineteenth century.

The first half of the nineteenth century was an extraordinary era by any measure. Britain became the first country in the world to be transformed by industry, as the ever-increasing production of iron, coal and textiles drastically altered its pattern of wealth and population. The former main cloth-making areas in East Anglia and the south were left behind by new towns springing up in Lancashire and Yorkshire, while iron-making moved from its old centres in Sussex and the Forest of Dean to coalfields in South Wales, the Midlands and Scotland. Britain's industrial base and technological innovations were instrumental in its success in finally seeing off Napoleon in 1815. Only a decade later possibly the most far-reaching revolution, the use of steam locomotives to pull wagons on railways, was well under way. Different forms of railway had been used in and around mines for centuries, and the ironmaster Abraham Darby had pioneered the use of iron rails in Coalbrookdale in 1767. By the beginning of the nineteenth century there were networks of railways, especially in the coal mining districts of North East England and South Wales, using either horses or gravity to move wagons of coal to wharves where it could be loaded on to boats. Railways were planned elsewhere and in 1799 the Lancaster Canal Company built a railway to link its canal with the Ashby Canal across the Ribble valley, while in 1809 there was an iron railway linking the Kirkby slate quarries to the Duddon estuary.

In 1804 the Cornish engineer Richard Trevithick designed the first steam locomotive to run on a railway for the coal mines at Merthyr Tydfil, and in 1809 he demonstrated an improved version on a circular track in London. Strangely enough this marriage of steam locomotion and railways didn't catch on immediately, and Trevithick went on to pursue other interests. However, by the 1820's it was becoming clear that the canal system couldn't cope with the volume of traffic generated by industrial expansion, especially in the north west, and longer distance railway lines were planned, particularly a line between Manchester and Liverpool. There was no automatic presumption that steam locomotion would be used on this, or on the more famous Stockton to Darlington line. Odd though it may seem, these lines were originally conceived of as public highways, rather like the turnpikes, where people would pay a toll to the company which built the line so that they could pop their own horse-drawn wagons on the rails. This idea did not last. The development of reliable steam locomotives and the totally unforeseen demand from the public to travel on lines which had been envisaged as another means of moving coal and goods led to the railway revolution. For the first time ever the movement of people and goods on land was freed from the physical limitations of horses and other draft animals, and this in turn led to a gradual turnaround in the way communications in Britain were regarded. For centuries rivers, estuaries and the sea had been seen as highways, especially for heavy goods. After the coming of the railways, people gradually forgot the role these waterways had played in transport. As a result of this collective amnesia, it is often claimed that Furness was isolated before the railway arrived, whereas this was not necessarily the case, given its good communications by sea with the rest of the country.

The many rapid changes in the early nineteenth century led to almost intolerable strain on the old political and social order and the ruling classes were in constant apprehension that revolution was only a hair's breadth away. The rise of mechanised industries had ruined the livelihood of many traditional workers, and in 1812 more soldiers were needed to quell the 'Luddites' who attacked mills and smashed machines than were used in Spain to fight the French. After the end of the Napoleonic Wars, 400,000 demobilised soldiers and sailors swelled the ranks of those looking for work and the Corn Laws, which protected landowners by keeping wheat prices high, caused near starvation amongst the poor. In August 1819 a peaceful demonstration at St Peter's Fields Manchester, calling for votes for all and repeal of the Corn Laws, was broken up by soldiers resulting in what became known as the Peterloo Massacre. The government of Prime Minister Lord Liverpool responded with repression, banning the early trades unions and equating demands for reform with treason. As the economy picked up in the 1820's, the threat of revolution receded, yet there was now a large industrial working class whose employment was precarious and who mostly lived in cramped and insanitary conditions.

Despite this industrialisation, the way Britain was governed had barely altered since the time of Queen Anne. Only freeholders of land worth more than 40sh a year had the vote, and this vote was either given to local aristocrats or sold to the highest bidder. Parliamentary constituencies had not changed either, so that medieval boroughs which were now deserted hamlets returned MP's while huge new towns like Manchester had no representation. 1830 saw the return of riots, sparked by high prices and unemployment, and widespread demand for 'Reform', especially universal male suffrage and the abandoning of the property qualification for MP's. William 1V's Prime Minister, Lord Grey, introduced successive bills for electoral reform but these were rejected by the House of Lords, and more riots ensued. Finally in 1832, after the Scots Greys announced they would not stop a planned march from Birmingham if it remained peaceful, and after some desperate political manoeuvring, a watered down Reform Bill was passed by the Lords. Governments still had to find a way to deal with the unprecedented phenomenon of mass urban poverty, and it was from the Poor Law Amendment Act of 1834 that Ulverston's grimly imposing workhouse was born.

If national government hadn't changed for over a century, it has to be said that in the 1830's local government in Ulverston was even more archaic. Ulverston borough had never gained 'incorporation', that is, it had never been granted a formal constitution and borough seal. The town was governed by a combination of ancient manorial courts and the 'vestry', or parish ruling body, also known as the 'Four and Twenty' since it was made up of twenty four sidesmen. This self-selecting group, mostly of rich farmers, dealt with church business, with education, which included responsibility for Ulverston Grammar school, and with relieving poverty. The whole question of poverty, or 'pauperism', in Furness is complex. It seems that poverty increased with the population in the early nineteenth century although it was never on the scale of the new urban industrial centres. The vestry raised local rates to provide support for paupers, either in the form of a top-up for very low paid workers with wives and children (the equivalent of modern working tax credit), or to maintain the 'poor-house', which since 1753 had been in Neville Hall. The vestry tried hard to distinguish between the 'deserving' and the 'undeserving' poor, and tended not to let into the poor-house everyone who applied to go there. In practice, most people did their best to avoid Neville Hall, so its inhabitants were usually very old, infirm, very young or married couples who were totally destitute.

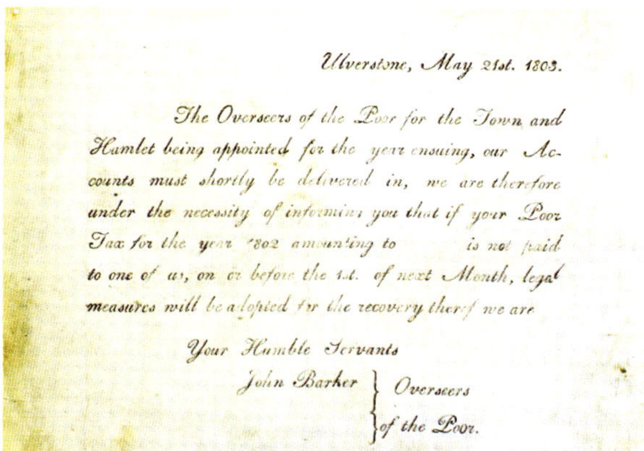

Ulverstone, May 21st. 1803.

The Overseers of the Poor for the Town and Hamlet being appointed for the year ensuing, our Accounts must shortly be delivered in, we are therefore under the necessity of informing you that if your Poor Tax for the year 1802 amounting to is not paid to one of us, on or before the 1st. of next Month, legal measures will be adopted for the recovery thereof we are

Your Humble Servants

John Barker } Overseers of the Poor.

A notice demanding payment of 'Poor Tax' in 1803.
Cumbria Archive and Local Studies Centre, Barrow-in-Furness.

The Act of 1834 brought an end to the system in which the vestry could make decisions based on their local knowledge. For the purposes of dealing with poverty, parishes were to be grouped into Unions run by an elected Board of Guardians who adhered to regulations devised by central government and based on two principles. The first was that able-bodied men could only get help if they gave up their homes and went into the workhouse, and the second was that conditions should be worse for someone in the workhouse than for the poorest labourer outside. In 1836 the Ulverston Union, comprising all the parishes in Lonsdale north of the sands, was formed, its guardians elected and William Cavendish of Holker Hall, Earl of Burlington, the leading landowner in Furness, became its permanent chairman. Although this new union had three existing workhouses, in Ulverston, Dalton and Colton, it was pretty obvious that they couldn't cope with everyone who was in need of help. When the Guardians petitioned for an amendment to the new Poor Law, the government's response was to direct them to build a bigger workhouse, and a huge building on the Gill was the result. Even so, the system as planned never worked in practice. In 1850, for example, when there were 198 unfortunates in Ulverston workhouse, over a thousand people were receiving some form of out-relief. More detail about the Ulverston Union workhouse can be found in June Whitehead's '*Lost Children: Ulverston Workhouse in the Nineteenth Century*' (Handstand Press 2006). Although the system may have provided a basic safety net for the sick, the mentally incapable, abandoned children, orphans and old people, it would not be far-fetched to say it was a system which criminalised misfortune and a net which was widely feared.

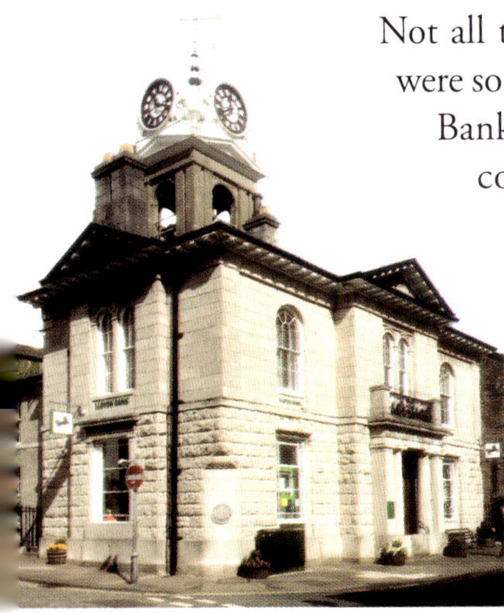

The former Ulverston Savings Bank, designed by Kendal architect George Webster.

Not all the changes in Ulverston between 1832 and 1851 were so gloomy. In 1838 the elegant new Ulverston Savings Bank (now the Lloyds Bank building), where the thrifty could deposit their money and which had been originally founded in 1816, was built on the corner of Market and Union Street to a design by the Kendal architect George Webster. In the same year the first North Lonsdale Agricultural Show was held outside the town, reflecting interest in advances in animal breeding and husbandry. A National School, paid for by local subscriptions to give poor children an education, was founded on the Ellers in 1834. Later, a sign of growing literacy and appetite for information was demonstrated by the appearance in 1847 of the first newspaper in Furness, Stephen Soulby's *'Soulby's Ulverston Advertiser and General Intelligencer'*.

While Quakers were not as dominant in industry as formerly, they were still active and the fine building on the corner of Queen and Cavendish Streets was built as a Temperance Hotel in 1851 through the good work of a local Quaker, Hannah Goad. The Theatre Royal and Assembly Rooms housed its very own 'Athenaeum', or literary and scientific society, with a museum mostly of natural history specimens, some of which had been donated by Sir John Barrow. To cater for less refined tastes, according to Dorothy Ashburner in *'A Story of the Growth of Ulverston'* the Victoria Concert Hall, whose faded splendour can still be seen on Mill Street, was built in 1850 as a music hall. The crowning glory for the less temperate who enjoyed sport and a bet was the wrestling match for the Championship of England held at the Flan How wrestling ring in October 1851. The event attracted thousands of people from as far away as Liverpool, Manchester and London to see Robert Atkinson of Sleagill beat William Jackson of Ennerdale. While the presence of such crowds from outside Furness, a phenomenon inconceivable before the spread of the railway, might have been gratifying, it would have highlighted the fact that Ulverston was not yet connected to anywhere by rail. Indeed, it is around this time, after the opening of the Furness Railway (discussed in the next chapter), that people in Ulverston seem to have become uneasy about the future of their town in a rapidly changing world.

This underlying concern is reflected in letters and articles from *'Soulby's Ulverston Advertiser'* collected by Jack Layfield in his book on the Sir John Barrow monument (Handstand Press 2005). It's not hard to see parallels between the story of this monument and that of numerous modern projects which start off in a rush of enthusiasm and then nearly founder on the rocks of financial reality. The generally undisputed view in the Advertiser was that Sir John Barrow, who died in 1848, was a shining example of how someone could rise from humble beginnings to great eminence if they were prepared to develop their natural talents by hard work and by adhering to a strict moral code. The son of a tanner from Dragley Beck, John Barrow was educated at Ulverston's Town Bank Grammar School, and after a colourful early career which included working in an iron foundry and taking part in a whaling expedition, he obtained his big break, a post in Lord McCartney's embassy to China. A gifted linguist and capable civil servant whose backroom skills were vital in the naval war against Napoleon, he eventually rose to become a permanent Secretary to the Admiralty, a founder of the Royal Geographical Society and the driving force behind expeditions to map the source of the Niger and find the North-West passage. His story is admirably told in Fergus Fleming's *'Barrow's Boys'* (Granta 1998).

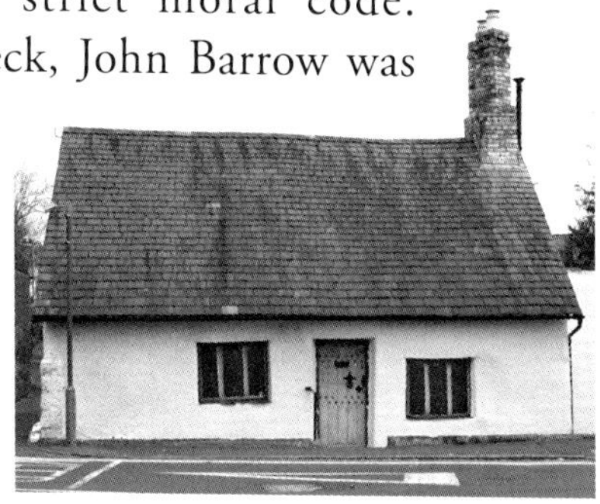

Birthplace in Dragley Beck of Sir John Barrow.

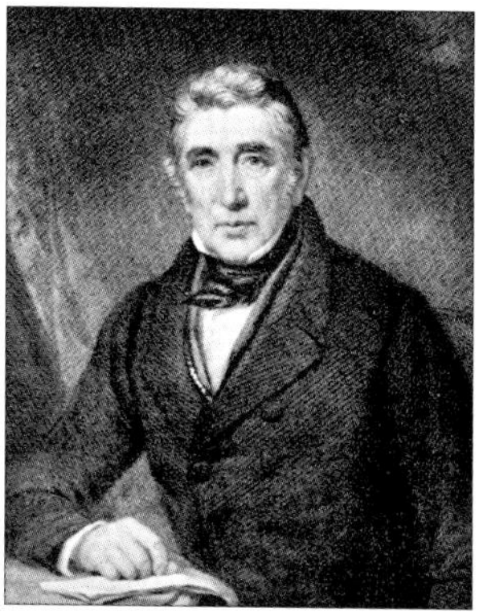

Sir John Barrow. North Lonsdale Magazine

On his death in 1848 there was a strong movement in Ulverston to build a suitable memorial to him. Some of the reasoning was high-minded: a memorial would inspire young people to emulate this famous son of the town; and moreover if it was built in the form of a tower it would also have a practical use, perhaps as a lighthouse, an observatory, a telegraphic station or a navigational aid. Some arguments were pragmatic in that people also wanted to attract Lake District tourists to Ulverston. A plaintive letter of March 1850 went so far as to say, *'Ulverston, in itself, possesses little or no attraction, either for the excursionist, the man of science, the scholar or the romantic pedestrian'.* Subscriptions were raised from the town, and in 1850 Trinity House, the body in charge of lighthouses, contributed £100 and gave permission for a tower to be built on Hoad Hill, but there were further calls for the townspeople to shake off their apathy and dig deeper into their pockets to build this attraction.

The building of the monument got off to a flying start in May 1850 when what seems to have been the entire town population processed up to the top of Hoad to witness the laying of the foundation stone and to listen to speeches and to poetry which made up in noble sentiment what it lacked in sophistication. Thereafter misfortunes dogged the project. The building was nearly finished in February 1851 when it was struck by lightning and damaged. There were calls for it to be repaired quickly and for the inside to be fitted out in order to tempt the many foreigners who would surely travel on to the Lake District after visiting London for the 1851 Great Exhibition of Industry. Like the 2012 London Olympics, the Great Exhibition confounded the doom-mongers and became the wonder of its age. It was visited by millions, their journeys in many cases only made possible by the railway, yet one suspects that just as in 2012 the anticipated tourist boom in Ulverston never materialised. In March 1853 the monument was still a shell and there were wrangles between the Barrow family and the building contractor over costs. Vandals regularly caused 'malicious Damage' to the building and boys used it as a climbing frame, just as their modern counterparts did during its restoration in twenty first century.

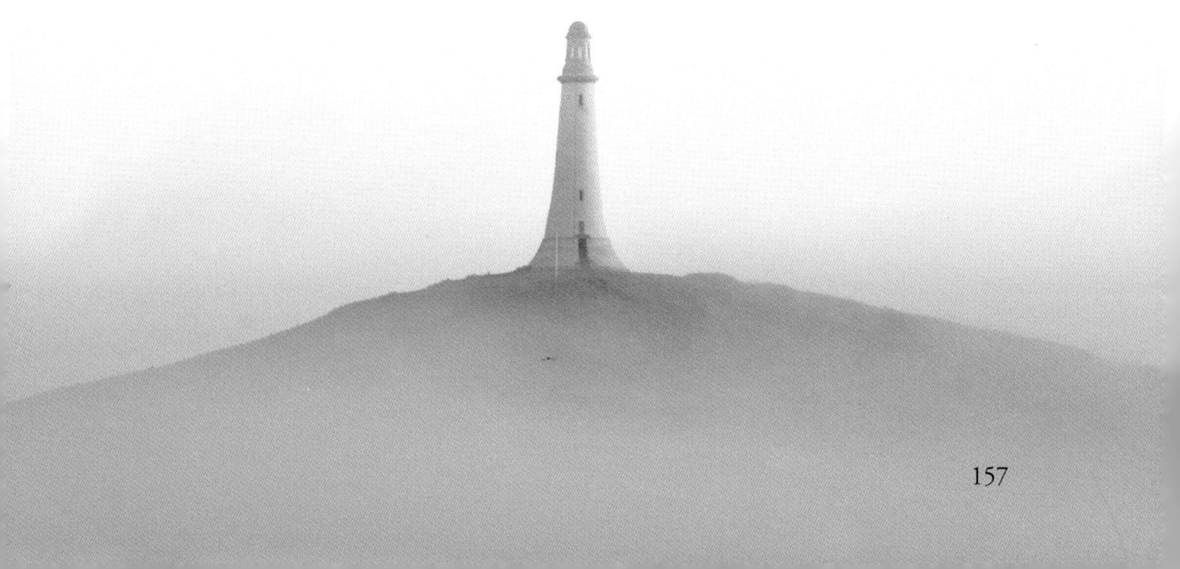

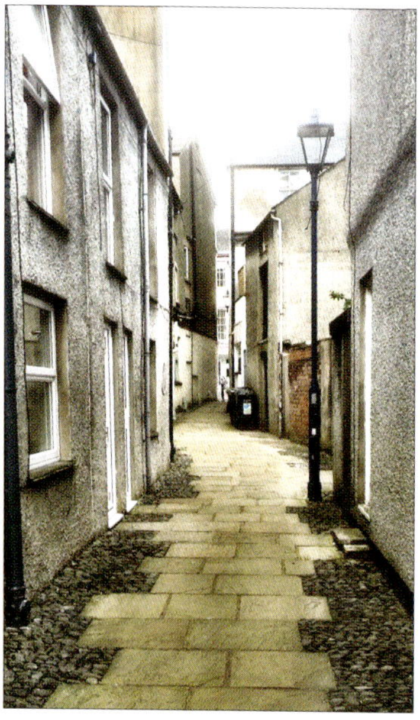

A surviving Ulverston lane showing just how close the buildings were to each other in the 19th century.

There is an intangible sense that all was not as it should be in Ulverston. Earlier complimentary accounts of the town's cleanliness give way to a damning report in 1854 from an Inspector from the General Board of Health. In his opinion houses were too close together, windows were too small, flagged floors encouraged damp, privies, cesspits and middens were too close to houses and water pumps and there was no proper sewerage system. No wonder diseases flourished and death rates were high. Earlier, in 1848, letter writers to Soulby's Ulverston Advertiser argued over whether covering the town's streams, which acted as sewers, had been such a good idea since it encouraged the build-up of waste. In JD Marshall's view, by the early 1850's the attention of Ulverston's tradesmen, gentry and landowners was focussed less on improving the town, in particular its local government, and more on what was happening elsewhere in Furness, namely the coming of the railway.

• XI •

ULVERSTON AND THE RAILWAYS

While the outlook for Ulverston in the early1850's may have seemed uncertain, by the end of the century the town had nearly doubled in size after the coming of the railway and new industry. With the opening of the line to Carnforth in 1857, Ulverston was connected to the national railway system which had grown rapidly, if in a piecemeal fashion, since the success of early lines like the Manchester to Liverpool railway.

Steam locomotion on railways had become the force behind a second industrial revolution, driving economic growth. The construction and operation of railways increased demand for the coal and iron they had originally been designed to carry, and other countries soon wanted their own railways, so before long Britain was manufacturing track and locomotives for the world. Railways not only shrank Britain in terms of many times faster journey times but also brought with them features we take for granted today, from the acceptance of Greenwich Mean Time throughout the country to dodgy train catering. Given that all of Britain's railways were built by private companies who needed to raise capital from shareholders and pay out dividends, it was not inevitable that they should be built in Furness, and the history of their development was far from straightforward.

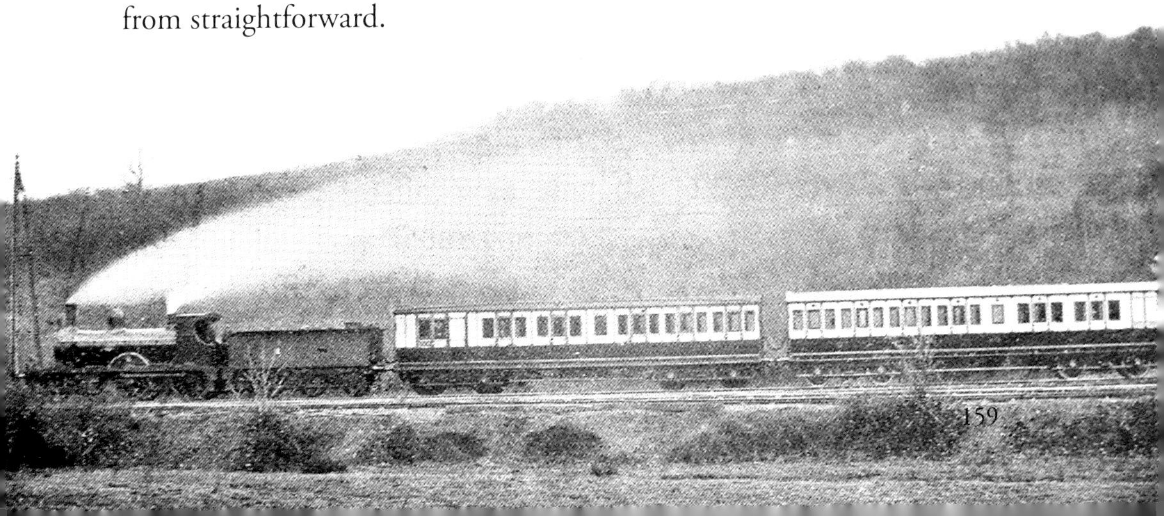

Readers who would like more than the following précis should consult the experts in Leslie Gilpin's *'The Ulverstone and Lancaster Railway'* (Cumbria Railways Association 2008) and Michael Andrew's *'The Furness Railway'* (Barrai Books 2012).

Landowners in the nineteenth century lucky enough to be sitting on deposits of coal and other sought-after raw materials made substantial sums of money, and those in Furness were no exception. The two main landowners were the owner of the Kirkby slate quarries, William Cavendish Earl of Burlington, who was very involved in the district, and the Duke of Buccleuch, holder of the manor of Ulverston, who was largely an absentee landlord. No railway project would ever get off the ground without their permission, and although adventurous was the last word one would use to describe Burlington's approach to business, he and his agents were instrumental in building the first railway in Furness, the aptly named Furness Railway. The Furness Railway Bill, which received Royal Assent in May 1844, was originally a modest project involving a railway, not necessarily using steam locomotion, to carry slate from the Kirkby quarries to jetties at the hamlet of Barrow, with a branch coming in from outside Dalton to carry iron ore. Not all iron ore merchants, suspecting high tolls for carriage, were in favour of a railway, and for Burlington the jury was out on how successful it would be although he, Buccleuch and their business connections were the first investors in the Furness Railway Company. In the event, the Furness Railway board decided to use steam locomotives, and in making the railway's headquarters at Barrow sowed the seeds of Barrow's future expansion. The railway exceeded Burlington's expectations. Within a few years of its opening in 1846 more haematite and slate was being carried by rail and shipped from Barrow than was being sent through the canal at Ulverston, a town in which Furness Railway owners were losing interest. The shift away from Ulverston as the commercial centre of Furness was accelerated by the discovery in 1850 of the huge Park haematite deposit near Askam. Ore production shot up and now the Furness Railway could transport masses of high quality ore to ships at

Barrow for export to furnaces in South Wales. Burlington and Buccleuch collected their share of royalties from every ton of ore mined and of tolls for every ton carried to Barrow by rail. Indeed, a condition of Buccleuch's leases for ore mines on his land was that the ore should be carried by the Furness Railway. A further blow to Ulverston's pre-eminence came when the ore merchant and investor H W Schneider, who had the lease of the Park deposit, built a modern iron-smelting works at Hindpool outside Barrow. These works, profiting from Bessemer's steel-making process which used phosphorus-free haematite pig-iron, became the biggest iron and steel plant in Europe and led to the creation of a large new industrial town.

William Salmon's naive assertion in his 1849 history of the Ulverston Canal that the expense of taking iron ore to ports was 'not materially lessened by the Furness Railway', and that in future more ore would be shipped down the canal where vessels were not damaged by high loading chutes as they were at Barrow, now seems laughable. His confidence in increased business at Ulverston canal, bolstered by the engineering feat of Collins Weir, which was built in 1847/48 to persuade the Leven channel to stay on the Ulverston side, was misplaced if understandable, since he had already seen railway schemes involving Ulverston come to nothing in the 1830's. These schemes appear impossibly grandiose to us today, even when a proposal to build a bridge from Barrow to outside Lancaster pops up at regular intervals. They were largely based on two assumptions. The first was George Stephenson's belief that Shap summit was an obstacle to the viability of a west coast railway line linking England and Scotland, and the second was that the construction of embankments carrying railways across Morecambe Bay and the Duddon sands would lead to the reclamation of thousands of acres of land for agriculture, an enormous carrot where landowners were concerned. The idea of a line to Scotland along the north-west coast and passing through Furness was raised in 1836, and the following year George Stephenson himself appeared and briefly surveyed a possible route across Morecambe Bay and up to Whitehaven. He suggested building embankments from

Lancaster to Humphrey Head, from the Cartmel peninsula to Sandhall via Chapel Island, and across the Duddon sands. An even more ambitious scheme proposed an embankment topped by a railway right across Morecambe Bay to Rampside with a branch line to Ulverston. Confident in the engineering prowess of their age, many people in Ulverston were all for these schemes, and ore merchants, tradesmen and gentry wanted Burlington to lend his weight to the cause. He thought the latter plan in particular was 'very wild', and others doubted whether either phenomenally expensive scheme would make money, especially as there had been passenger steamer services between Furness and the Fylde coast since 1835. Steam locomotives which could conquer Shap were developed, and the two ideas were dropped for the time being.

Salmon's dismissal of the railway is also maybe not so surprising since he was writing in 1849 after the spectacular 1848 end to the first bout of railway mania. Rather like the bursting of the dotcom bubble, the value of shares in many railway schemes fell through the floor, ruining thousands of investors. Against this background, along with the failure of various other proposals for Ulverston and the hostility of some ore merchants to the Furness Railway because of its high tolls, it is debatable whether a railway would have reached Ulverston at all if it hadn't been for John Brogden and his sons. A Cheshire man, Brogden had made a pile of money from railway and general contracting, and had a finger in many pies including providing horses to local authorities and cleaning Manchester's streets. An early investor in the Whitehaven to Kirkby Ireleth line, he also had railway contracts all over the country and was a director of the South-Eastern Railway from 1846 until 1850 after which he turned his attention back to Furness. Brogden acquired leases for ore mines at Stainton and shares in the Ulverston Mining Company, one of the Kennedy businesses, and bought Lightburne House which his son, another John, made his home.

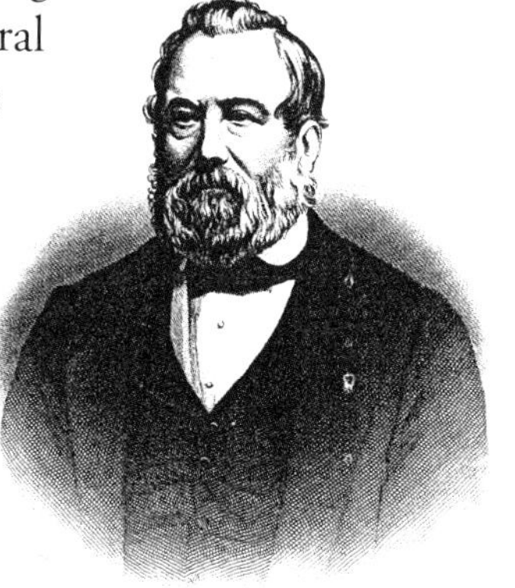

John Brogden 1798-1869
by Joseph Richardson.

Brogden's master plan was for a railway from Ulverston to the main line at Carnforth so that he could transport ore directly to furnaces in land-locked South Staffordshire. Although the Furness Railway as a company wasn't interested in building such a line, some of its shareholders like Burlington and Buccleuch put money into Brogden's scheme, since it meant that if they extended the Furness line to Ulverston, they would have a mainline link they hadn't risked all to build. The Ulverston and Lancaster Railway Bill received assent in July 1851, but work did not begin on the line until 1853, and it was only then that the Furness Railway pushed ahead with extending their line to Ulverston, a troublesome project which was completed in April 1854. Their station, nowadays a car showroom, was on the edge of town and 113 feet above sea level, not exactly helpful to the Ulverston to Lancaster Company.

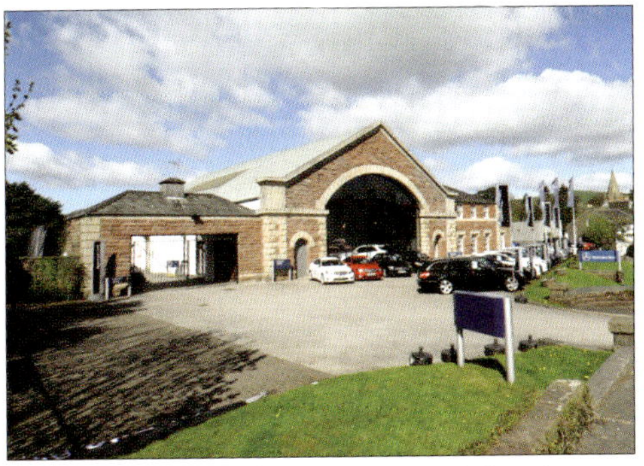
The first Ulverston Railway Station as it is today.

By modern standards the line to Carnforth was a daunting undertaking, and it was fortunate that the civil engineer James Brunlees, an expert on bridges and embanking marshy ground, was on board. First of all, a great embankment was built to take the line from a junction with the Furness Railway down to the shore at Plumpton, with a bridge over the canal thrown in for good measure, and then more embankments were constructed, notably along the shore of the Cartmel peninsula and between Grange and the Kent viaduct. The ambitious viaducts over the Leven and Kent estuaries rightly attract our admiration today, yet these embankments were also a considerable achievement, given that a day's work was often washed away by the next high tide. Once it was decided that iron would be better than wood for constructing the viaducts, building the Leven viaduct was contracted to the firm of W & G Galloway who established a foundry towards the foot of the canal, which Brogden now owned. An added complication was that a moveable section had to be incorporated into the viaduct so that ships could still reach the port at Greenodd. This was ordered from another of Brogden's pies, an ironworks in Tondu, Glamorgan. The engineers invented a new kind of pile which could be driven down into the sand by jets of water, a piece of civil engineering history. All this ground-breaking engineering and grinding hard work might still have come to nothing as spiralling costs taxed even Brogden's deep pockets. Fortunately, another company, the South Durham and Lancashire Union Railway, announced their intention to build a railway from Barnard Castle to Tebay. This would mean that if the Ulverston to Carnforth line was completed, there would be a direct connection between Furness and iron smelters on the east coast, so Burlington and Buccleuch were moderately happy to stump up more money for Brogden to finish his line. Despite setbacks, including the ramming of the Leven viaduct by the schooner 'Sarah Jane', it opened for goods traffic at the end of August 1857. While spectacular lines like the Settle to Carlisle attract all the plaudits, the construction of the Ulverston to Carnforth line has to be counted as one of the unsung feats of Victorian railway engineering.

Engineering triumph or not, the Ulverston and Lancaster Railway didn't live up to Brogden's expectations in terms of carrying iron ore away from Furness. The traffic was more coke from Durham coming the other way, a factor which encouraged Schneider to build an ironworks at Barrow. Neither was there much passenger traffic at first except to and from Ulverston on market day. The line was taken over in 1862 by the Furness Railway Company which had already built a line in 1859 between Broughton and Coniston to carry slate, copper ore and that growing source of income, tourists. To solve the problematic moving section of the Leven viaduct, the Furness Railway Company persuaded those with interests in the

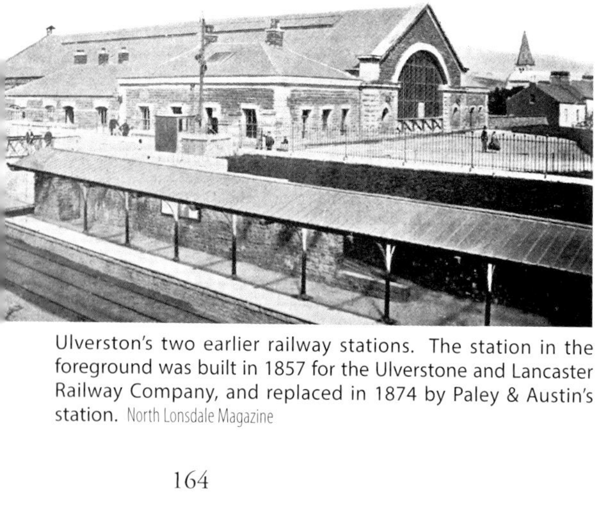

Ulverston's two earlier railway stations. The station in the foreground was built in 1857 for the Ulverstone and Lancaster Railway Company, and replaced in 1874 by Paley & Austin's station. North Lonsdale Magazine

port of Greenodd that a railway would be preferable to the sea channel. This line, built in 1867-9 from Plumpton through Greenodd and Haverthwaite to Lakeside, was another route for tourists making for Lake Windermere.

There is a school of thought that the arrival of these railways led to a period of stagnation in Ulverston in the 1860's when the population hardly grew. The railway certainly led to a sharp decline in shipping using the Ulverston canal even though Brogden had built a new basin when the railway bridge made the old one inaccessible for schooners. This was accompanied by a decline in ship-building in Ulverston and, tellingly, the custom house was transferred to Barrow in 1862. A canal-side ironworks where pig iron was converted into wrought iron only lasted until 1861, and cotton manufacturing in the town ceased in the 1870's, a consequence of the drying-up of cotton imports in the American Civil War and because smaller mills in outlying areas could not compete with larger more efficient mills in the main Lancashire cotton towns.

In the mid-1860's Ulverston was condemned by the Registrar General's office for its shockingly high death rate, which was driven more by unhygienic living conditions than by poverty, since, even with the loss of some businesses, apparently there was plenty of well-paid work around and prices were reasonable. One argument is that Ulverston was becoming neglected and falling behind the times because leading Furness landowners and industrialists were now concentrating on Barrow where Gladstone himself opened the huge new docks in 1867. Moreover, the townspeople were bickering amongst themselves, with some obstructing the formation of a local health board, as laid down by the Public Health Act, which would have the authority to clean up the town by building sewers.

A lack of focus on Ulverston might also have been compounded by the departure from Conishead Priory in the 1840's of the Braddylls, the last of the major local traditional landowning families. Thomas Braddyll, who had incurred vast debts rebuilding the Priory, was unable to recoup his losses from developing mines in the Durham coalfield and went bankrupt. Thomas Braddyll's father had been instrumental in getting

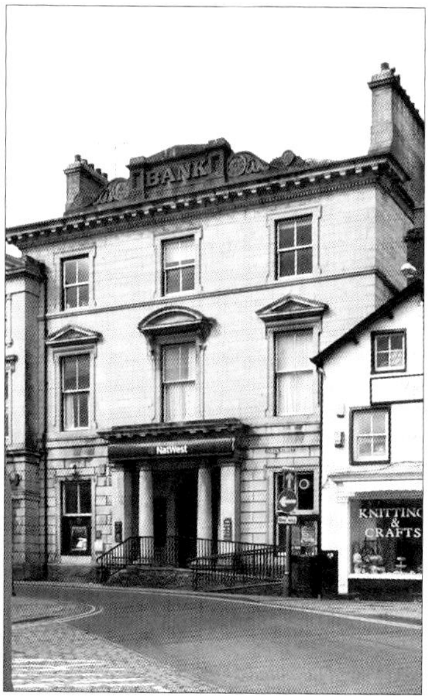

The former Lancaster Bank in the Market Place.

the canal built, and now it might seem that there was no influential family from the gentry to put Ulverston first.

This picture of stagnation is not the full story, and investment in Ulverston did not come to a full stop in the 1860's. While it is rightly said that it was the building of the North Lonsdale Iron and Steel Company's ironworks alongside the canal in the mid-1870's which kick-started Ulverston's Victorian expansion, by 1870 there had been considerable re-building in the town centre. In 1865 the Lancaster Bank built a smart new banking hall, now occupied by the NatWest bank, at the top of Market Street, and by this year the row of small buildings on the western side of King Street towards Mill Street, visible in 18th century paintings, had been replaced with the buildings we see today. At some point in the 1860's the building now housing the Oxfam shop on the corner of Daltongate and King Street was constructed on the site of a smaller building, also seen in earlier Georgian paintings. In 1866 the parish church of St Mary's was renovated, although the loss it entailed of historic features like the box pews is now more a cause of lamentation than rejoicing among historians.

In 1871 Ulverston finally gained a local government board, and it was decided that a purpose-built market hall was required to replace the crush of assorted carts in the historic market place. This hall wasn't finished until 1875 and was about three times larger than the current market hall which occupies part of its site. By this time, the Drill Hall, now the Red Rose Social Club, had been built on Victoria Road for the 10th Lancashire Royal Volunteers, and Ulverston had a new railway station, the result of investment by the Furness Railway. Designed by the Lancaster architects,

Paley and Austin, it was built in 1873-4, with the old Furness Railway station becoming a goods only station. This fine station is still in use, and traces of its former glory can be found in its cast-iron canopies and Italianate clock tower. There have been various attempts to find alternative uses for some of the now empty station buildings, including 'Buffers', a night club which was a favourite late night venue for many years.

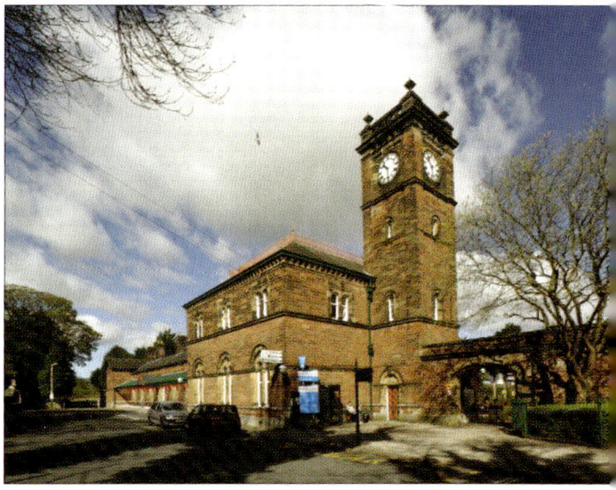

Paley & Austin's fine railway station.

Although there was resistance to the formation of a local government board, the 1870's saw the appearance in Ulverston of the philanthropic public-spiritedness we associate with more high-minded Victorians. In 1871 a Dr Henry Barker pointed out that Ulverston needed a cottage hospital, not least because of all the accidents arising from the increased use of machinery in industry and agriculture. The following year a hospital was built on Newton Street, and from 1899 annual parades to raise money for this worthy cause became a feature of town life, a tradition which lives on in the Ulverston Carnival. The land for the hospital was donated by Myles Kennedy, whose family were becoming increasingly influential in Ulverston. The Kennedy iron ore firm had hit the big time after discovering a massive new ore bed at Roanhead, and profits from these mines enabled Myles Kennedy to build a grand house at Stone Cross at the top of Daltongate in 1874. It was also Myles Kennedy and another local ore family, the Ainslies, who were major shareholders in the North Lonsdale Iron and Steel Company when it was incorporated in October 1873. With the 'blowing in' of the company's first two modern iron furnaces in May 1876, Ulverston was set for another phase of growth. Between 1871 and 1881 the town's population increased by more than two thousand as workers migrated into the area from other iron-working areas, especially Staffordshire. The town spread beyond its medieval core, an entirely new settlement was built in South Ulverston and new industries were established.

This dramatic growth can easily be seen when we look at the 1890 Ordnance Survey map. On the southern edge of town Lightburne House, having changed hands several times to become the County Hotel, no longer looks out over park land. Buildings have gone up towards the railway on what is now Victoria Road, and Hartley, Oxford and Cox Streets have been built, while more houses appear on Princes Street towards the station. Similarly to the north of town a whole clutch of new streets including Sun and Star Streets, Hoad Terrace and Garden Terrace have sprung up, and moving south-east towards the parish church, Beech Bank and Ford Park Crescent have been laid out. Ford Park and Ford Park House, named after Ford Ainslie who died in the Crimean War, make an appearance, and the previously empty area between the town centre and Ratten Row has filled up with Burlington, Ainslie, Casson, Cavendish and Newton Streets. Towards the canal, the triangle of land between Sunderland Terrace, Quay Street and Ratten Row is built over, and yet more new streets, including Byron Street, Towers Street, the Devonshire Road, Dale Street and Bailey Street are creeping over the area between Quay Street and the railway. In the centre of town the gardens on the south side of Market Street have disappeared under New Market Street and Brogden Street, with the new market hall between these recent thoroughfares. A link with the past has gone with the demolition of Neville Hall and the construction of a Police Station and Court in its place. Meanwhile in 'South Ulverston' North Lonsdale Road, with its Methodist Chapel, Post Office and Empress Hotel, together with Kennedy and Steel Streets are in place.

When we look at the shoreline the impact of the ironworks on the area hits home. What was a small curved stretch of shore between Hammerside Hill and Sandhall is now a jumbled mess of mud and sand dominated by Beaconsfield and Ainslie Piers built on slag banks, and by a new Furness Railway line heading off towards Conishead Priory. This line, running from a junction with the Ulverston to Lancaster railway at Plumpton, crossing the canal on a unique sliding bridge and going right through the ironworks, was opened for goods traffic in 1882 and for

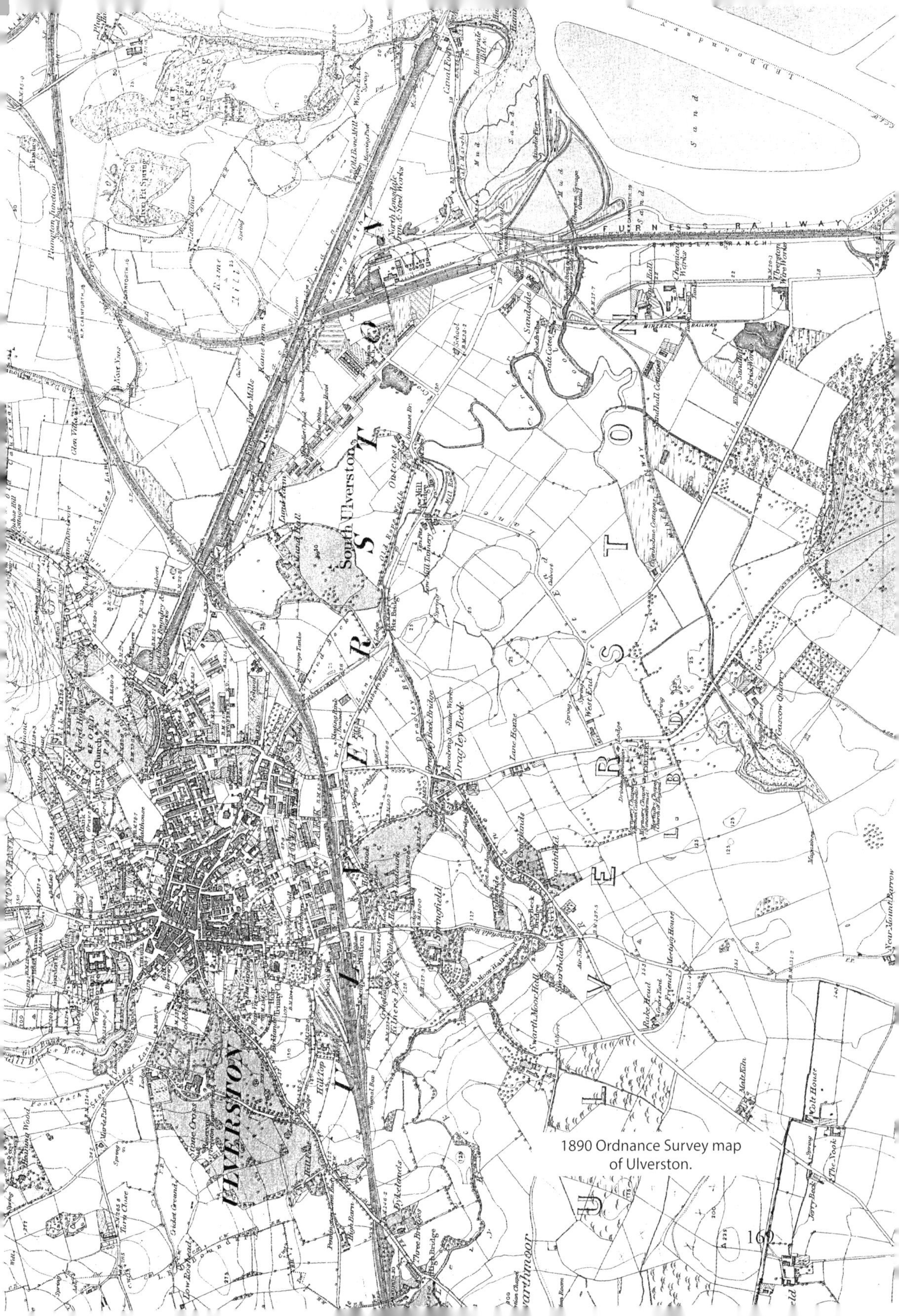

1890 Ordnance Survey map of Ulverston.

passengers to Conishead Priory, now a 'hydropathic hotel', in 1883. It was intended to run through Bardsea and all the way to Barrow, but this never happened, which is why we can still see its embankment coming to an abrupt stop in a field beyond the former Priory station. Before the line was built, iron ore from the Furness mines and coke from Durham for the iron works had to be taken along a hazardous spur plunging from the Ulverston to Lancaster line near the bridge over the canal down to canal side sidings, and iron could be taken out the same way or shipped from Beaconsfield Pier. Limestone for the ironworks came from Plumpton and along a mineral line from Gascow quarry, now the Bardsea Caravan Park, and yet another line served the Sandhall brickworks, lying south of Sandhall itself, whose products were much in demand for the brick-lined furnaces. Indeed, in 1890 the whole flat area south of the canal was industrialised, with different businesses served by a network of railways.

As well as the ironworks dominating the skyline with their massive furnaces, the brickworks and Gascow quarry, there was a chemical works at Sandhall and a wireworks close to the brickworks. The chemical works had been set up in 1876 by a Yorkshire industrialist, S A Sadler, to refine pitch and other tar products using tar carried from his coke ovens in North Yorkshire on the trains which brought coke for the ironworks. The chemical works had its own siding off the mineral line, as did the wireworks, nothing of which remains now except for a brick chimney sticking up incongruously in land which has returned to rural peace. In 1890 this area was not the only source of growth, since the map shows how other older industrial sites in and around the town were being put to new uses. After Low Mill ceased spinning cotton it was probably used as a bobbin mill and then briefly as a brush factory before being converted in 1875 to a large and successful tannery which remained in operation until 1972.

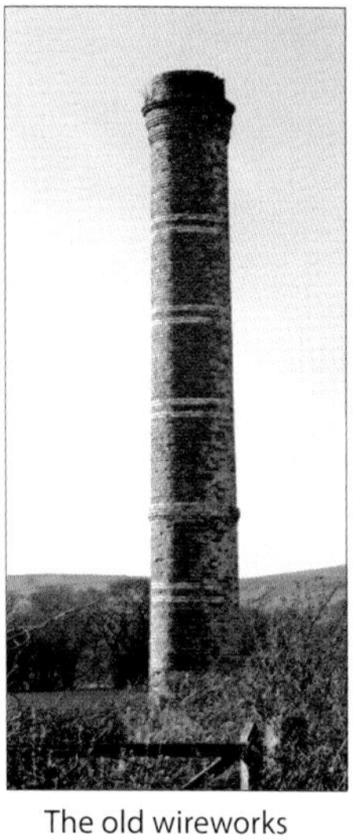

The old wireworks chimney at Sandhall.

The site of the puddling furnace just below the new basin on the canal was taken up in the 1870's by the Furness Paper Mills, and a foundry and engineering works replaced the slate and timber depot at Canal Head. Dragley Beck's iron foundry was succeeded by a revolving shutter works, while part of the large mill on the Ellers became a candle factory, making candles for iron ore miners.

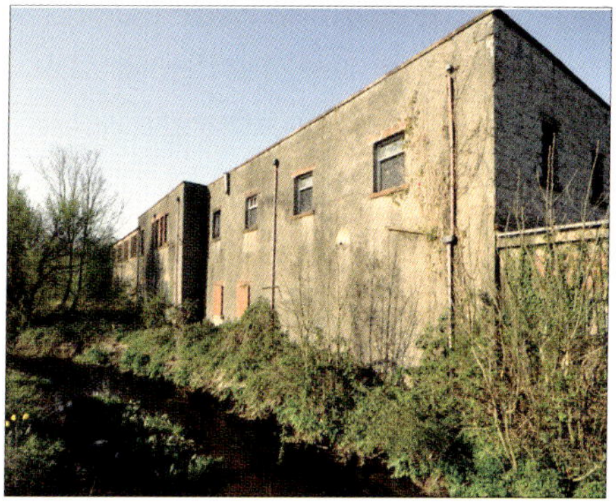

All that remains of the former tannery on the site of Lundbeck Cotton Mill.

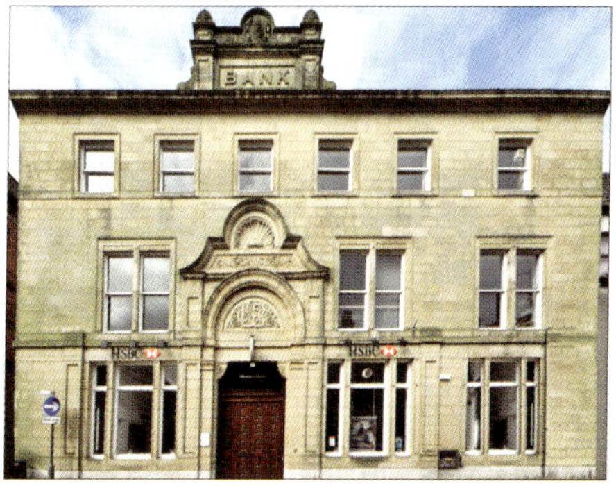

The former Cumberland Bank on New Market St.

The industrial activity and the wealth it generated created a legacy in Ulverston of the self-confident public buildings we associate with the later Victorian period. These include the frontage of the Co-operative Society buildings on lower Market Street, and the Cumberland Bank (now the HSBC) on New Market Street.

An example of the Victorian urge to tidy things up is the Victoria Road Auction Mart which was built in 1878 to end the old-fashioned practice of selling livestock out in the open in the Gill or the Market Place. This building, now partly occupied by the Ulverston Brewing Company, goes

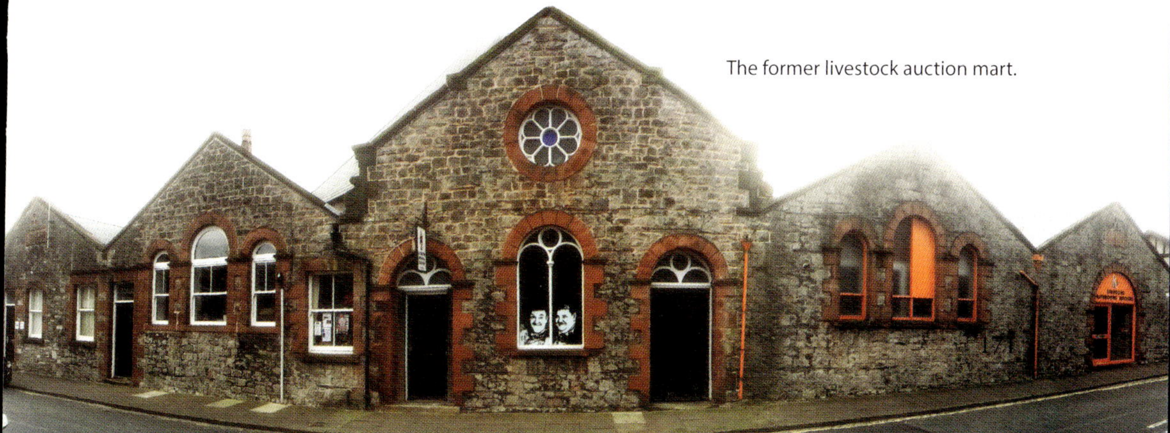

The former livestock auction mart.

well beyond the utilitarian in its surprisingly elegant design. The carved stone over the separate entrance for sheep (the stone over the other entrance, maybe for cows, has been defaced) echoes the stones over separate entrances for boys and girls in schools from the same era.

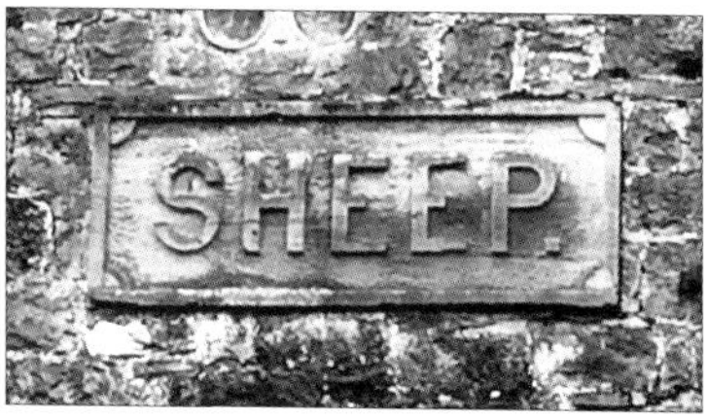

One such school in Ulverston was the now re-modelled National School on the Ellers, which was enlarged in 1884. While the town never seems to have lacked a multiplicity of small private schools, other schools were founded in accordance with legislation encouraging free education for the children of the poor. Although primary education was not made compulsory until 1889, the 1870 Education Act allowed for elected local school boards which could raise taxes to pay for non-church schools. A school board was formed in Ulverston in 1874, and in 1877 it opened its newly built board school always called the Dale Street School, although it was on Lund Road bang against the railway embankment in the newly developed area popularly known as the Honeypot. Church Walk Infant School, which had started as the vicar's project in 1855, had moved to a larger building by 1896, and in 1898 the foundation stone of the Higher Grade and Technical School, eventually to become the Victoria High School, was laid in Hart Street.

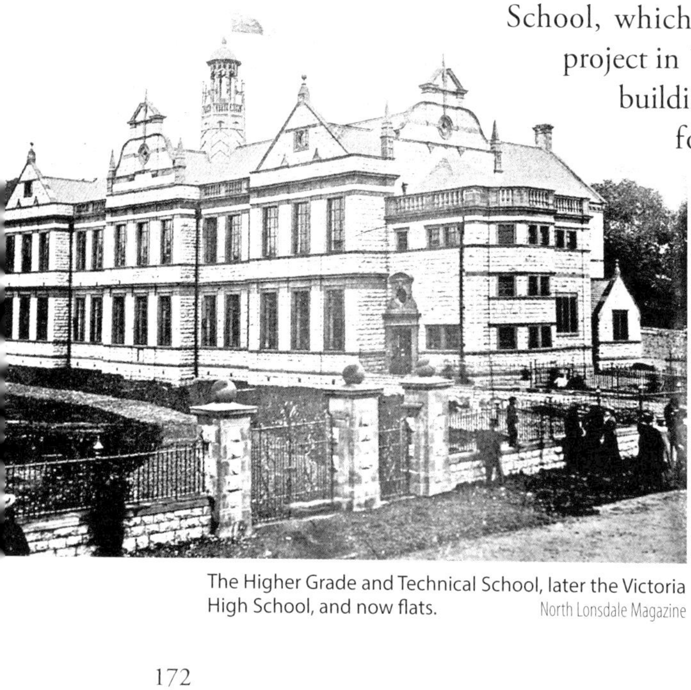

The Higher Grade and Technical School, later the Victoria High School, and now flats. North Lonsdale Magazine

Along with education, governments encouraged local authorities to pay more attention to public health. The 1875 Public Health Act required them to purify water supplies, provide sewage systems and appoint Medical Officers of Health to make sure this happened. A Rural Sanitary Authority for Ulverston was appointed in the 1870's, but in 1886 the Medical Officer of Health was unimpressed by Ulverston's cleanliness, and complained about shortcomings in 'scavenging' or human waste disposal. His words seem to have had some effect since the 1890 map shows a sewage outfall at the base of Beaconsfield Pier, suggesting that efforts were being made to clean up the town.

A picture of Ulverston in its later Victorian heyday can be found in Mannex & Co's '*History and Directory of Furness and Cartmel*' of 1882. While admitting that 'in commercial importance it has paled before the light of its youthful rival, Barrow', it states that Ulverston is a 'wealthy and thriving town' with 'elegantly furnished' shops and good hotels. It still harks back to the past in the observation that the new Beaconsfield pier might be 'the nucleus of other extensive works which may bring a revival of Ulverston's former prosperity as a port'. The directory lists a huge range of small businesses in the town, from fourteen Bakers and Confectioners and ten Booksellers, Printers, Stationers and Bookbinders through eighteen Drapers to forty one general 'Shopkeepers and Provision Dealers', a vivid reminder of a world where there was a shop on nearly every residential street. Bringing these lists to life, Jennifer Snell's *'Lost Ulverston'* (Jennifer and Maurice Snell 2008) recounts many fascinating tales about the town and its inhabitants around this time.

The temptation to look back with nostalgia on Ulverston re-invigorated by new industries and embracing Victorian improvements in the late nineteenth century has to be balanced by acknowledging that the flipside of prosperity for some was poverty for many others. June Whitehead's book on children in the Ulverston workhouse shows how overcrowding was endemic in the 1870's and 1880's, partly because of the large numbers of children who found themselves there. Some were orphans while others may have been left by their parent or parents while they moved around looking for work, perhaps as a result of the agricultural depression in these decades. As late as 1891 children were still being sent back to their 'original' parishes from which their parents had migrated, presumably because they had done the Victorian equivalent of getting on their bikes to find a job. Mannex's Directory seems to see no contradiction between the need for a larger workhouse because of the great increase in 'paupers' and the depiction of Ulverston as a wealthy town. Families like the Kennedys may have provided treats for workhouse children, yet Ms Whitehead illustrates the stigma and petty meanness pervading the system. In the celebrations for Queen Victoria's Diamond Jubilee in 1897 children in the town were given china commemorative mugs, while those in the workhouse were given cheaper enamelled versions, and the grim new children's department, built in 1897-8, looked a lot less prepossessing than even the new Auction Mart.

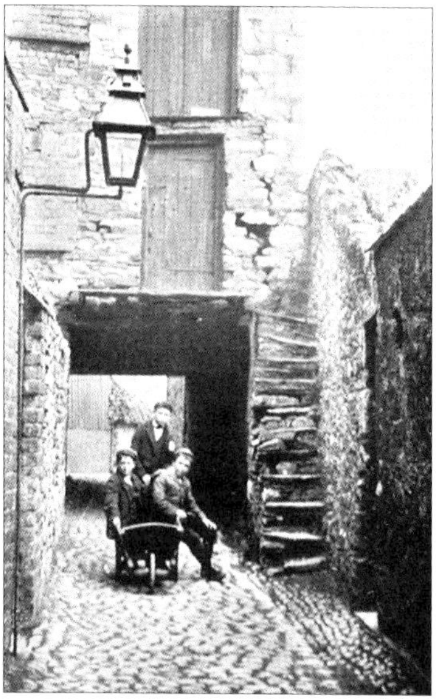
A cobbled ginnel off Soutergate, showing older buildings in a poor state. Peter Lowe

Physical conditions might not have been much better for some families outside the workhouse. Unlike more prestigious town centre buildings and solid middle-class houses like those on Hoad Terrace, some poorer housing put up in this period had a relatively short shelf life. Late nineteenth century small houses on Quay Street and on Brewery Street, for example, have disappeared without a trace in the twentieth century. This makes it hard for us to imagine how crowded and insanitary parts of the town, away from the leafy outskirts, must have been, although Ulverston can have been no different from other comparable towns, and a lot more salubrious than contemporary cities.

It was a place which demonstrated that one need not be trapped by one's origins. Just as the previous century saw John Barrow rise above humble beginnings, the end of the nineteenth century saw the births of two men who were to be at the heart of contrasting twentieth century spheres. The first was Norman Birkett, the son of a draper, who rose in the law to become one of the judges at the Nuremburg Trials, and the second was Arthur Stanley Jefferson, better known as Stan Laurel. Between the extremes of wealth personified by the Kennedy family and of poverty exemplified by workhouse children were other Ulverstonians whose unexpected talents enriched the town's life. Foremost among these must be Edwin Woodburn whose family had owned the Town Mill since 1835. Not only was he a celebrated pole-vaulter at the Flan Sports, he also found time to practise as a sculptor, carving the four faces, representing either the four seasons or the four ages of women, which can still be seen on the corner of the former mill's front facing wall.

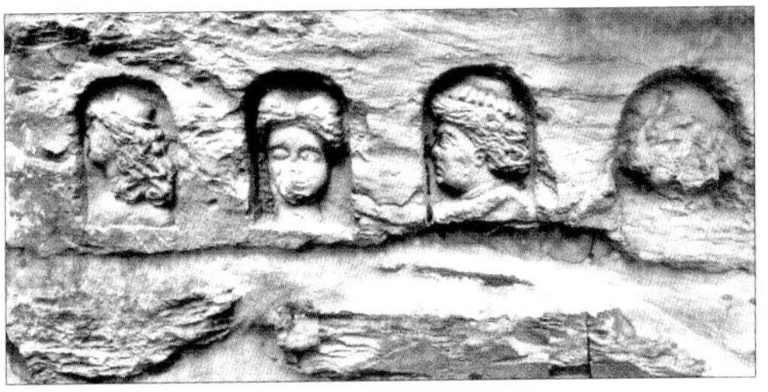

The heads carved by Edwin Woodburn on the Town Mill.

A bustling slice of the Victorian world, Ulverston celebrated the ageing queen's Diamond Jubilee in 1897 with parties and a massive bonfire. The pace of change in the second half of the nineteenth century might have seemed fast to some, yet no-one could have foreseen that so much of what had been built in the previous fifty years would be swept away in the next century.

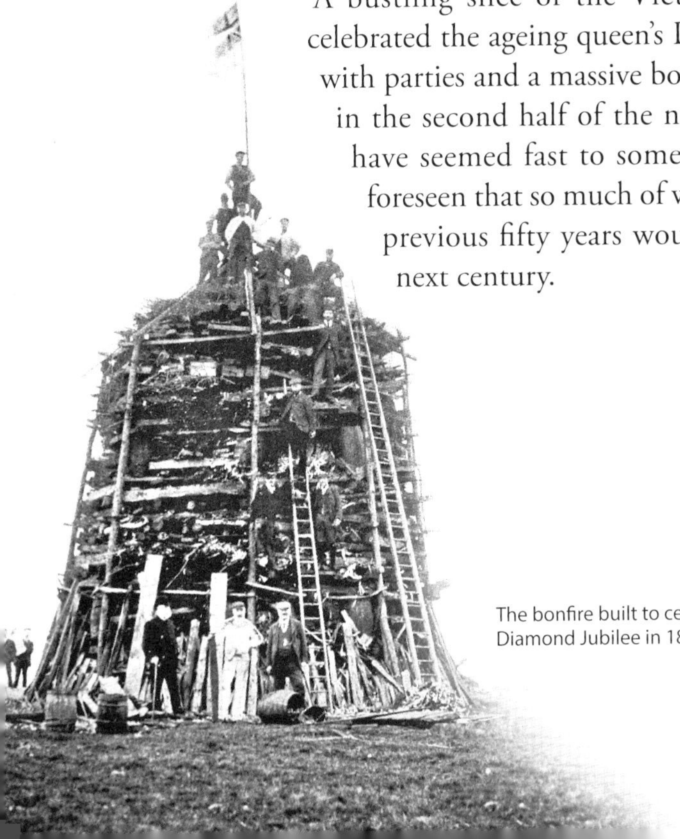

The bonfire built to celebrate Queen Victoria's Diamond Jubilee in 1897. North Lonsdale Magazine

• XII •

Modern Ulverston

On a July evening in 2011 hundreds of people poured into Ulverston's Coronation Hall for a public meeting. There was standing room only as Robinsons, owners of the now closed brewery on Brewery Street, outlined their plans for its future. On a site where beer had been brewed since 1775 and where the local firm R & P Hartley had made their famous beer 'straight from the wood', Robinsons planned a wholesale demolition, the erection of a concrete and glass structure and the excavation of an underground car park, in the hope that a major supermarket chain would lease this construction. Robinsons' developers faced the hostility of shop-keepers, business leaders and locals who argued that this would be a gross over-development on an unsuitable site, and that the last thing Ulverston needed in difficult economic times was another supermarket and the loss of more of its historic fabric. A commonly expressed sentiment among opponents to the 'supermarket' was 'we don't want to turn into a town like any other'. In the weeks following the meeting, supporters of Robinsons were equally passionate. Ulverston couldn't live in the past. A national retailer with competitive prices would revitalise a dying town centre and why should Ulverstonians have to trail to Barrow for a weekly or fortnightly shop that wouldn't break the bank? While war was waged in the local papers and social media, their heated arguments obscured the fact that both sides had something fundamental in common: a deep desire for Ulverston to survive as a viable town in the twenty first century with all its new challenges.

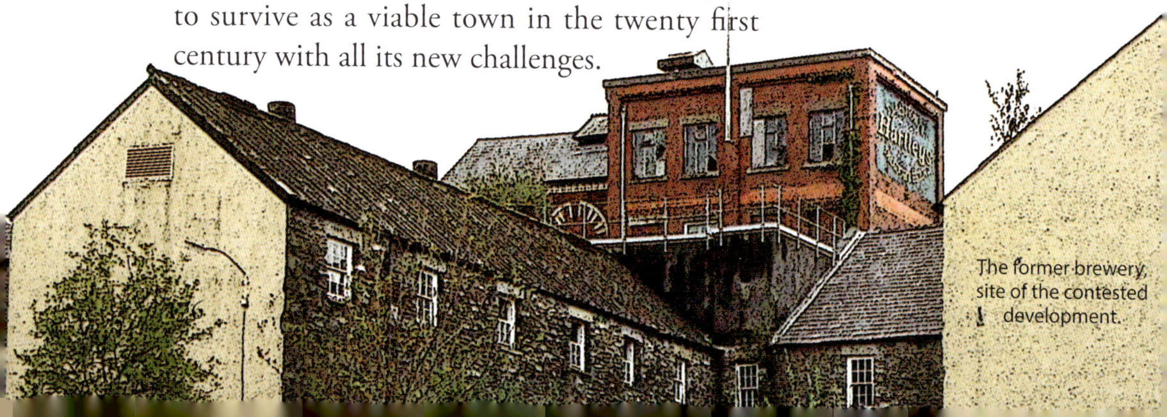

The former brewery, site of the contested development.

Buffeted by external economic and political forces throughout the twentieth century and into the millennium, Ulverston has seen many such clashes as its citizens and their elected representatives struggled to find a role in a Furness now dominated by Barrow. The result, for good or ill, is a town which has lost chunks of buildings in its centre, been sliced in half by a main road and ballooned round the edges with housing estates. In the 1990's you could still find traditional general grocers in the town centre; now changing shopping and leisure habits have seen the loss of independent bakers, butchers and greengrocers, not to mention public houses, and any Ulverstonian will tell you how quiet market days are compared with only twenty years ago. At the same time, as old industries like the iron works have disappeared, new ones have replaced them, and nowadays there is cautious optimism that Ulverston's industrial and manufacturing base has a future. Since there is a wealth of material available for twentieth century Ulverston, in this final chapter I will focus on the changing face of the town, highlighting areas such as the slum clearance of the 1930's which have not been fully covered elsewhere.

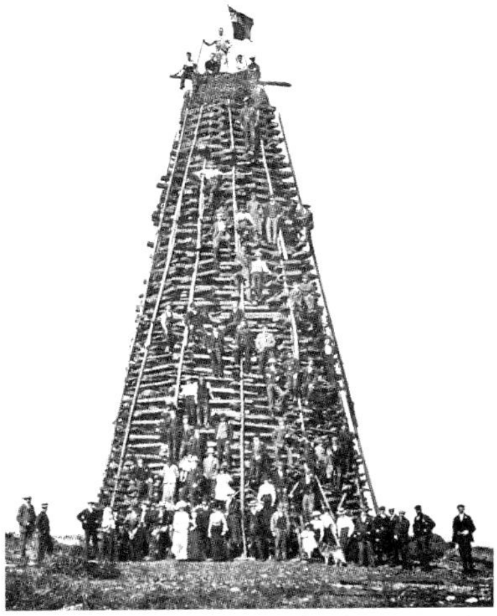

The immense bonfire built for the coronation of Edward VII in 1902. North Lonsdale Magazine

Although councils and planners were responsible for many of the changes in Ulverston, some have come about because of disastrous fires which even the town's hard-working fire brigade, based on the Ellers since 1885, could not control. One of the most destructive was the burning down on October 9th 1911 of the County Hotel, formerly Lightburne House and before that Little Croft, the home of Thomas Sunderland. *'Lost Ulverston'* gives a lively account of this enormous conflagration with its scenes of guests escaping down a ladder and crowds of spectators watching the action as flames lit up the whole neighbourhood.

The building was judged beyond repair and the site was used for a new Post Office and the public hall with which the council commemorated the coronation of George V (1910 -1936). Myles Kennedy laid the foundation stone of the Coronation Hall in June 1914, but its building was interrupted by the great cataclysm of the twentieth century, the First World War, which Britain joined an hour before midnight on August 4 1914.

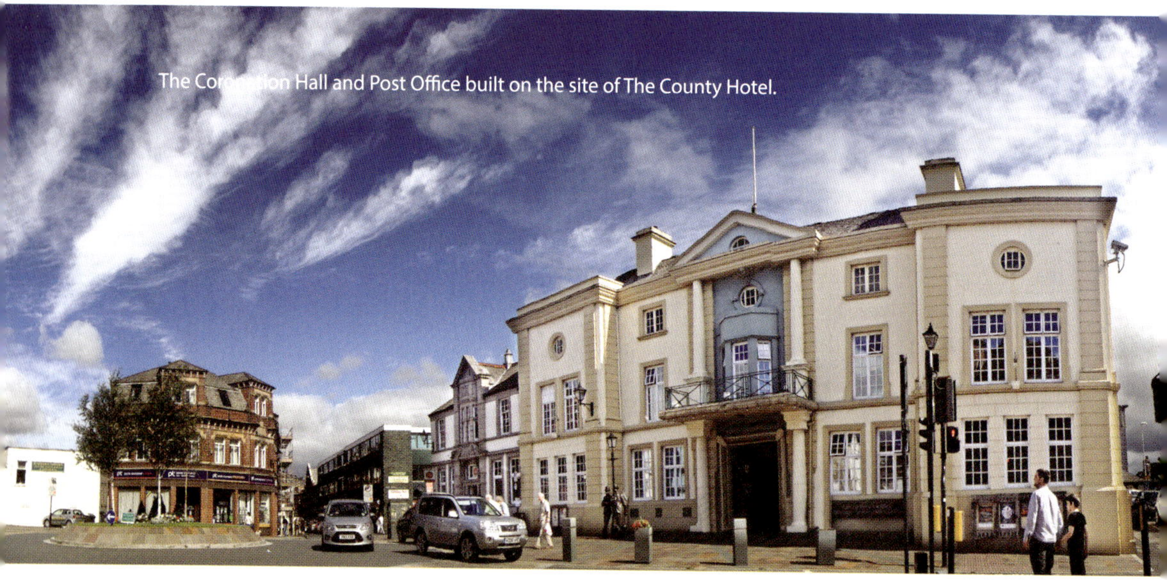

The Coronation Hall and Post Office built on the site of The County Hotel.

Local papers for July 1914 reveal how sudden this crisis was for people in Furness. The North West Evening Mail's coverage of international news was mostly concerned with the imminent danger of civil war in Ireland, and it was only on July 25th that a small column mentioned the trouble between 'Servia' and Austria, and on July 27th that the headline 'European War Cloud' appeared. It is also clear that some people in Ulverston were carrying on with lives which bore little resemblance to the idyllic pre-war summer of popular myth. The court reports in the paper of July 30th tell the story of an unfortunate who was sentenced to a month's hard labour in Lancaster prison for sleeping rough, and the harrowing tale of a mother whose drunken wife-beater of a husband starved her of money for rent and threatened her with a razor. Within a few days, these stories must have seemed small beer as the seriousness of the coming war was brought home. On August 4th the local Territorials were called up, and soon soldiers were guarding the viaducts over the Kent and Leven estuaries, recruiting offices were set up in Queen Street and the Drill Hall, and the North Lonsdale Agricultural Show was cancelled. On August 12th, soldiers from the area were billeted at Dale Street School and the Victoria Grammar School before leaving Ulverston station early one morning to guard the Great Western Railway at Slough. Here Ulverston suffered its first fatality, when Sergeant John Tindall, son of the Ulverston police inspector, was hit by a train. The stories of many of the Ulverston men who marched off to the Great War, and the one hundred and seventy one who didn't come back, are told by John Hutton in *'Kitchener's Men'* (Pen and Sword Military 2008). Ulverston's dead were honoured on a war memorial which was unveiled on May 13th 1921 and which still stands at the top of Market Street. A more idiosyncratic thank you to those in Ulverston and the surrounding district who had lent money for the war effort through the War Savings Committee was a tank. It must have been quite a sight in the narrow streets as it was driven from the station to a plinth in Ellers Square, where Market Street ended and the Ellers began, remaining there for seventeen

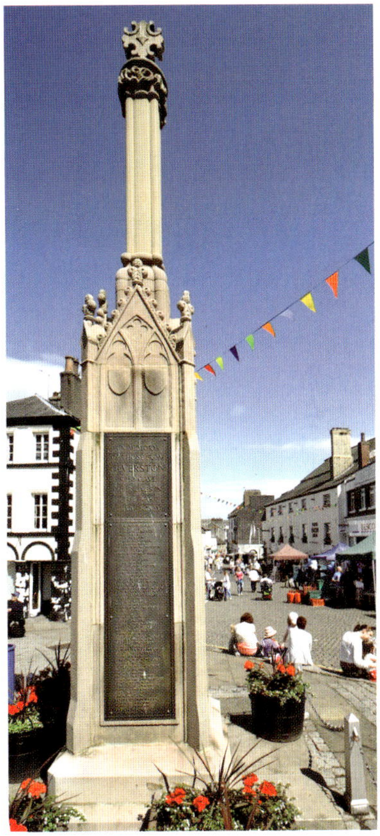

Unveiled in 1921, the war memorial stands at the top of Market Street.

years before being scrapped. This area is now under the County Road roundabout, but it is still sometimes referred to as 'Tank Square'.

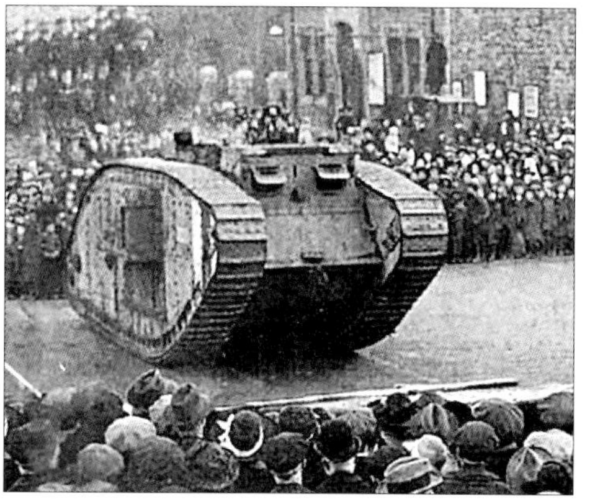

The 26 ton Mark IV tank arriving in its new home in 1920.

Because men and women from all walks of like had made great sacrifices in the war, after 1918 there was a strong urge to create a better and more equal society. It was only in 1918 that every man over twenty-one, and some women, gained the vote for general elections, and the 1834 Poor Law was still in force. Dorothy Ashburner in her book *A Story of the Growth of Ulverston* mentions the 'Guardians Riot', when attempted protest marches from Lindal and Dalton to Ulverston, where the Poor Law Guardians still met, were beaten back by police. The Poor Law was only superseded in 1929, when the Local Government Act abolished the system and and transferred responsibility for Public Assistance to county councils and county boroughs. Unfortunately, efforts to improve people's lot came up against harsh economic realities and government debt. Traditional British heavy industries like coal and steel production found that foreign competitors, who could produce more cheaply, had taken over many markets, and workers began to lose their jobs. In the Furness iron and steel industry, where cheaper Spanish haematite was imported in the 1920's, the number of iron miners employed began to fall. The coast road between Ulverston and Barrow was built in 1923/4 to provide relief work for men without a job. The picture in agriculture wasn't rosy either. Farm workers faced wage cuts as cheap foreign food started coming into the country, and the Agricultural Wages Board, set up in 1924 to standardise wages, put an end to the busy hiring fairs in Ulverston. The Wall Street crash of 1929 and the ensuing Depression worsened the plight of heavy industry. One furnace at the North Lonsdale Iron and Steel works had already closed down in 1927, and in 1932 the business merged with the Millom and Askam Iron works. Production of pig iron moved to Millom, and none is recorded as having been made in Ulverston between 1932 and 1936. Although a blast furnace was working between 1937 and 1938, an explosion in 1938 put an end to Ulverston's pig iron production for ever, and there are several reminiscences which describe the desolation felt by those left unemployed in the town in the 1930's. One bright spot was a new factory, built in 1934 by Fred Broome, a retired wealthy textile machine designer and manufacturer, to provide jobs by producing 'Ulvex', a combination of cashmere and silk. This Morecambe Road factory, with its distinctive roof typical of northern weaving sheds, can still be seen today, although sadly Mr Broome died in 1936 and 'Ulvex' died with him.

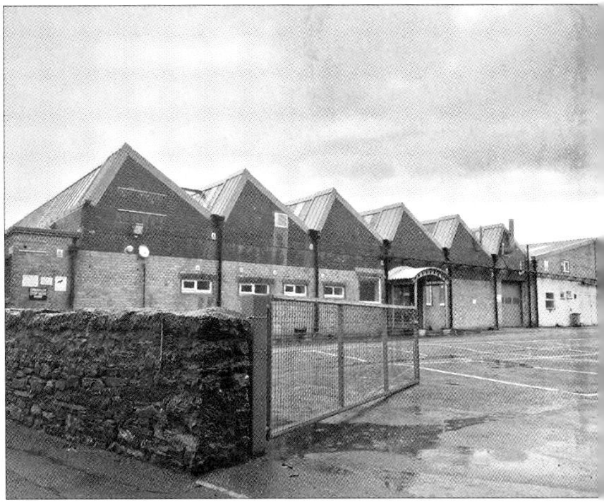
The former Ulvex factory on Morecambe Road.

Clearly, the picture in Ulverston during these inter-war years wasn't one of unremitting gloom, and Henry Birkett's description of the disbelief with which townspeople saw the poverty of some evacuees in the Second World War shows that conditions were nothing like as bad as in the larger northern centres of heavy industry. This was the golden age of cinema, and as early as 1922 Ulverston's first cinema, the Palladium, was built on Victoria Road, where the rose garden is now, to be followed by the Art Deco Roxy on Brogden Street in 1937. Electricity came to the town in 1926 following a heated debate over whether Ulverston should reject this innovation since it was going to be generated in Barrow. Another fire in 1935 destroyed the Market Hall which was rebuilt and still houses the indoor market today. One feature noted by Henry Birkett was the way 'multiple shops' arrived to replace former family-run businesses in Ulverston. Obviously referring to Woolworths, he describes how an older building on Market Street was partly knocked down to create 'an exact copy of their thousand other stores', and how 'Old Ulverstonians did not welcome a change that made their town at one with any other town', sentiments uncannily similar to those expressed today. It is maybe a sign of our times that the former Woolworth's building is now a Tesco Express. In contrast, Dorothy Ashburner recalls that in the 1930's many shops were still small and dark, and makes particular mention of the 'Li'l Bacca Shoppe' with its two doors. All that remains of this tiny shop, originally next to the Piel Castle, is its sign which has been moved up the street.

Undoubtedly, one of the biggest changes of the 1930's was the demolition and rebuilding of Quebec Street, formerly Ratten Row, the building of new streets of council houses in the Honeypot for those displaced by the demolition, and more demolition to widen the road junction where Quay Street, Quebec Street and Swan Street met.

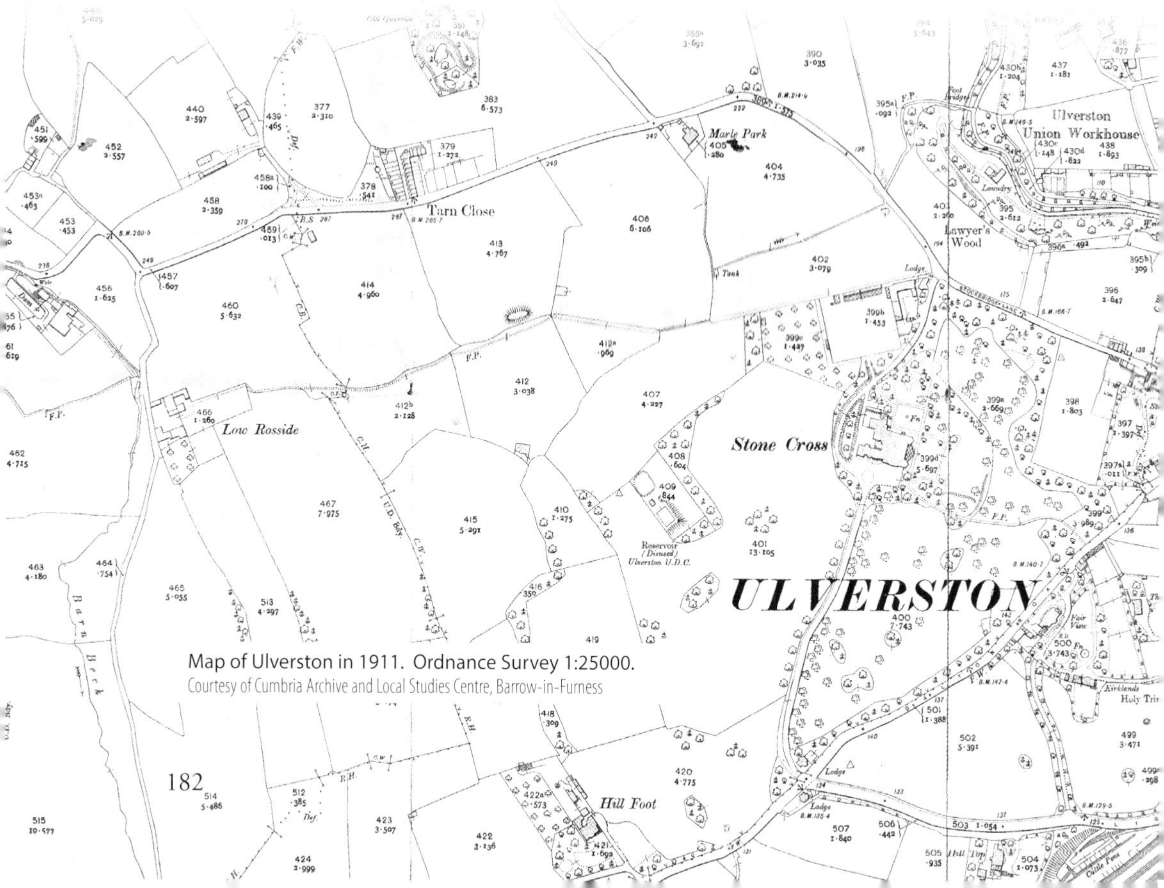

Map of Ulverston in 1911. Ordnance Survey 1:25000.
Courtesy of Cumbria Archive and Local Studies Centre, Barrow-in-Furness

Decent housing for workers was an important issue after 1918, and while we can say that bad housing in Ulverston wasn't on the scale of slums in the major cities and land had been released to build solid terraces, a fair number of late Victorian sub-standard dwellings still existed. What is noticeable when we compare John Wood's 1832 plan of Ulverston with the 1911 Ordnance Survey 1:2500 map is the way that by 1911 substantial buildings had been divided many times over to make what must have been tiny dwellings. In 1832 the stretch of Ratten Row between its junction with Swan Street and its junction with the Ellers had about twenty dwellings on one side and seven on the other.

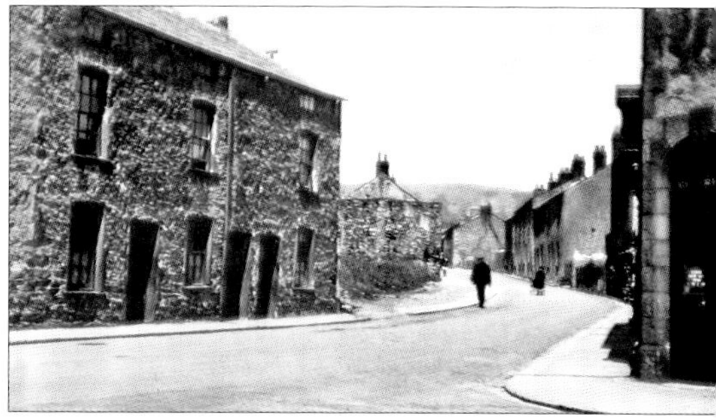

Ratten Row in 1936. A gap shows where demolition of the street may already have begun. Courtesy of Peter Lowe

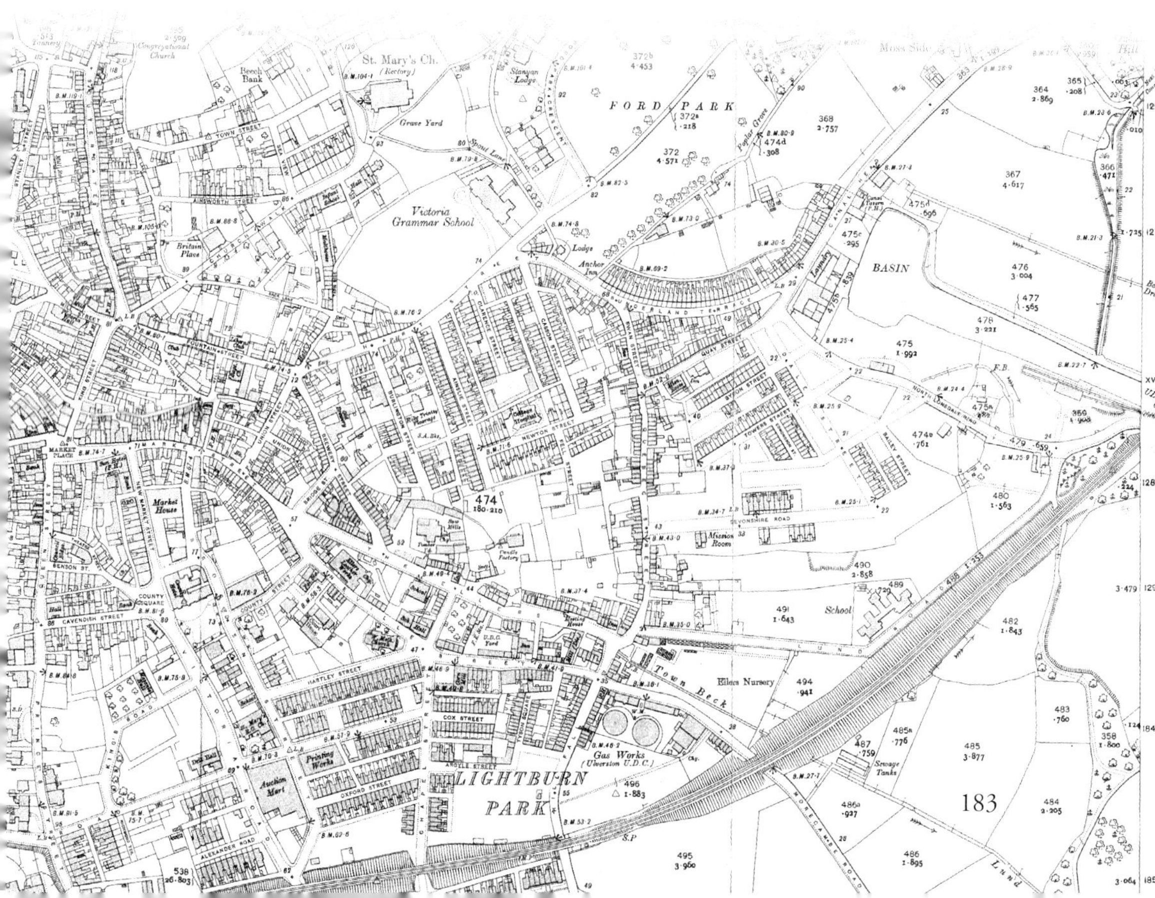

By 1911 the twenty dwellings seem to have become over forty, and the seven, with the addition of new building, over twenty five. The trend continues on Swan Street with the Parsonage and nearby buildings divided up, to create in one case an alley of what must have been weeny houses at right angles to the road. It has been noted before that the triangle of land between Swan Street, Sunderland Terrace and Quay Street had one building on it in 1832; by 1911 it was a clutter of houses and yards, so that Sunderland Terrace was built up on both sides. From 1919, governments passed Housing Acts which gave local authorities responsibility for developing new housing, and promised them subsidies for new houses. The Housing Act of 1924 gave councils substantial grants, and it was probably because of this that Ulverston gained its first council houses on Lund Road in 1924. However, it was the ambitious Act of 1930 obliging councils to clear all slum housing which led to the demolition of Ratten Row/Quebec Street. In Barrow Records Office there is a mass of material relating to the 'slum clearance' efforts of Ulverston Urban District Council, showing how seriously the council was taking this responsibility, and what an uphill struggle it could be.

As well as identifying Quebec Street as the main slum to be cleared, the council also designated as slums part of the Swan Street, Quay Street and Sunderland Terrace area together with various other pockets, among them Paradise Yard off Daltongate and houses on Stanley Street and the Ellers. In proportion to Ulverston's size at the time, the demolition of Quebec Street and building all the new houses was a major undertaking. To add to the headache of allocating new houses without causing ructions, the council had to deal with people helping themselves to timber, cisterns and lead piping from demolished buildings in what was described as 'wholesale pillage'. Nowadays we may regret the razing to the ground of a street containing buildings which, even though they had been divided up, might merit listing in later decades. On the other hand, a glimpse into the horrible state of the houses is given by the council's insistence that all the tenants' furnishings had to be 'gassed' or fumigated to get rid of vermin before they could be moved into the new houses.

Along with 'slum clearance', the council planned to widen the rebuilt Quebec Street and then Swan Street and Quay Street. It was this latter intention which bought them into conflict with the redoubtable Miss Florence Appleyard, Confectioner and Tobacconist, of 3 Sunderland Terrace, which stood in front of the present day flats opposite nos. 6 and 8 Sunderland Terrace. In one of those hidden episodes of Ulverston's history, the archives preserve the running battle between Miss Appleyard and Mr Poole, the long-suffering Town Clerk, a ding-dong correspondence which began in February 1937 and continued well into the Second World War, with Miss Appleyard fighting tooth and nail to prevent her property being knocked down. Other owners of properties in this area were almost as troublesome, demanding unreasonable sums in compensation and then insisting that their claims went to 'arbitration'. In spite of this, some demolition on Swan Street had taken place before the war intervened, leaving the gaps which Henry Birkett likened to bomb damage.

In contrast to the summer of 1914, very few people were caught on the hop by the immediate crisis which led Britain to declare war on Germany at 11am on Sunday September 3rd 1939. Since 1938 the country had been hoping for peace while preparing for war, and plans swung into action in Furness even before the formal declaration. As if in anticipation of the coming storm, on August 25th Lord Balniel, the local MP, delivered a stirring speech to the Ulverston and District Garden and Allotment Holders Association in the Coronation Hall, and on Friday 1st September the first evacuees from Salford arrived in Ulverston to be swept up by an obviously well-prepared reception system. The next day, ever-optimistic football fans flooded into local grounds for the first matches of the new season. War rendered the results academic: these were also the last matches of the shortest season on record. With National Service being quickly brought in, the Barrow shipyards going on a war footing, preparations for rationing being made and ARP posts being established in Ulverston, on Wednesday September 6th Ulverston Urban District Council still found time for a long discussion about a footpath across Church Fields. One doesn't know whether to wonder at the Council for worrying over such a minor detail, or to admire their determination not to let Hitler dictate every agenda.

Such determination was needed in the upheaval of the next six years when Barrow was a target for bombers, and there were fears that the vital train line across the Leven estuary into Furness would suffer the same fate. As German bombing escalated from September 1940, Ulverston itself came to be seen as relatively safe, a perception which led to the arrival, from more vulnerable areas, of new industries, which in turn were to contribute to its renewed post-war manufacturing base. After the bombing of Coventry, Armstrong Siddley took over the now disused Paper Mill buildings on the canal, and used the site for repairing and refitting aero engines, while Fred Broome's 'Ulvex' factory on Morecambe Road was used by Ashley Accessories, originally based in Liverpool, to manufacture electrical components for the military. One wartime arrival is still going strong today. In 1940 Robert Oxley was producing capacitors for the military, and having been told by the Ministry of Aircraft Production to move somewhere safer after the Blitz, in 1942 he started production in the building on Market Street which now houses the Oxfam shop. Wartime labour shortages led to hard working conditions: at Armstrong Siddely workers were brought in from Lancaster to work twelve hour shifts seven days a week.

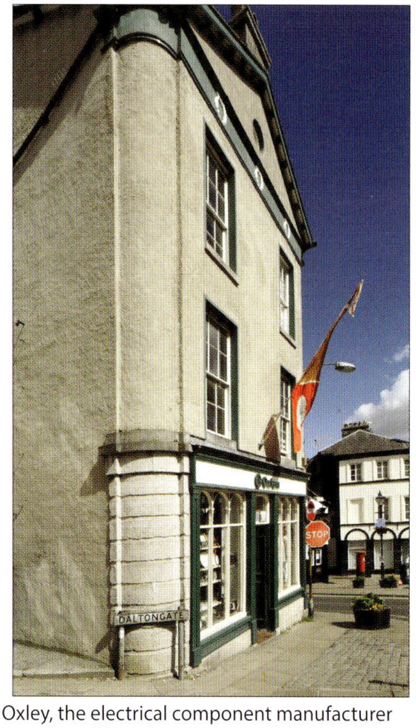

Oxley, the electrical component manufacturer were based here from 1940 until the mid-fifties.

It is worth mentioning here three men born in Ulverston who made outstanding personal contributions to the war effort and its aftermath. The first two, Francis Arthur Jefferson and William Basil Weston, were both awarded the Victoria Cross. 'Frank' Jefferson, a fusilier in the Lancashire Fusiliers, was taking part in the Battle for Monte Cassino in May 1944 when two German tanks counter-attacked. Single-handedly he picked up an anti-tank gun and ran forward in a hail of bullets to knock out one tank and force the other to retreat. He lived to tell the tale and to inspire generations of schoolchildren at the Ulverston Victoria High School through the Jefferson Cup. The story of Basil Weston, a lieutenant in the Green Howards, does not have a happy ending. Badly wounded at an enemy bunker entrance in the attack on Meiktila, Burma, in March 1945, to save his comrades he pulled the pin on his grenade to destroy those in the bunker and himself. Although not a military hero, the third man, William Norman Birkett, later ennobled as the first Baron Birkett of Ulverston, is rightly regarded as one of Ulverston's greatest sons. As well as being one of the finest criminal lawyers of the first half of the twentieth century and a noted Methodist preacher, he served as a Liberal MP in the 1920's and 1930's, and became a judge in 1941. Famous for the speaking skills which swayed juries in favour of his seemingly doomed clients, in 1945 he was asked to be the British alternate judge at the Nuremberg Trials. Although he didn't have a vote in the proceedings, his fellow judges could not speak highly enough of his contribution to their discussions and to the final judgement. Unlike Sir John Barrow of the previous century, who might have been a little keen to brush over his origins, Lord Birkett never forgot his roots in Ulverston and the north. He came to open the new library in Ulverston in 1961, and his final service to the Lake District, days before his death in February 1962, was a speech in the House of Lords in which he successfully opposed a bill which would have allowed Manchester to drain water from Ullswater to use in the city.

Only a few years after the end of the Second World War, when memories of those dark days were still fresh, Henry Birkett published his history of Ulverston. Whilst he acknowledges that there was no undoing the changes brought about by the war, his enduring image is of a close-knit market town peopled by independent-minded characters who all knew each other. Before County Road was built, the town centre in Mr Birkett's day had a feeling of closeness, with many features familiar to him which have now disappeared. Among these are the Workhouse, the Mill Pond and the Tannery buildings at the top of Stanley Street, the Rose Garden next to the Coronation Hall, the old Rectory on Swan Street and the row of houses on the other side of Sunderland Terrace, not to mention the narrow streets and buildings where the County Road roundabout and empty spaces of car parks are now. Most of the family-run shops he championed have also long gone. These include his own County Stores, now Poole Townsend's premises, and Atkinson's, the booksellers, stationers and printers, whose King Street shop is now 'Pretty Things', and who produced postcards of Ulverston in their printing works, now a charity shop, on Upper Brook Street.

We tend to place the blame for all the changes which might have Henry Birkett spinning in his grave squarely on the shoulders of planners in the 1960's, a decade which was particularly hard on anything Victorian, and when councils wanted to knock down the old and embrace a modern concrete future. It is instructive therefore to look at the Development Plan for Ulverston, drawn up as early as 1951, which foreshadows many of the developments in housing, industry and roads which we think of as more typical of the 1960's.

This plan is quite critical of some of Ulverston's older housing, and seems to regret that it is in scattered pockets preventing it from knocked down in one fell swoop. It gives a cautious seal of approval to later Victorian housing, although some of it is described as rather small, probably meaning houses like those on the former Brewery Street as it ran towards the Ellers. It is maybe no coincidence that it was in the 1950's that work started on the Croftlands housing development, spreading upwards from Priory Road and hugely increasing the town's size. New areas of more suitable modern housing would be needed because of Ulverston's industrial development and, if we read between the lines, because of intentions to widen the A590. The plan notes that while a considerable number of people travelled to Barrow every day to work in the ship yards, a trend still evident today, since the war important new industries had arrived in Ulverston as a result of the efforts of local authorities and government departments. One of these new industries was 'chemicals', which must be a reference to the arrival of Glaxo, a stroke of fortune for industry in the town. Glaxo took over the iron works site in 1948, when only the refining foundry, which closed in 1949, was still working. The massive blast furnaces were demolished, and Glaxo started manufacturing antibiotics. Since 1951 Glaxo has been through several incarnations as it has expanded to become GlaxoSmithKline, the major international pharmaceutical company, and although it has had its ups and downs in Ulverston, it now has new plans for the site, which are mentioned later in this chapter.

It is when the plan talks about the A590 'Trunk' road between Greenodd and Barrow that it is most interesting. It points out that this road is used by heavy and outsize loads and is 'quite inadequate' for the purpose, since through Ulverston it follows a narrow and winding route which includes two right-angled bends and one of the main shopping streets. Not surprisingly Ulverston's role as the local market town made the congestion even worse, and 'conditions were particularly bad on market days'. The proposed solution, back in 1951, was largely what we see today, a dual-carriage way between Canal Head and Stone Cross to provide a free flow for east-west through traffic, with the proviso that it should be done as economically as possible. Even though the plan's proposal did not come into fruition until the mid-1960's onwards, it is no surprise that it generated more controversy than practically any other development because of all the attendant destruction and the way it divided the town. In fairness, it's hard to see where else a relatively economical east-west route could go. It's noticeable in Ulverston how the transport decisions of one century caused problems for the next. The people who built the canal could not have foreseen that it would be an obstacle to building a railway, and Brogden could not have anticipated the invention of the internal combustion engine and the twentieth century explosion in road traffic. By 1951 the canal lock gates had been concreted up, the last boat having left in 1945, but the canal water was used by Glaxo and both the canal and the railway stood in the way of any other route for a by-pass. Well before the bulldozers started work in 1965 the planners in 1951 had sealed the fate of the Ulverston which Henry Birkett knew.

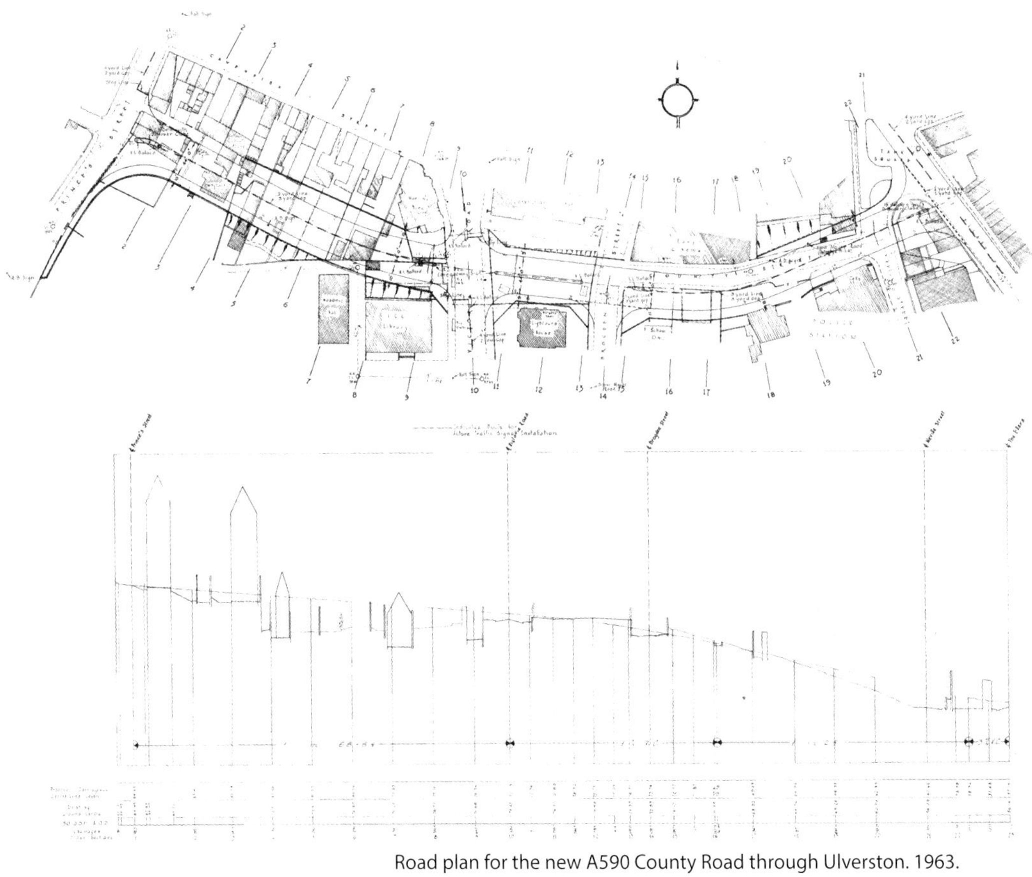

Road plan for the new A590 County Road through Ulverston. 1963.

In the 1960's demolition, not all of it necessary to build the widened A590 or County Road, destroyed a significant amount of historic Ulverston. In 1961 small houses on the Ellers, together with the remains of the mill and associated works, were knocked down to build the bungalows there today, and in 1965 most of the old Market Hall with its fish stalls facing New Market Street also went under the wrecking ball to be replaced with the Coniston House office block. In the same year Stage I of the road building saw the Rose Garden next to the Coronation Hall obliterated, although when the Palladium on Victoria Road was demolished in the following year, a replacement garden was planted on its site. As the sixties wore on the houses on the other side of Sunderland Terrace came down, and the road ploughed towards Ellers (or 'Tank') Square, until by 1969 Stage II saw the wiping out of most of Brewery Street, all of Bridge Street (which ran parallel to Union Street between Market Street and Brewery Street) and all the buildings on the triangle of land between Bridge Street, Brewery Street and the Ellers. Elsewhere there was a widespread clearance of older buildings on Hill Fall, of the old Rectory and other houses on Swan Street, and of part of the Theatre Royal building.

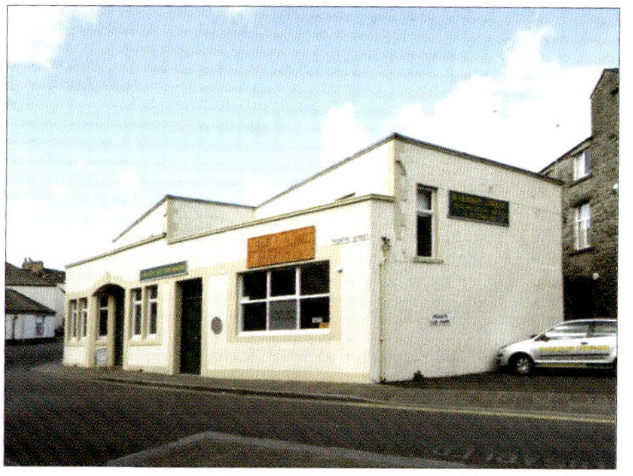

All that remains of the Theatre Royal in County Square

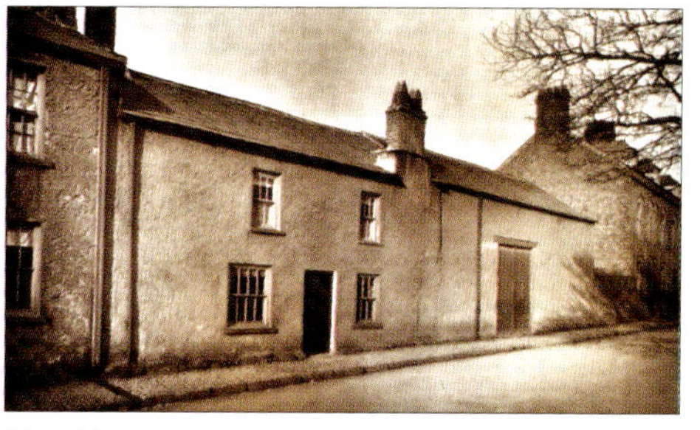

The old parsonage on Swan Street, lost in the demolition mania of the 1960's. Chronicles of Ulverston

The creation of County Road created havoc in Ulverston but the bottom line is that there was no other easy way to provide a route through to Barrow. If the town centre was congested in 1951, it would be many times worse by the end of the century. More questionable is the decision of the council in the early 1970's to demolish part of the town centre to create the Buxton Place car park. In April 1971 it was noted that the 'greater part of the Council's Capital Allocation for 1971-72 is allocated specifically for Buxton Place car park' and the council made haste to buy the land and buildings including the former 'Old Curiosity Shop'. Only the listed building still standing marooned in the car park was spared, and an area which would nowadays probably be regarded as a gem worthy of preservation was gone, leaving barely a trace.

When County Road was built, the death of Ulverston was predicted, probably not for the first time and certainly not for the last. In the early 1970's the town lost two traditional industries in the Tannery at Low Mill and the Town Mill itself. The final insult for many was the local government re-organisation of 1974 when Furness officially ceased to be part of Lancashire and was bundled into a new country, Cumbria. At the same time, Ulverston lost its Urban District Council, and came under the Kendal-based South Lakeland District Council. Although there had been historical links with Kendal dating back to the early Middle ages, Ulverston was reluctant to relinquish control over local matters to the new district council with its competing priorities. The positive news is that, as in the past, Ulverston's industry has managed to continue reinventing itself. As iron-making, weaving, cotton-spinning, ship-building and tanning have come and gone, pharmaceuticals and hi-tech industries, especially those engaged in LED lighting technology, have come in their place.

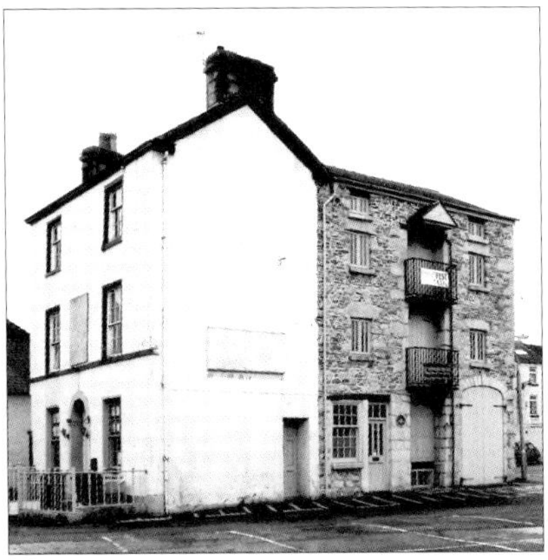

All that remains of old buildings in Buxton Place, demolished in the 1970's to make a car park. Lynn Shamal

Following expansion through the 1980's and 1990's, the future of GlaxoSmithKline's Ulverston site, the town's largest single employer, began to look uncertain and in 2002 four hundred redundancies were announced. Happily this uncertainty was dispelled in 2013 when GSK announced that Ulverston had been chosen as the location for a brand new biopharmaceutical manufacturing plant predicted to generate new skilled employment. The growth of other modern industrial concerns continues apace. Among these are Oxleys, which moved out to Priory Park in the 1950's and which continues to design and manufacture electronic and electro-optic systems and components. Two other companies, Marl, now in part of the former Ashley Accessories factory, and Forge Europa, opposite the station approach, are successfully competing in the field of LED technology. A new factory has been built close to the former Tannery for Tronic, now owned by Siemens, which manufactures subsea connection systems for the oil and gas industry. Another has been developed next to Booths supermarket for Tritech, a high-technology Marine Electronic Equipment Manufacturer.

Unfortunately flourishing local industry doesn't necessarily translate into a flourishing town centre. Hand wringing over the decline of the high street has not altered people's preference for shopping in supermarkets or online rather than walking round independent shops and traditional markets. The coming of Booths supermarket sounded a death knell for the last of the traditional grocers like Gillams and Rogers & Tyson which had served generations of Ulverstonians. The latest recession in particular has hit Ulverston's town centre hard. Nevertheless, members of the community put a huge amount of effort into keeping the town centre alive, and in the 1990's attempts at regeneration led to Ulverston building on its talents and history to become a 'festival town'.

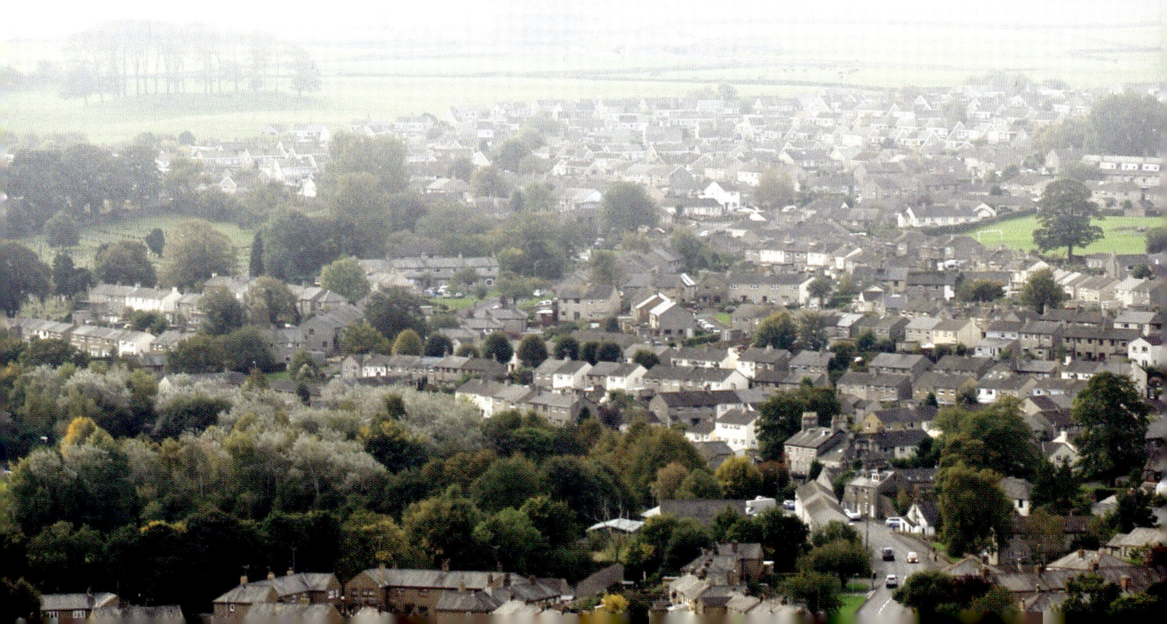

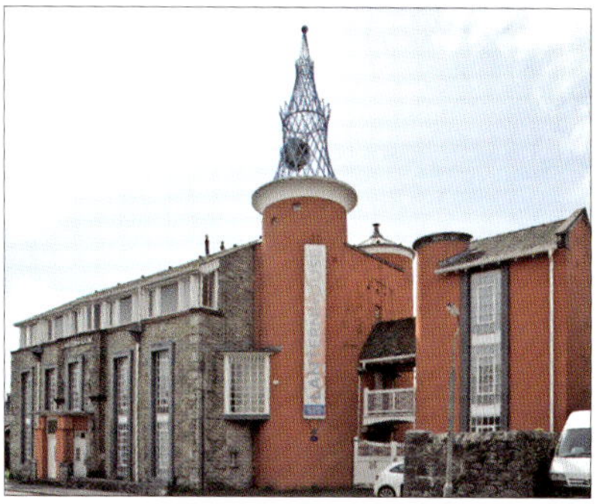

Lantern House - the home of the arts organisation Welfare State International from 1999 to 2006.

In the days of the Royal Theatre Ulverston was thought of as the cultural capital of Furness, and there has always been an interest in music and arts in the town with a tradition of people coming together for the annual Carnival Parade. In the 1970's Ulverston's cultural life was given a boost by the arrival of the Renaissance Theatre Trust. The trust had formerly run Her Majesty's Theatre in Barrow, and took an office in Theatre Street to organise school tours, plays and musical tours around the county, before moving in 1974 to what became Sting in the Tail in Fountain Street. From here the trust promoted visits to Ulverston by the best touring companies, including the English National Ballet, the English Touring Opera and the Royal Shakespeare Company. The trust also invited Welfare State International into the area, and encouraged them to settle in Ulverston in 1979. Welfare State International, a radical and innovative company of artists specialising in spectacular and unusual celebratory community events, gave impetus to the festival town idea. They instituted the Lantern Procession which ends the town's Charter Festival held every September. Festivals such as the Dickensian Festival at the end of November, Furness Folk and Tradition, the International Music Festival and the Walking Festival continue to attract visitors from within Furness and further afield. Enterprising groups have been encouraged to set up new festivals, like the 'Another Fine Fest' inspired by Ulverston as the birthplace of Stan Laurel.

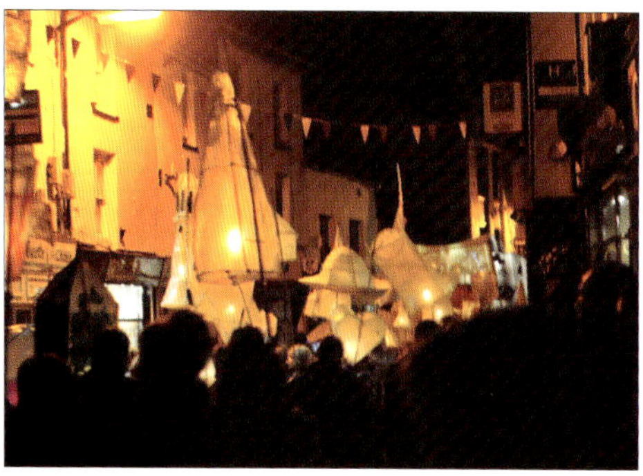

The annual Lantern Parade held each September during the Charter Festival.

Keeping a market town alive comes down in no small part to the efforts of local people. Stringent cuts in government funding threaten even the future of the iconic Coronation Hall, Ulverston's cultural and entertainment centre, but the well of affection for the town means that few residents are indifferent to its fate, and it has a Town Council which reflects this feeling. This sense of purpose was demonstrated in the restoration of the Sir John Barrow monument, which is owned by the Town Council. By 2003 the monument was suffering structurally, not helped by inadequate repairs in the previous century, and it had to be closed to the public. In 2008 the Town Council won a large sum from the Heritage Lottery Fund towards restoration, and through heroic fund-raising the Friends of the Sir John Barrow Monument made up the shortfall. On August 22nd 2010, hundreds of people climbed up to the monument in the sunshine to see Sir Anthony Barrow, the 7th Baronet of Ulverston, officially re-open the much-loved landmark. This culmination of hard work and dedication was rounded off by a spectacular firework display in the evening, and the beautifully restored monument is a fitting tribute both to Sir John Barrow and to the people of Ulverston, who throughout their town's long history have made it such a distinctive place.

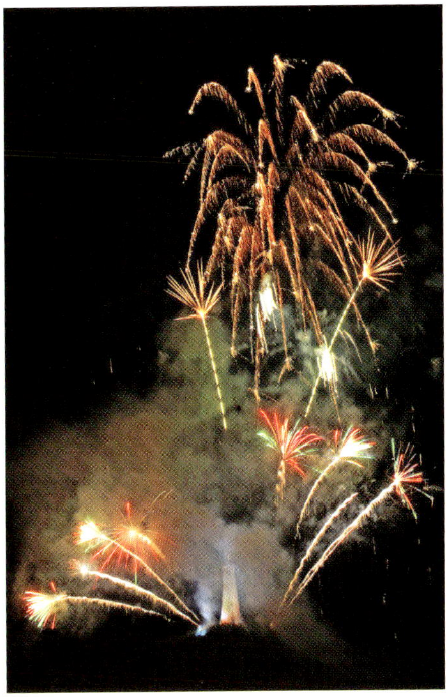

The spectacular firework display in August 2010, the culmination of hard work and dedication marking the re-opening of the Sir John Barrow monument

How this distinctiveness will be preserved in the future is open to question. Over the centuries many reminders of Ulverston's history have been lost, and discovering more about its past could become harder as the town changes shape and evidence gets buried further and further under successive layers of re-development. A case in point is what has happened to Neville Hall and its associated buildings. First the manor house was demolished in Victorian times to be replaced with the Police Station and Courts. Now with the imminent closure of the police station, these buildings will probably be sold, knocked down in turn and replaced by new housing. The mill on the Ellers, perhaps the site of the manor's medieval grain mill, is gone, and Robinsons Brewery, focus of the hotly

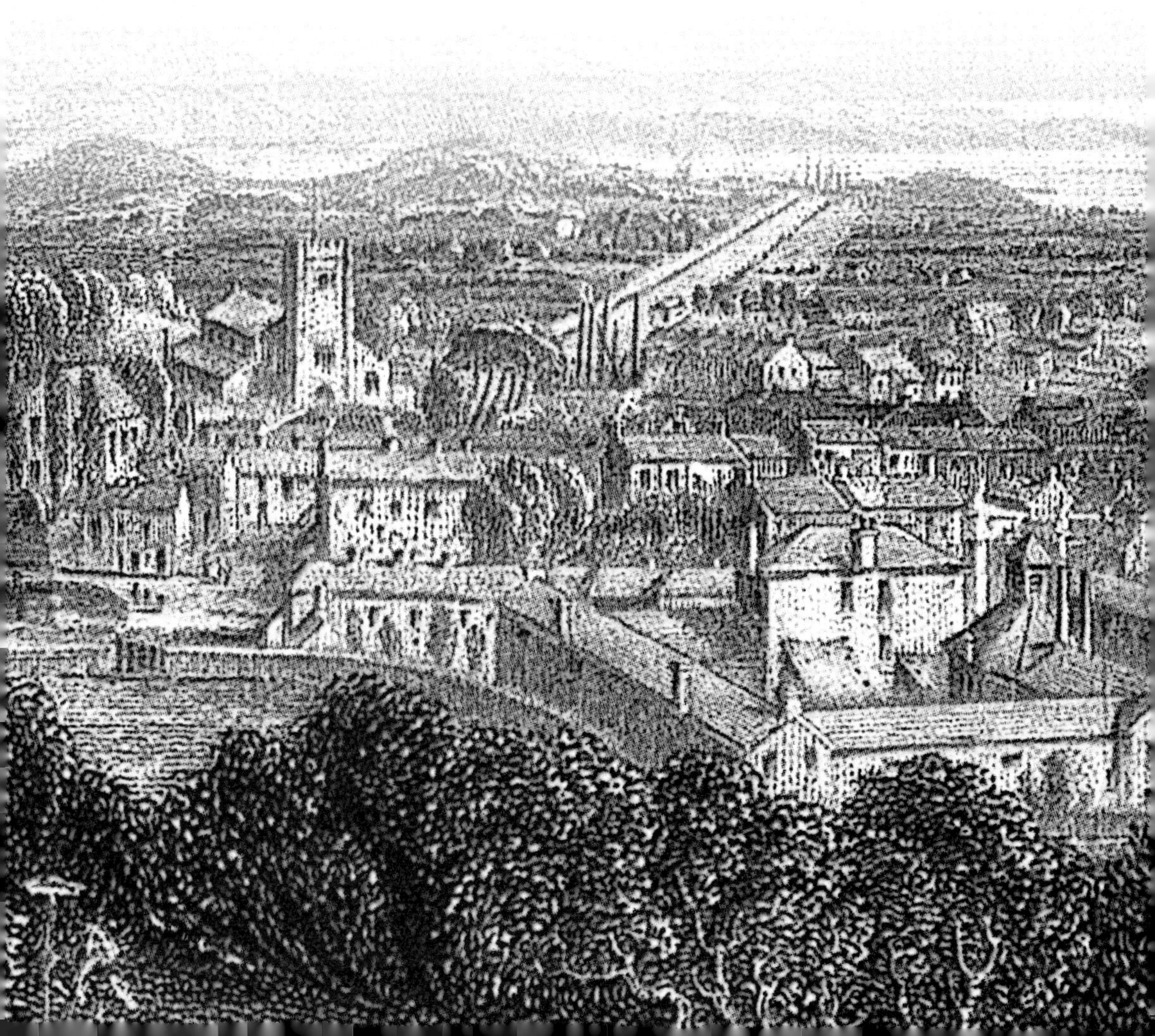

contested supermarket controversy, was itself most likely built on part of the original manor complex. At the time of publication planning permission has been granted for this development, and if it is built according to the plans submitted, the old line of Brewery Street will go and any evidence of pre-eighteenth century buildings will also disappear.

There is always a tension between preserving what remains of Ulverston's historic fabric and the demands of the twenty first century. It has to be hoped that any new developments will take the interest in Ulverston's past into account, and allow archaeological investigation so that features which contributed to the town's uniqueness are not completely lost to future generations.

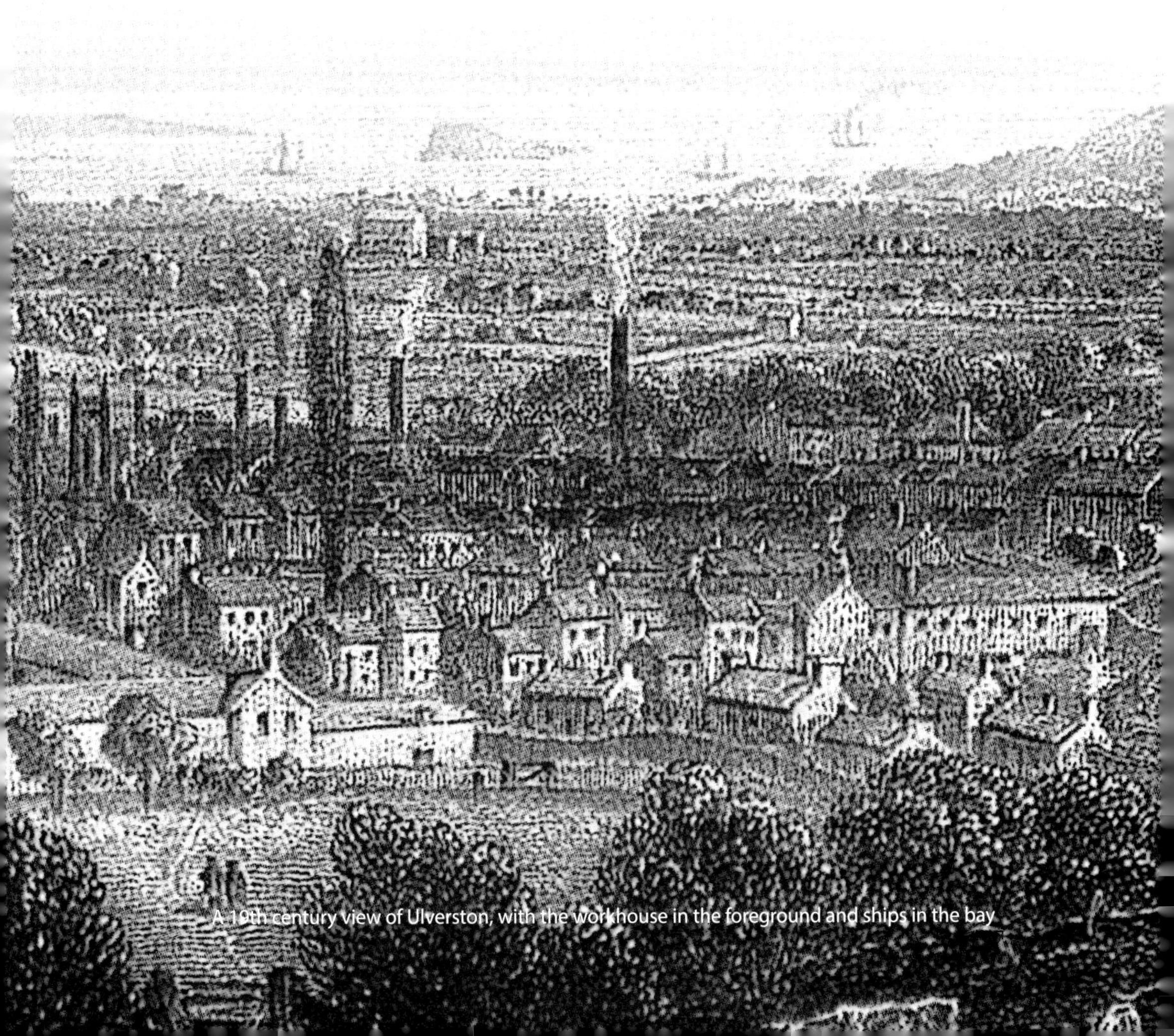

A 19th century view of Ulverston, with the workhouse in the foreground and ships in the bay

Index

D

E

F

G

H

I

J

K

L

M

U

V

W

Y

Select Bibliography

The Victoria History of the Counties of England. Ed William Page

A History of Lancashire Vol II 1908 Reprinted Dawsons of Pall Mall 1966

A History of Lancashire Vol VIII 1914 Reprinted Dawsons of Pall Mall 1966

Andrews, Michael *The Furness Railway* Barrai Books 2012

Ashburner, Dorothy *A Story of the Growth of Ulverston* Dorothy Ashburner 1993

Barber, Henry *Furness and Cartmel Notes* James Atkinson 1894

Bardsley, Charles Wareing Endell *Chronicles of the Town and Church of Ulverston* James Atkinson 1885

Barnes, F *Barrow and District: An Illustrated History* 2nd Edition Barrow-in-Furness 1968

Barrowclough, David *Prehistoric Cumbria* The History Press 2010

Birkett, Henry F *The Story of Ulverston: A Short History* Titus Wilson 1949

Crosby, Alan *A History of Lancashire* Phillimore 1998

Dickinson, J C *The Land of Cartmel: A History* Titus Wilson & Son 1980

Dickinson, Steve *The Beacon on the Bay* 2002

Donald, M B *Elizabethan Copper* Red Earth Publications 1994

Fell, Alfred *The Early Iron Industry of Furness and District* Hume Kitchin 1908, Cass 1968

Fell, Alfred *A Furness Military Chronicle* Ulverston, Kitchin & Co 1937

Fell, John *Pedigree of Fell of Daltongate* Kerby and Endean 1882

Fleming, Fergus *Barrow's Boys* Granta Books 1998

Gilpin, Leslie R *The Ulverstone and Lancaster Railway* Cumbrian Railways Association 2008

Holmes, Sarah E *The Paradise of Furness* Handstand Press 2012

Hutton, John *Kitchener's Men* Pen and Sword Military 2008

Layfield, Jack *Ulverston Canal and the Construction of Collins Weir* Jack Layfield 2007

Layfield, Jack *The Sir John Barrow Monument* Handstand Press 2005

Lowe, Peter and Carol Bennett *Images of England: Ulverston* Tempus 2006

McKeever Rob *An Ulverston Anthology* Furness Peninsula Press 2010

and Jack Layfield *The Industrial Archaeology of South Ulverston* Furness Peninsula Press 2004

Marshall, J D *Furness and the Industrial Revolution* James Milner Ltd 1958

Park, James *Some Ulverston Records* James Atkinson 1932

Parkinson, Anne C *A History of Catholicism in the Furness Peninsula 1127 – 1997* CNWRS University of Lancaster 1998

Penney, Norman (ed) *The Household Account Book of Sarah Fell* Cambridge University Press 1920

Rollinson, William *Life and Tradition in the Lake District* Dalesman Books 1981

Ross, Isabel *Margaret Fell: Mother of Quakerism* Longmans Green & Co 1949

Satchell, John *The Kendal Weaver* Kendal Civic Society/Frank Peters 1986

Snell, Jennifer *Lost Ulverston* Jennifer and Maurice Snell 2008

and Jack Layfield *Down Memory Lane*

Tiplady, Suzanne and Kevin Baverstock *The Parish of Satterthwaite A Social History* Saetrpress 2014

Walton, James E *A History of Dalton-in-Furness* Phillimore 1984

Waterhouse, John *The Stone Circles of Cumbria* Phillimore 1985

West, Thomas *Antiquities of Furness* new ed. William Close, Ashburner 1805

White, Andrew *A History of Kendal* Carnegie 2013

Whitehead, June *Lost Children. Ulverston Workhouse in the 19th Century* Handstand Press 2006

(Also documents relating to Kendal in British History Online)